IN THE PRESENCE OF OUR LORD

IN THE PRESENCE OF OUR LORD

THE HISTORY, THEOLOGY, AND PSYCHOLOGY OF EUCHARISTIC DEVOTION

FATHER BENEDICT J. GROESCHEL, C.F.R.,
AND JAMES MONTI

Our Sunday Visitor Publishing Division
Our Sunday Visitor, Inc.
Huntington, Indiana 46750

Nihil Obstat: Francis J. McAree, S.T.D.
Censor Librorum

Imprimatur: ✠Patrick Sheridan, D.D.
Vicar General, Archdiocese of New York
December 5, 1996

The Nihil Obstat and Imprimatur are official declarations that a book or pamphlet is free of doctrinal or moral error. No implication is contained therein that those who have granted the Nihil Obstat and Imprimatur agree with the contents, opinions, or statements expressed.

International Standard Book Number: 0-87973-920-7
Library of Congress Catalog Card Number: 96-71769

Cover design by Peggy Gerardot

PRINTED IN THE UNITED STATES OF AMERICA

Dedicated to the great saints and *beati* of Eucharistic devotion, among them:

Paul of Tarsus	Clare of Assisi
Augustine of Hippo	Juliana of Cornillon
John Chrysostom	Rose of Lima
Francis of Assisi	Margaret Mary Alacoque
Thomas Aquinas	Elizabeth Ann Seton
Thomas More	Thérèse of Lisieux
Alphonsus Liguori	Gemma Galgani
Peter Julian Eymard	Katharine Drexel

ACKNOWLEDGMENTS

We wish to express our gratitude to all those who have helped us in bringing this book to fruition, but in particular to Monsignor James O'Connor, who generously took the time to evaluate our manuscript; to Father Richard Brown, who courteously assisted us in preparing the manuscript; to the Secretary General of Bishop José Higinio Gomez Gonzalez, OFM, of the Diocese of Lugo, Spain, for most graciously providing us with information essential to our presentation of Lugo's long history of Eucharistic adoration; to Father Edward O'Neill, who translated our correspondence with the Diocese of Lugo; to Sister Ilia Delio, OSF, who patiently located for us valuable documentation in the library of St. Bonaventure University; to Mrs. Pat Forton of the Apostolate for Perpetual Adoration for sending us a number of very useful items regarding perpetual exposition; to the staff of the Corrigan Memorial Library of St. Joseph's Seminary for making available to us their marvelous collection of books and periodicals; and to the staff of the Irvington Public Library (New York) for obtaining for us two important interlibrary loans for our project. Finally, we wish to thank all those who by participating in nocturnal adoration societies, parish holy hours, apostolates of perpetual adoration, and indeed all forms of Eucharistic worship — even a short visit before the tabernacle on the way home from work or school — bear witness to the living presence of our Redeemer in the Blessed Sacrament.

* * *

We are also grateful to those publishers and authors who have given us permission to excerpt material from their works. Among them are: Veritas Publications, *The Holy Eucharist: From the New Testament to Pope John Paul II*, by Aidan Nichols, © 1991, used by permission; The Liturgical Press, *Blessed and Broken: An Exploration of the Contemporary Experience of God in Eucharistic Celebration*, by Ralph A. Keifer, © 1993, reprinted by permission of The Liturgical Press; P.J. Kenedy & Sons, *Autobiography of St. Thérèse of Lisieux*, © 1958, reprinted by permission of "The Official Catholic Directory"; Cambridge University Press, *In Breaking of Bread: The Eucharist and Ritual*, by P.J. Fitzpatrick, © 1993, reprinted with

* * *

For the benefit of the reader, it should be pointed out that a work of this kind necessarily requires relying on various sources that invariably do not agree completely, for instance, on the spelling of proper names, dates of events, and sometimes even on the specifics of events. We have tried to use the most reliable sources but realize that many "facts and figures" are still the subject of debate and speculation among the experts.

TABLE OF CONTENTS

PRELUDE

Let everyone be struck with fear,
the whole world tremble,
and the heavens exult
when Christ, the Son of the living God,
is present on the altar in the hands of a priest!
O wonderful loftiness
and stupendous dignity!
O sublime humility!
O humble sublimity!
The Lord of the universe,
God and the Son of God,
so humbles Himself
that He hides Himself
for our salvation
under an ordinary piece of bread!
See the humility of God, brothers,
and *pour out your hearts before Him*
                    (Ps. 62:8 [V 61:9])!
Humble yourselves
that you may be exalted by Him
                    (cf. 1 Pet. 5:6; James 4:10)!
Hold back nothing of yourselves for yourselves,
that He Who gives Himself totally to you
may receive you totally!
                    — Saint Francis of Assisi

(From "Letter to a General Chapter," in *St. Francis of Assisi: Writings for a Gospel Life*, Regis J. Armstrong, OFM Cap., Crossroad Publishing Co., New York, 1994)

INTRODUCTION

For the two thousand years of its history, the center of the life of the Church founded by Jesus Christ has been, as it had to be, the sacrament He initiated the night before His death when He said to the Apostles, "Do this in memory of me." As His own sacrifice, the Paschal Mystery of the Messiah has been repeated by the Church in an essentially mysterious way in the Liturgy of the Eucharist. In Western Christianity this celebration of the Paschal Mystery has been called "the Mass" since the fourth century. And as part of that sacred mystery the followers of the Savior have been mysteriously fed the life of grace by consuming His Body and Blood, fulfilling these awesome and mysterious words of the Lord: ". . . unless you eat the flesh of the Son of man and drink his blood, you have no life in you . . ." (Jn 6:53). It remains a painful mystery to me how those dedicated to being disciples of Christ can prayerfully read the words of our Lord and not be filled with an insatiable desire to receive this divinely given nourishment called since ancient times the Banquet of the Lord or Holy Communion. It should be a surprise to no one that the Eucharist, called more affectionately the most Blessed Sacrament, has been and will ever be the center of life of the Catholic and apostolic Church.

For at least a thousand years a popular and spiritually effective response to the Paschal Mystery of Christ's life, death, and resurrection, the mystery by which all who are saved come to eternal life (even those who innocently do not know Him), has been the devotion to the presence of Christ in the Eucharist. Even apart from the time of the actual celebration of the Eucharist great saints and poor sinners in the Catholic Church have prayed, worshiped, wept, and rejoiced before the Blessed Sacrament. Since the time of Saint Francis and Saint Thomas Aquinas in the thirteenth century there has not been a single Catholic saint for whom this devotion to the Eucharist has not been an integral part of the spiritual life. In fact the devotion itself is rooted in the teachings of the Church Fathers, and may have arisen in practice by the end of the sixth century. From Saint Clare of Assisi and Saint Juliana, who proposed the Feast of Corpus Christi in the thirteenth century, to such great

Christians of our time as Mother Teresa, Dorothy Day, and the Baroness Catherine de Hueck, devout women have been outstanding in their devotion to the presence of the Lord in the Blessed Sacrament. Whether I am visiting the Dominican Sisters of Hawthorne in their home for those dying with terminal cancer, or I am at Mother Angelica's convent with its TV stations abutting the Chapel of Eucharistic Adoration, I am aware of the very special call that this devotion makes to devout women.

Despite this "cloud of witnesses" there have always been critics. Some of these have been devoted to the Eucharist themselves but have been annoyed or even alarmed by excesses or rather by what they see as eccentricities of devotion. Some of the most distinguished liturgists of our time have sought to bring this devotion into line with the rest of Christian piety and its response to the revelation of God's love for us in the Paschal Mystery.[1] Their concerns will be considered and, hopefully, wisely used in this book.

Others have displayed in varying degrees a distasteful or even frightening hostility to the Eucharistic Presence and to the devotional piety it so obviously inspires. As we shall see, attacks on the Eucharist and the presence of Christ that it presents to believers have inspired cynicism, mockery, blasphemy, sacrilege, and even physical attack. This dark side of the human response to the presence of Christ is in itself intriguing and provides a horrifying echo of the cries of the evil spirits often reported in the Gospels, "What have you to do with us, Jesus of Nazareth?" (Lk 4:34). Since no account of Eucharistic devotion is complete without this dark side, we shall also consider its meaning and its various degrees and expressions in these pages.

Different from these hostile attitudes but certainly disturbing to the many devout Catholics is an obvious minimizing of Eucharistic devotion by some clergy and religious educators. This deliberate effort to minimize or even eradicate devotion to the Real Presence of Christ in the Blessed Sacrament is observable on all sides. One hears complaints everywhere. "The Eucharist is not even in our parish church but in a two-by-four room down the hall!" Young Christians and especially those who might think of a vocation to the priesthood or religious life respond very enthusiastically to this devotion when made aware of it. But many say that even though they attended church regularly or went to Catholic school they have never heard of the Real Presence. One discouraged seminarian reported the big joke in his seminary to me: "The only real presence are the ones you get for Christmas."

An example of well-intentioned but disastrous misrepresentation of the Holy Eucharist is to be found in a popular article in which the author reduces a church to a dining room. He writes in *U.S. Catholic* in 1970, "The essential things in the church are something to eat and the people to eat it. . . . In a sense it is they, not a spoken formula, which makes Christ present."[2] The amazing thing about this article is that it was popularly received and represented a point of view that had much currency right after the Vatican Council. It still determines much of the architecture of churches, which come more and more to resemble steak-and-stein type eateries. This point of view incredibly ignores two thousand years of Catholic history, the writings of all the Fathers and Doctors of the Church, and particularly dispenses completely with the piety that was inspired by the liturgical reform. The author of this article must have studied the encyclicals *Mediator Dei* and *Mystici Corporis Christi* of Pope Pius XII when he was in the seminary. Apparently he completely dispenses with these monumental documents of liturgical history. Without being too critical of this author I think it is not unjust or uncharitable to point out that he reflected a point of view that was very popular at that time but that from this perspective really looks hackneyed.

It is worth noting that this same magazine twenty-five years later carried a remarkably positive article on the perpetual adoration of the Eucharist by a writer from the Catholic Worker Movement. This devotion, which requires a continuous presence of adoring Christians before the exposed Eucharist, is now observed in hundreds of parishes. We will later discuss the experience of the parish community of Sacred Heart Cathedral in Winona, Minnesota.[3] Nevertheless, skepticism and even hostility to the devotion to the Eucharistic Presence of Christ is still very widespread in the Catholic Church in the United States and other English-speaking countries.

The members of the Church — laity, religious, and clergy — are confused and intimidated by this sad state of affairs. This book is meant to provide information, encouragement, and, where needed, ammunition in the present conflict over devotion to the presence of Christ in the Holy Eucharist. It is not written at the level of the professional theological discourse, but it does provide instruction on the official teaching of the Church and refers to useful theological sources. Because this is a devotion that took root in the first millennium of the Church and flourished in the Middle Ages, the history of Eucharistic worship is thoroughly and interestingly described in the second part of this book by James Monti, a very competent researcher on theological and liturgical subjects and author of the fascinating work *The Week of Salvation: History and Traditions of Holy Week* (Our Sunday Visitor, 1993). These origins are often completely unknown in an age suffering from a bad case of historical and cultural amnesia.

What Is Devotion?

Although this book is meant to provide a summary of the theology and history of belief in the Real Presence, it is above all about devotion, or a loving response. At its best, religious devotion is what Saint Paul so beautifully describes in 1 Corinthians 11 as "charity." Loving devotion is when theology and psychology come together. Devotion (a word meaning dedication of one's being) is the place where the word of God planted by the Divine Sower of the parable takes root in the life and being of the believer. Too little attention is paid to devotion by many contemporary scholars, considering that it is the grass roots of all religious experience. Without devotion there would soon be no clergy or theologians or church officials, because there would be no one to come to church and pay the bills and supply the payrolls. In a time of threadbare and basically ineffective religiosity, with a growing wasteland of dull intellectualism on one side, and a wacky New Age return to poorly understood anthropological symbolism on the other, a serious look at the most powerful and popular of all Catholic devotions is certainly a worthwhile endeavor. And if someone is disinclined to promote this form of piety, he might at least refrain from disturbing the very large number of faithful who do find great meaning and love of God and His children in the presence of the loving Savior. Finally, this book is meant to be an act of grateful dedication along with being a determined defense. The Church in its devotion to the Eucharistic Presence echoes the cry of the children of Israel when they were surrounded by people who did not understand them or accept their unique faith and pure worship. "For what great nation is there that has a god so near to it as the Lord our God is to us. . . ?" (Dt 4:7).

If devotion to the presence of Christ in the Eucharist is important to your spiritual life, if you want to explain, defend, or encourage this prayerful form of piety that so powerfully expresses the Paschal Mystery, then this book is written for you. If on the other hand you feel left out or are puzzled by this devotion that means so much to others but has little meaning in your life, then you may find profit in this book as well.

FATHER BENEDICT GROESCHEL

ENDNOTES

1. See Fr. Hans A. Reinhold, *The American Parish and the Roman Liturgy*, 1958, pp. 10-13, 67.
2. Rev. Henry Fehren, "Where Is the Dining Room?" *U.S. Catholic*, Sept. 1970, Vol. 35, p. 41.
3. Jerry Daoust, "Could you not wait one hour with me?" *U.S. Catholic*, Jan. 1995, Vol. 60, pp. 33-36.

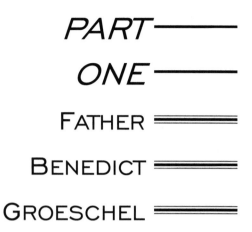

PART——
ONE——
FATHER
BENEDICT
GROESCHEL

Chapter 1

The Mystery of the Eucharist

The sacrament of the Holy Eucharist is one of the seven mysterious signs that offer the life-giving and unmerited relationship of parental love with God to the whole being of the broken and bent human creature. These seven powerful and fundamentally incomprehensible realities are the work of the only one who could possibly have made them, the God-man, given when He lived among us. They bring together eternity and time, divinity and humanity, and consequently can only have been made by Him who walked the earth but who, in His own words, "descended from heaven" (Jn 3:13). Each of these seven signs brings the free and loving help of the Triune God to us human beings who experience in the most painful way the burden of human nature as it now exists. This is a nature good but wounded, seeking eternity but captured in time, drawn irresistibly to life but trapped in the web of death. Each of these signs — Baptism, Confirmation, the Holy Eucharist, Reconciliation (or the forgiveness of sins), the Anointing of the Sick, Holy Orders (or the conferral of the power of ministry), and Matrimony — finds its own foundation in the New Testament. The reader would do well to review the second section of the new *Catechism of the Catholic Church* to learn about these sacraments. These seven gifts are in some ways similar to the gifts of nature, such as sight, hearing, and memory, all profoundly mysterious; and ultimately the sacraments are even more mysterious, because they are founded in eternity. That is to say that they are essentially supernatural realities. Please be well aware that a good deal of contemporary writing on the sacraments is calculated to diminish, disguise, or even deny the supernatural element in sacraments.

"I Love a Mystery"

A half century ago there was a radio program, *I Love a Mystery*, which told about the wicked goings-on of some bad guys who were defeated each week by Jack, Doc, and Reggie. I loved this program because in the end we listeners always had the opportunity to try to solve the mystery with their help. I transferred this love to the objective study of the mysteries of nature that are the subject of science. It didn't matter to me if these were questions in biology, physics, psychology, or astronomy. I loved them all. What a great thrill it is for me even now to live in the age of discovery for the science of astronomy. Almost every day one can read of the latest theory or discovery scientists are making in astronomy. I know that the beginning of all these mysteries is the greatest of natural mysteries, the unsolvable one: What was there before this wonderful machine of the cosmos began billions of years ago? This is the natural mystery that crosses over into the world beyond matter: Where did it all come from? I love to soar from the details of subatomic particles and the organization of DNA molecules to the clouds of galaxies that hang like great star cities in the empty stretches of the cosmos. I memorized these words from Psalm 102 as cited in Hebrews when I was a teenager, and I still frequently go over them in my mind: "Thou in the beginning, O Lord, didst found the earth: and the works of thy hands are the heavens. They shall perish, but thou shalt continue: and they shall all grow old as a garment. And as a vesture shalt thou change them, and they shall be changed: but thou art the selfsame, and thy years shall not fail" (Heb 1:10-12 [Douay-Rheims edition]; see Ps 102:25-27 [101:26-28 in Douay-Rheims]).

Writing of the origin of the universe, Dr. Robert Jastrow, professor emeritus of astronomy at Columbia University, put the mystery of the cosmos in scientific terms but acknowledged that the question goes over into theology. He had discovered that the exploration of the mystery of existence must always lead to that infinite Reality religious people call God:

Consider the enormity of the problem. Science has proven that the Universe exploded into being at a certain moment. It asks, What cause produced this effect? Who or what put the matter and energy into the Universe? Was the Universe created out of nothing, or was it gathered together out of pre-existing materials? And science cannot answer these questions, because, according to the astronomers, in the first moments of its existence the Universe was compressed to an extraordinary degree, and consumed by the heat of a fire beyond human imagination. The shock of that instant must have destroyed every particle of evidence that could have yielded a clue to the cause of the great explosion. An entire world, rich in structure and history, may have existed before our Universe appeared; but if it did, science cannot tell what kind of world it was. A sound explanation may exist for the explosive birth of our Universe; but if it does, science cannot find out what the explanation is. The scientist's pursuit of the past ends in the moment of creation.

This is an exceedingly strange development, unexpected by all but the theologians. They have always accepted the word of the Bible: In the beginning God created heaven and earth. To which St. Augustine added, "Who can understand this mystery or explain it to others?" It is unexpected because science has had such extraordinary success in tracing the chain of cause and effect backward in time. We have been able to connect the appearance of man on this planet to the crossing of the threshold of life, the manufacture of the chemical ingredients of life within stars that have long since expired, the formation of those stars out of the primal mists, and the expansion and cooling of the parent cloud of gases out of the cosmic fireball.

Now we would like to pursue that inquiry farther back in time, but the barrier to further progress seems insurmountable. It is not a matter of another year, another decade of work, another measurement, or another theory; at this moment it seems as though science will never be able to raise the curtain on the mystery of creation. For the scientist who has lived by his faith in the power of reason, the story ends like a bad dream. He has scaled the mountains of ignorance; he is about to conquer the highest peak; as he pulls himself over the final rock, he is greeted by a band of theologians who have been sitting there for centuries.[1]

The truly great scientists have never run away from mystery or naïvely thought they could solve all mysteries. The following well-known observation of Albert Einstein summarizes the attraction of natural mystery and opens the door to the next and even greater realm of mysteries, those of faith: "The most beautiful experience we can have is the mysterious. It is the fundamental emotion which stands at the cradle of true art and true science."[2]

A Beginning of Wonder

While I would enjoy just taking you on a spectacular journey through the mysteries of natural science, some solvable and (as Jastrow has indicated) others unsolvable, like the origins of the universe, ever to be wrapped in darkness, such a journey would finally leave you unfulfilled. Modern man has finally been brought to the humbling but intelligent realization that he can't know everything, that his mind is not the measure of everything in the heavens and on earth, especially in the heavens.

This realization brings us to the greatest mysteries, those of faith. For the person willing and gifted by God to fly on the wings of faith in divine revelation, the truly greatest mysteries appear over the horizon of this world when one is lifted up to see all experience by the light of endless day. People ask me in an almost bewildered way, "How can you be a believer in God and still be a psychologist?" I answer with an even greater bewilderment, "How could I possibly be a psychologist and not believe in God?" I have observed the incredible complexity of the human being, of memory and intelligence, of emotion and intuition, of love and hate, of emotional slavery and freedom — all in an hour spent with a single human being. And I have never met a person who wanted anything but real life. Some were tired and wounded by this half-life that we lead now. But all, without exception, yearned for a fuller, more real, unending life of joy and love. They deeply desired unending life, especially those who did not believe that such a life was possible.

This thought brings us to the really great mystery, the incredible source of all things, the Maker and final goal of atoms and stars, of flowers and of the human mind. This Being calls to us. He calls us by what He gives and takes, by what we have and by what we long for. But He also calls to us by sounds, by words spoken to Abraham, Moses, the prophets, to Zechariah, Joseph, and finally in a crescendo to a young girl named Mary. And all of these people said "yes" to the voice that called them. Thus does the greatest mystery enter the world.

This word, "mystery," simply means that which is really there but cannot be seen or understood. We only know that a mysterious reality is there by its effects that we can in some limited way experience.

In a recent discussion of the meaning of mystery, Professor Sixto Garcia of St. Vincent's Regional Seminary in Boynton Beach, Florida, made an important observation that I think will help us in the appreciation of mystery. We often think a mystery is that which is simply puzzling to the mind because one lacks the facts that would make the matter clear. So some people enjoy what is called a "murder mystery." This is not what we mean by the theologically mysterious, Dr. Garcia pointed out. I was relieved to hear this because I loathe murder mysteries. The good professor then launched into a fervent Latino discussion of divine truth being mysterious because it is infinite. This is of course what Saint John of the Cross meant when he wrote with equal Hispanic gusto:

> Such is faith to the soul — it informs us of matters we have never seen or known, either in themselves or in their likenesses; in fact nothing like them exists. The light of natural knowledge does not show us the object of faith, since this object is unproportioned to any of the senses. Yet, we come to know it through hearing, by believing what faith teaches us, blinding our natural light and bringing it into submission. St. Paul states: *Fides ex auditu.* [Rom. 10:17] This amounts to saying that faith is not a knowledge derived from the senses, but an assent of the soul to what enters through hearing. . . .
>
> Faith, manifestly, is a dark night for man, but in this very way it gives him light. The more darkness it brings upon him, the more light it sheds. For by blinding it illumines him, according to those words of Isaias that if you do not believe you will not understand, that is, you will not have light. [Is. 7:9][3]

The greatest mystery brings time and eternity together, this life and the world beyond, a reality that all human hearts long for or will long for as death approaches. The ultimate expression of this mystery is Christ, the Word of God, a Word without beginning or end, but spoken in time. Do not go near the sacraments without falling on your face before the mystery of Christ (it is my guess that Catholics who have trouble with the Church's teaching on the Holy Eucharist have never really fallen on their faces before Christ, or perhaps they once did but now have forgotten what it meant to do so). The following powerful lines from Venerable John Henry Newman, the luminous theologian and intellect of nineteenth-century England who was named Pope Leo XIII's first cardinal, eloquently state the necessity for a profound and personal faith in order for anyone to cope creatively with the Christian revelation and especially with the Eucharist:

> I come then to this conclusion; — if I must submit my reason to mysteries, it is not much matter whether it is a mystery more or a mystery less, when faith anyhow is the very essence of all religion, when the main difficulty to an inquirer is firmly to hold that there is a Living God, in spite of the darkness which surrounds Him, the Creator, Witness, and Judge of men. When once the mind is broken in, as it must be, to the belief of a Power above it, when once it understands, that it is not itself the measure of all things in heaven and earth, it will have little difficulty in going forward. I do not say it will, or can, go on to other truths, without conviction; I do not say it ought to believe the Catholic faith without grounds and motives; but I say that, when once it believes in God, the great obstacle to faith has been taken away, — a proud, self-sufficient spirit. When once a man really, with the eyes of his soul and by the power of Divine grace, recognises his Creator, he has passed a line; that has happened to him which cannot happen twice; he has bent his stiff neck, and triumphed over himself. If he believes that God has no beginning, why not believe that He is Three yet One? if he owns that God created space, why not own also that He can cause a body to subsist without dependence on place? if he is obliged to grant that God created all things out of nothing, why doubt His power to change the substance of bread into the Body of His Son?[4]

We see then that the experience of faith in God leads to the other mysteries, and Newman selects the Eucharist to illustrate these. There are many mysteries that lie between the Divine Being and the mystery of the Eucharist, mysteries too numerous for us to mention here but well developed in the first two sections of the *Catechism of the Catholic Church* on the creed and the sacraments. While it is an almost irresistible impulse to write of these mysteries, we must confine ourselves to the mysterious Eucharist.[5]

The Church Receives and Gives the Sacraments

Along with giving the Good News of Salvation to the world by certifying and publishing the New Testament and preserving the teaching Christ gave to the Apostles, the celebration and distribution of sacraments is the essential duty of the Church. The source of all supernatural grace and the fountain of the sacraments is the life of Jesus the Messiah from the announcement of His miraculous conception in the womb of the Virgin Mary to His return to the Father, when He ascended beyond the time and place of the material cosmos to a domain of being that eye has not seen nor has it entered into our minds to think (cf. 1 Cor 2:9). A theological shorthand for this central element of human history is the "Paschal Mystery." This term encompasses all historical events from the coming of the Son of God to this race of thinking animals, to His mysterious passage beyond death to life without end.

In his powerful study — *The Mysteries of Christianity* — Matthias Scheeben, the nineteenth-century theologian, has summed up the need for a sense of mystery quite eloquently:

> The greater, the more sublime, and the more divine Christianity is, the more inexhaustible, inscrutable, unfathomable, and mysterious its subject matter must be. If its teaching is worthy of the only-begotten Son of God, if the Son of God had to descend from the bosom of His Father to initiate us into this teaching, could we expect anything else than the revelation of the deepest mysteries locked up in God's heart? Could we expect anything else than disclosures concerning a higher, invisible world, about divine and heavenly things, which "eye hath not seen, nor ear heard," and which could not enter into the heart of any man? And

if God has sent us His own Spirit to teach us all truth, the Spirit of His truth, who dwells in God and there searches the deep things of God, should this Spirit reveal nothing new, great, and wondrous, should He teach us no sublime secrets?

Far from repudiating Christianity or regarding it with suspicious eyes because of its mysteries, we ought to recognize its divine grandeur in these very mysteries. So essential to Christianity are its mysteries that in its character of truth revealed by the Son of God and the Holy Spirit it would stand convicted of intrinsic contradiction if it brought forward no mysteries. Its Author would carry with Him a poor recommendation for His divinity if He taught us only such truths as in the last analysis we could have learned from a mere man, or could have perceived and adequately grasped by our own unaided powers.[6]

Your head should now be reeling with the thought of all of these mysteries. If it is not, go back and read the last paragraphs over again slowly because you missed what was being said. You can never sufficiently deal with the mystery of the Eucharist or the particular subject of this book, the devotion to the presence of Christ in this sacrament, unless you have a vibrant sense of mystery and have an awesome awareness of the incredible reality of this sacrament.

Running Away from Mystery

A person may do many things with what is assumed to be a mystery. Most of the time we ignore mysteries. They are frightening, or they will take too much time, or they will disturb our artificially ordered universe. The astronomer Robert Jastrow, whom we cited earlier, observes that scientists particularly dislike and are traumatized by mystery. This eminent scientist gives away the secret of why scientists refuse to grapple with the mystery of creation. Jastrow describes the shock that the discovery of the mysterious origin of the universe at a single moment of time and in a single place was to the scientific community. It presented questions that science could not answer. Jastrow describes it this way: "When that happens, the scientist has lost control. If he really examined the implications, he would be traumatized. As usual when

faced with trauma, the mind reacts by ignoring the implications —
in science this is known as 'refusing to speculate' — or trivializing
the origin of the world by calling it the Big Bang, as if the Universe
were a firecracker."[7]

The famous experimental psychologist B.F. Skinner shortly
before his death wrote in an autobiographical piece that for years
he had pretended to be an atheist because he did not know what to
do with God. Finally, as the end of his life approached, he expressed
his conviction that God exists, and even returned to the radical
Protestantism of his youth.[8] All those years this very bright man
had been doing what so many others do — he was running away
from mystery by pretending it did not exist.

Unlike Skinner and many others, some of us could not run
away from these mysteries. When I am asked why I became a priest,
I have to confess that at a very distinct moment in the second grade,
in the parish church of Our Lady of Victory in Jersey City, I knew
that I was supposed to be a priest. A vocation, a mysterious call,
was there from that moment. I did not become a priest because of
an intuition of mystery but because of a grace or gift from God. It
was there. Bang! But this vocation — or conviction (it is clearer and
more permanent than any other conviction I have ever had) —
opened my mind to mystery and to the need to explore mysteries of
faith.

I was delighted to add to the mysteries of the material world
studied by science the world greater than nature studied by philosophy and theology. The history of religion is filled with the accounts of people, some great, most like myself, just ordinary souls,
who had an eye on both worlds. As I approach the end of my visit to
this planet, I am grateful that I was aware of both dimensions of
reality and was blessed by Providence to experience the search for
truth in the two domains of science and faith.[9] But as a child I was
unaware of the distinction. I just loved strange places, peculiar
things, eccentric people, museums, zoos, planetariums, and of
course, churches, temples, synagogues, and anywhere else that
people were calling upon the Author of nature and grace. Consequently, it is no surprise that very early I discovered the mystery of
the Eucharist and began an exploration that continues to this very
day. I will trace out this exploration for you and in doing so will

review the basic teachings of Catholic Christianity on the mystery of the Living Bread come down from heaven (Jn 6:51).

A Child's View of the Mystery of the Eucharist

The Dollhouse ✱ One of my earliest memories, when I was about four years old, is that of being carried to church on Sunday by my father because we were late for Mass and it was faster that way. The Church of Corpus Christi in Hasbrouck Heights, New Jersey, is a building with arches and nooks and a great place for a lover of mystery. On the way back home my father explained that Jesus lived in the golden box in the center of the altar, and that in a few years I would be able to receive Him in Holy Communion. I tried for months to look into the golden box, but it had a white veil over it. The best way I could deal with this puzzling presence was with an analogy (I did not know the word). The inside of the box must be like the dollhouse my cousin Julie had. There must be a tiny bed, a chair, a desk, and a light. For a couple of years I lived comfortably with this explanation, the theory of the dollhouse. I was disappointed at not being able to see either Christ or the inside of the house because of the white veil. This analogy contains the error of thinking that Christ's presence is a local presence. Working on this primitive theory, one may arrive at the idea that Christ's presence is localized, and then comes the absurd notion that He is in the literal sense a prisoner in the tabernacle, or if you drop the Eucharistic Bread, the Host, He will get hurt. This theory had to be replaced.

The Shadow ✱ My materialistic theory went out the window in first grade when Sister Longinus explained that Christ was invisible. He was there but not seen. Now this was a big improvement, since I was unsatisfied with the dollhouse theory myself and, like all inveterate explorers, knew there had to be a better explanation. Almost all children my age in the early 1940s spent Sunday afternoon at five o'clock being terrified by a program called *The Shadow*. We listened, mesmerized, to the adventures of Lamont Cranston, who was a very good guy with the ability to make himself disappear while remaining present and even able to speak. Orson Welles provided the spooky voice, and it all seemed very real to me. No doubt about it — the original *Shadow* was Jesus. He had given us the little white Communion wafer so that we could keep track of where

He was. Since you could pray to Him anywhere, He was not bound to the Host, but it helped you to know that He was present. I prepared to receive my first Holy Communion and was well instructed that His presence, even His Body and Blood, was contained mysteriously in the Host (I tactfully avoided using *The Shadow* theory when Father Ed examined me for my first Communion). Since I loved mystery, First Communion was a great day for me, with the exception that I felt disappointed insofar as my behavior did not improve as much as I had hoped when I started to receive Holy Communion every week. I was really comfortable with *The Shadow* theory, although at bottom it was unsatisfactory like the dollhouse theory because Lamont Cranston's body actually disappeared and Jesus' Body was really there. I suppose that I was accidentally involved in the notion, long ago rejected by the Church, that Christ's presence in the Eucharist is only spiritual.[10]

Although the author of *The Shadow* was not presenting a Eucharistic theology, and *The Shadow* could move things around, somehow my use of this image could have left me with the view of some of the Protestant reformers, that is, that Christ's presence is only spiritual, not physical or permanent. They thought that the presence departed after Holy Communion. It is interesting to note that Luther did not accept this theory and neither did the divines of the then new Anglican Church.

Substance and Accident ✳ I remember quite clearly the dawn of abstract reasoning — the ability to deal with ideas that philosophers call universal concepts. I think I became really aware of this new ability in the Museum of Natural History. I realized that all flying creatures from the prehistoric flying reptiles (such as pterodactyls) to hummingbirds belong to a single great classification. They did not look alike, but they were all birds, or at least they were becoming birds.

It was not long before this ability to reason abstractly was applied to the mystery of Christ's Body. Several different sisters, who taught us so carefully, spoke about substance and accidents, and that in the Eucharist by the power of God the substance of bread and wine were changed into the Body and Blood of Christ. They said that the accidents — the appearances — remained the same, veiling, as it were, the Real Presence of Christ. I had a problem grasping substance until Mother Dolorita brought in a green orange and an orange-colored orange. Both were real oranges but one was missing its orange appearance. It looked like a misshapen lime. I grasped then that orangeness is a substance. It makes a thing (an orange, in this case) capable of producing other oranges. The color orange is just an accident or an appearance — an orange was still an orange if you painted it blue. I recall even now the burst of intellectual pleasure that came to me when I had solved the mystery of the Eucharist — with the help, I was told, of Saint Thomas Aquinas. I even memorized one of Saint Thomas's hymns for the Feast of Corpus Christi. *Lauda Sion* had so much theology tucked away in its verses that I memorized it. The following is an old translation essentially the same as that found in an English missal I had at the time. You'll learn much from carefully contemplating these lines:

Lauda Sion[11]

Sion, lift thy voice and sing;
Praise thy Saviour and thy King;
Praise with hymns thy Shepherd true.
Strive thy best to praise Him well,
Yet doth He all praise excel;
None can ever reach His due.

See to-day before us laid
The living and life-giving Bread,
Theme for praise and joy profound.
The same which at the sacred board
Was by our incarnate Lord,
Giv'n to His apostles round.

Let the praise be loud and high;
Sweet and tranquil be the joy
Felt to-day in every breast;
On this festival divine,
Which records the origin
Of the glorious Eucharist.

On this table of the King,
Our new paschal offering
Brings to end the olden rite.
Here, for empty shadows fled,

Is reality instead;
Here, instead of darkness, light.

His own act, at supper seated,
Christ ordained to be repeated,
In His memory divine;
Wherefore now, with adoration,
We the Host of our salvation
Consecrate from bread and wine.

Hear what holy Church maintaineth,
That the bread its substance changeth
Into flesh, the wine to blood.
Doth it pass thy comprehending?
Faith, the law of sight transcending,
Leaps to things not understood.

Here, beneath these signs are hidden
Priceless things, to sense forbidden;
Signs, not things, are all we see:
Flesh from bread, and blood from wine,
Yet is Christ in either sign
All entire, confessed to be.

They too who of Him partake,
Sever not, nor rend, nor break,
But entire their Lord receive.
Whether one or thousands eat,
All receive the selfsame meat,
Nor the less for others leave.

Both the wicked and the good
Eat of this celestial food;
But with ends how opposite!
Here 'tis life, and there 'tis death,
The same, yet issuing to each,
In a difference infinite.

Nor a single doubt retain,
When they break the host in twain,
But that in each part remain,
What was in the whole before.
Since the simple sign alone
Suffers change in state or form,

The signified remaining one
And the same for evermore.

Lo! upon the altar lies,
Hidden deep from human eyes,
Bread of angels from the skies,
Made the food of mortal man:
Children's meat, to dogs denied:
In old types foresignified:
In the manna heav'n-supplied,
Isaac, and the paschal Lamb.

Jesu! Shepherd of the sheep!
Thou Thy flock in safety keep.
Living Bread! thy life supply;
Strengthen us, or else we die;
Fill us with celestial grace;
Thou, who feedest us below!
Source of all we have or know!
Grant that with Thy saints above,
Sitting at the feast of love,
We may see Thee face to face.

Amen. Alleluia.

I studied with a good deal of enthusiasm the teaching of the Church on the mysterious words of the institution of the Eucharist and their interpretation. The Last Supper was obviously central, and the words "... this is my body ... this is my blood ..." (Mt 26:26-28), when literally interpreted, left no room for any other way to approach this mystery. These words became the center of my religious perception and life — that is, along with the words "... unless you eat the flesh of the Son of man and drink his blood, you have no life in you ..." (Jn 6:53). From that time to this day I have never doubted that the Eucharist is really, though mysteriously, the Body and Blood of Christ.

Corpus Christi ✹ Since I was a very active altar boy, I became quite familiar with every aspect of the Liturgy — even solemn pontifical Mass, when the elderly and venerable Archbishop Thomas Walsh would come to celebrate it at the Dominican motherhouse in Caldwell, New Jersey. But my favorite day of all was Corpus Christi, which the sister told us the French called the Feast of God, *le fête Dieu.* We practiced for weeks and knew in Latin all the hymns Saint Thomas Aquinas had written for the celebration. Each one was different and had a beautiful melody of its own with the most poetic Latin phrases: *Pange Lingua, Adoro Te Devote, Lauda Sion, Tantum Ergo.*[12] Then there was *O Salutaris,* excerpted from one of Saint Thomas's other Eucharistic hymns. There were newer hymns too — *Ave Verum, Panis Angelicus,* and even in English, "Soul of My Savior." Most of these were sung in parts with music written by great composers. We practiced for weeks before the feast, and I made my way up to the great position of crossbearer, leading the procession when I was an eighth grader. The whole school and much of the parish participated. The pastor carried the golden monstrance containing the Blessed Sacrament under a canopy borne by the leaders of the parish. The little children walked slowly behind the cross dropping baskets of rose petals on the paths, making a carpet of flowers. The old Italian people made a beautiful carpet of rose petals with the designs of different colors before the door of the church.

Mother Dolorita gave me strict instructions not to disturb the petals because only the crossbearer and the pastor walked down the center of the path. Everyone else retreated to the side of the path. When I got to the carpet of roses, unnoticed I walked several feet without touching the ground — by a preternatural gift (smile). I was at the pinnacle of my ecclesiastical career. Everything has been downhill since, because now I know the price you have to pay to give yourself completely to God. I did not understand this when I was the crossbearer.

Later on in life I would hear of the great Corpus Christi processions in Europe. In Toledo, Spain, I came across the elaborate preparations being made weeks before Corpus Christi. The huge monstrance weighing hundreds of pounds would be carried solemnly through miles of canopied streets. The whole city was being scrubbed. We will return later to the significance of these great cultural events and how they contribute to (or in rare instances detract from) the devotion to the Blessed Sacrament. Anyone who doubts the possibility of the presence of Christ in the Eucharist being a focal point for all kinds of beautiful, social, and cultural activities, including a fervent appeal for social justice to the poor, ought to attend a Eucharistic Congress like the one held in Philadelphia in 1976. All that any one of these hundreds of thousands of people sees is the appearance of bread and wine, but all profoundly respond to the teaching of faith that the Body and Blood of Christ are with them — all, regardless of social stations or position in the eyes of the Church or the world.

What Is for Real?

If there was anything that one learned in religious education and by participating in the life of the Church in the mid-twentieth century it was that the consecrated bread and wine of the Eucharist really contained the Body and Blood of Christ. He is totally present in each particle of bread and drop of wine. That was the most obvious conclusion of this mystery. One did not speak above a whisper in the presence of the Eucharist. We were taught to genuflect (or bend the knee) every time we passed the tabernacle. If by accident in distributing Communion a Host fell to the ground, the spot was marked with a cloth, and after Mass the priest would carefully wash this spot. The linens of the altar were meticulously washed three times and beautifully ironed, and the brass doors of the tabernacle gleamed. Religious communities often had their own special ceremonies of devotion. The Dominicans made the most profound bow resembling something you might see in the Orient. The Capuchins genuflected by putting their faces to the floor. Certain convents of cloistered nuns held a vigil of perpetual adoration, with sisters praying before the tabernacle or the monstrance with the exposed Sacrament for many hours every day, or even perpetually, that is, day and night.

I recall my first visit to the Blessed Sacrament Monastery, a convent of cloistered nuns in Yonkers, New York, when I was just ordained. A charming old Irish sister with a clover-sweet brogue, Sister Ann Marie, took care of all the external business of the convent including the sacristy. She was one of a very intrepid but largely unknown band of extern, or "out," sisters who represent cloistered convents. I asked her if it were true that the nuns kept vigil all night. She answered with that familiarity with the sacred that is characteristic of the friends of God, "O Father, they give the Lord no peace; they're at Him night and day."

In the piety of that time stories abounded about great acts of reverence or even mysterious signs that surrounded the presence of Christ. The point of all of these accounts was that Christ is really present veiled in the bread and wine. Some were historical, some were accounts of miracles like the bleeding Host of Bolsena, some were legends like animals that knelt before Saint Anthony when he carried the Blessed Sacrament, and some were powerful myths like Lord Tennyson's rendition of the Holy Grail story. For the contemporary reader to have some feeling of the reverence and certitude of faith that surrounded the sacrament, the following account of the Hapsburg King Charles II is worth including.

In February of 1685 King Charles II of Spain took a large group of courtiers and ordinary folk on royal procession out into the country for what we would call a royal picnic. As they were making their way out of the city the cortege met a priest who was crossing the same road carrying the Blessed Sacrament to a poor sick gardener. The priest was only accompanied by an acolyte carrying a candle. When the king discovered that the priest was carrying the sacrament, he stopped the carriage and knelt on both knees to adore Christ in the Eucharist. Then the king entreated the priest very respectfully to enter the royal carriage and sit in his place with the acolyte. Shutting the door with the new occupants inside, the king then took the reins of the carriage in his own hand and drove the horses on foot the whole length of the road, which was long and muddy.

When they reached the house of the poor gardener, the king opened the door and helped the priest down from the carriage; after kneeling again on the ground in worship, he rose and with his head uncovered followed the priest into the little cottage. During the whole ceremony that followed, the king remained in profound adoration. After the dying man had received the Blessed Sacrament, the king spoke to him very kindly and left him with a generous sum of money. He also promised that the gardener's only daughter, who was faced with becoming an orphan, would be assigned a suitable dowry. The king then brought the priest back to the church from which he had come. The priest was at least able to persuade the king not to walk along the road again, but as one further act of homage to the sacrament the monarch chose to ride in a separate carriage behind that carrying the priest. When they reached their destination the king accompanied the priest into the church and received the benediction that was customarily given to those who assist with the Communion of the sick. While all this was going on, the huge procession of noblemen and ordinary people had grown immensely, and there was much comment about the devotion of the king.[13]

This moving account, which is historical and not part of the reverent mythology of the Middle Ages, illustrates the fundamental belief in the Eucharist as the sacrament of Christ's presence with His Church, a belief common to both great wings of ancient Christianity in East and West. From the time of the Apostles and Fathers, the main body of the Church, at that time united (later divided between Rome and Constantinople), has held that the bread and wine of the Eucharist really contain Christ's Body and Blood.

The Earliest Witnesses — Apostles and Evangelists

It goes beyond the scope of this book to give the whole biblical and patristic foundations of the teaching that the Eucharist is really the Body and Blood of Christ. An excellent summary of the essential Christian teaching is given by my friend Monsignor James T. O'Connor in his most informative and readable book, *The Hidden Manna.*[14]

The Gospels give a full account of the institution of the Eucharist:

> Then came the day of Unleavened Bread, on which the passover lamb had to be sacrificed. So Jesus sent Peter and John, saying, "Go and prepare the passover for us, that we may eat it." . . . And they went . . . and they prepared the passover.
>
> And when the hour came, he sat at table, and the apostles with him. And he said to them, "I have earnestly desired to eat this passover with you before I suffer; for I tell you I shall not eat it until it is fulfilled in the kingdom of God." . . . And he took bread, and when he had given thanks he broke it and gave it to them, saying, "This is my body which is given for you. Do this in remembrance of me." And likewise the cup after supper, saying, "This cup which is poured out for you is the new covenant in my blood."
>
> — Luke 22:7-20; see also Matthew 26:17-29, Mark 14:12-25, and 1 Corinthians 11:23-26

These powerful Gospel texts must be seen in the light of two other equally powerful texts, one from the Gospel of Saint John, when Jesus speaks to the synagogue of Capernaum:

> "I am the living bread which came down from heaven; if any one eats of this bread, he will live for ever; and the bread which I shall give for the life of the world is my flesh."
>
> The Jews then disputed among themselves, saying, "How can this man give us his flesh to eat?" So Jesus said to them, "Truly, truly, I say to you, unless you eat the flesh of the Son of man and drink his blood, you have no life in you; he who eats my flesh and drinks my blood has eternal life, and I will raise him up at the last day. For my flesh is food indeed, and my blood is drink indeed. He who eats my flesh and drinks my blood abides in me, and I in him. As the living Father sent me, and I live because of the Father, so he who eats me will live because of me. This is the bread which came down from heaven, not such as the fathers ate and died; he who eats this bread will live for ever."
>
> — John 6:51-58

I.COR 1:26

The other text is from Saint Paul, 1 Corinthians 11:23-26: "For I received from the Lord what I also delivered to you, that the Lord Jesus on the night when he was betrayed took bread, and when he had given thanks, he broke it, and said, 'This is my body which is for you. Do this in remembrance of me.' In the same way also the cup, after supper, saying, 'This cup is the new covenant in my blood. Do this, as often as you drink it, in remembrance of me.' For as often as you eat this bread and drink the cup, you proclaim the Lord's death until he comes."

Those Who Took the Place of the Apostles

The latter text of Saint Paul not only indicates that the apostolic Church took very seriously the command of Christ to do this in His memory, but that it also recognized the bread and wine as His real Body and Blood. If one were to have any doubt about how the very ancient Church of the first two centuries interpreted these words, there are abundant quotations from Christian writings of this period proving the reality of the Body and Blood of Christ in the Eucharist. These are available in Monsignor O'Connor's book. A few of the most essential ones are included here.

Saint Ignatius of Antioch ✳ One of the most powerful testimonies comes from the last letters of Saint Ignatius, Bishop of Antioch (only one other bishop served in this city between Peter the Apostle and Ignatius). It was while in transit to Rome, the place of his eventual martyrdom in the year 107, that Ignatius wrote a series of splendid epistles to the various local churches. To the Christian Church of Smyrna he wrote to complain about those who did not receive the Eucharist: "Observe well those who are heterodox in respect to the grace of Jesus Christ that has come to us; see how they are opposed to the mind of God. Charity is of no concern to them, nor are widows and orphans or the oppressed, either those in prison or at liberty, or the hungry or the thirsty. They abstain from the Eucharist and from prayer, because they do not confess that the Eucharist is the Flesh of our Savior Jesus Christ, which suffered for our sins and which, in his goodness, the Father raised. . . . It would be better for them to show love in order [that] they [also] might rise."[15]

In his letter to the Church at Philadelphia, Saint Ignatius links the reality of the Body and Blood to the celebration of the sacrifice of Christ, thus giving very early testimony to the fact that the first Christians saw the celebration of the Eucharist as a sacrifice: "Be careful to observe [only] one Eucharist; for there is only one Flesh of Our Lord Jesus Christ and one cup of union with his Blood, one altar of sacrifice [Gk. *thusiasterion*], as [there is] one bishop with the presbyters and my fellow-servants, the deacons."[16]

Basing his teaching on 1 Corinthians 10:17, Saint Ignatius in his letter to the Ephesians urges the Christians to have only one assembly (this means not to break up), led by one bishop and with "breaking one bread that is the medicine of immortality and the antidote against dying that offers life for all in Jesus Christ."[17]

Without any credible evidence anti-Catholic writers often falsely maintain that belief in the reality of the Body and Blood of Christ and in the Eucharist as a sacrifice began in the Church in the fourth century, after Constantine declared Christianity to be the religion of the Roman Empire. It is alleged, completely without any historical foundation, that large numbers of pagan priests, put out of their jobs by the formal end of the Greco-Roman cult, became Christians in name only and brought their pagan belief in sacrifice with them.

Ignatius of Antioch and several other key patristic writers long before Constantine's edict in 313 clearly demonstrate the fallacy of this claim. No one who knows the writings of the postapostolic Fathers could honestly maintain that the idea of the reality of the Eucharist and its sacramental character came from pagan priests. Since many of these anti-Catholic writers are misled and confused about the Catholic teaching on the reality of the Eucharist, we need to be aware of and ponder the message of the early Christian writers.

Saint Justin Martyr ✽ In his famous *Apologia* dating from 150, Saint Justin Martyr, a philosopher who was converted around 135, wrote the following in the course of his description of the worship service of Christians:

> This word *Amen* in the Hebrew means "Let it be." And when the one who is presiding has given thanks, and all the people have cried out, those whom we call deacons give the bread and wine and water over which the thanksgiving was made [lit., "the eucharistized bread and wine and water"] to be received by each of those present, and then they carry it to those who are absent.
>
> This food we call Eucharist, which no one is allowed to share except the one who believes that our teaching is true, and who has been washed with the washing that is for the remission of sins, and unto regeneration, and so lives as Christ has handed down. For we do not receive these as common bread and common drink; but just as Jesus Christ our Savior, having been made flesh by the word of God, had both flesh and blood for our salvation, so likewise have we learned that the food over which thanks has been given by the prayer of the word which comes from him, and by which our blood and flesh are nourished through a change, is the Flesh and Blood of the same incarnate Jesus. For the Apostles in the memoirs composed by them and that are called Gospels have thus handed on what was commanded them; namely, that Jesus took bread, and when he had given thanks, said, "Do this in remembrance of me; this is my Body"; and that, in like manner,

having taken the cup and given thanks, he said, "This is my Blood," and gave it to them alone.[18]

Saint Justin points out that the devils have handed on a similar thing to be done in the mysteries of Mithras, but that there is a total difference between the two religious events.[19]

In another of his works Justin also calls the Eucharist a sacrifice. Writing in a dialogue with a Jew he names "Trypho," he cites the prophet Malachi (1:10-12), who states that a pure sacrifice will be offered in God's name among the Gentiles. Justin writes, "Already, then, did he prophesy about those sacrifices that are offered to him in every place by us Gentiles, speaking, that is, about the Bread of the Eucharist and the cup of the Eucharist."[20]

Saint Irenaeus ✳ Another important link with the time of the Apostles is Saint Irenaeus, Bishop of Lyons in France. He was born around the year 130 and tells us that as a boy he listened to the preaching of Saint Polycarp, Bishop of Smyrna, who was a disciple of Saint John the Apostle. He writes in his book *Against the Heresies*, condemning those who taught that the human body was not saved:

> Vain in every respect are they who reject the entire dispensation of God, and deny the salvation of the flesh, and spurn its regeneration, saying that it is not capable of incorruption. But if this flesh is not saved, then neither did the Lord redeem us by his Blood, nor is the cup of the Eucharist the Communion of his Blood, or the bread that we break the Communion of his Body. . . .
>
> When, therefore, the cup that has been mixed and the bread that has been made receive the Word of God and become the Eucharist and the Body of Christ, from which the substance of our flesh is increased and supported, how can they affirm that the flesh is incapable of receiving the gift of God, which is life eternal, which flesh is nourished from the Body and Blood of the Lord and is a member of him? . . . And just as the vine planted in the ground fructifies in its season, and as a grain of wheat falling into the earth and decomposing rises with manifold increase by the Spirit of God who contains all things and then, through the wisdom of God, serves for the use of men, and having received the Word of

God become the Eucharist, which is the Body and Blood of Christ; so also our bodies, having been nourished by this Eucharist and then placed in the earth and suffering decomposition there, shall rise at their time, the Word of God granting them resurrection unto the glory of God the Father.[21]

One of the most important aspects of the Eucharist is that it is a promise of eternal life. Here Saint Irenaeus reverses the argument to prove that the promise of Christ in the Eucharist must be real because the promise of eternal life it gives is true.

The Witnesses After the Persecutions

After the Council of Nicaea (325), as the Church was rising from three centuries in the catacombs, very great theologians who were likewise men of holiness of life and vast erudition proclaimed the whole Paschal Mystery with incredible intellectual power. They were very far from being the imaginary pagan priests turned pseudo-Christians described by some opponents of the Eucharist. We will mention only a few of the most illustrious. In the East there were three towering figures: Saint Cyril of Jerusalem, Saint Gregory of Nyssa, and Saint John Chrysostom, Archbishop of Constantinople. In the West among the bishops were Saint Hilary of Poitiers, Saint Ambrose (Archbishop of Milan), and Saint Augustine. Among priests we have Saint John Damascene in the East and Saint Jerome in the West. Time does not permit us to review the writings of all the Fathers of that time, but this is easily done by reviewing Monsignor O'Connor's book or any one of several serious studies of patristics, that is, the study of the Fathers.

Protestants and especially Evangelicals should realize that most of the theological underpinnings of their fundamental beliefs about Christ and redemption come from the very men whose names I have listed. Among these men are those who gave us the New Testament as a complete and certified document of divine revelation. The divinity of Christ, His virgin birth, His absolutely unique role as Savior and Lord are all proclaimed by their teachings and interpretations of the New Testament. Recently I spoke with a fine young man who had come from a devout family of Baptist missionaries. When he told me the story of his conversion to the Catholic faith, he said that he never even knew of the existence of these great bishops and theologians. He had no idea that the fundamental beliefs that he had as a devout Baptist were rooted in the writings of the same Fathers who had passed on the inspired writings and codified the Christian Scripture. These men took the words of Jesus at the Last Supper literally because that is how the Church in the time of the last living Apostles of Jesus had taken them. They strove, as Scripture scholars and teachers of any dedicated Christian denomination would do, to make a coherent and consistent teaching out of these mysterious words that Christ had left when He ascended into heaven. And all these Fathers of the Church, without exception, taught that the Christian Eucharistic worship was the representation of the sacrifice of Christ, and that the bread and wine of the sacred meal really became His Body and Blood.

Just a brief sample of statements by the Fathers after Nicaea is all that space permits us to include. I encourage again those who are interested to read further as I have indicated.

Saint Cyril of Jerusalem ✱ In the East Saint Cyril, Archbishop of Jerusalem (circa 315-386), wrote:

> The bread and wine of the Eucharist were simple bread and wine before the invocation of the holy and adorable Trinity, but when the invocation has taken place the bread becomes the body of Christ and the wine the blood of Christ. . . .[22]
>
> The seeming bread is not bread even though it is sensible to the taste, but the body of Christ, and the seeming wine is not wine, even though the taste will have it so, but the blood of Christ.[23]

As bishop of the city where the Eucharist was instituted, Saint Cyril gave the following instructions that clearly indicate the belief of the ancient Church in the reality of the sacrament: "Make your left hand a throne for your right, as for that which is to receive a king. And, hollowing your palm, receive the body of Christ, saying over it the 'Amen.' With due attention, sanctify your eyes by the sight of the holy body, and partake of it, taking care not to lose any part of it; for whatever you would lose would evidently be a loss to you from one of your own members."[24]

In another instruction Saint Cyril writes: "Tell me, if any one gave you grains of gold, would you not hold them with all care taking heed lest you should lose any of them and suffer loss? Will you not much more carefully be on your guard lest a crumb fall from you of what is more valuable than gold and precious stones? After you have made your communion in the body of Christ, draw near also to the cup of his blood, not stretching out your hands but bowing, and in an attitude of reverence and worship saying the 'Amen,' hallow yourself by partaking also of the blood of Christ."[25]

Saint Gregory of Nyssa ✸ Saint Gregory of Nyssa (335-394) sees a parallel between the Incarnation of the Son of God as a man and the transformation of the bread into the Body of Christ in the Eucharist. He speaks first of Christ eating bread when he lived in the world: "So, too, the Body into which God entered, by being nourished with bread, was in like manner identical with the bread. . . . This Body, by the indwelling of God the Word, has been changed to divine dignity. Rightly then do we believe that the bread consecrated by the word of God has been changed into the Body of God the Word. For that Body was bread in power, but it has been sanctified by the dwelling there of the Word, who pitched his tent in the flesh. The change that elevated to divine power the bread that had been transformed into that Body causes something similar now."[26]

Monsignor O'Connor explains that just as the union of the divine and human in Christ sanctified His humanity, so the union of bread and wine that Christ's own body assimilated when He was in this world united these earthly substances with the divine. And just as he assimilated bread and wine in this way during His earthly life, so now He assimilates the Eucharistic elements into Himself. He gives us life through Himself by this assimilation. This is a not a way in which we customarily think, but it is a fascinating parallel. Without belief in the reality of the Eucharist as the Body and Blood of Christ the parallel of assimilation makes absolutely no sense at all.[27]

Saint John Chrysostom ✸ Saint John Chrysostom, Archbishop of Constantinople (circa 350-407), in a homily on the words of Eucharistic institution at the Last Supper in Matthew 26, speaks most powerfully on the reality of the Body and Blood of Christ. No one can read this text by the great Patriarch of the East and deny for a minute that he believes in the Real Presence of Christ in the Eucharist. This text will be important later on when we are looking for evidence of belief that the presence of Christ in the Eucharist was seen as a personal presence in the early Church. Imagine the great bishop standing in the cathedral church of Constantinople before the altar and saying the following: "How many there are who still say, 'I want to see his shape, his image [Gk. *ton tupon*], his clothing, his sandals.' Behold, you do see him, you touch him, you eat him! You want to see his clothing. He gives himself to you, not just to be seen but to be touched, to be eaten, to be received within. . . . Let all of you be ardent, fervent, enthusiastic. If the Jews stood, shoes on, staff in hand, and eating in haste, how much more vigilant should you be. They were about to go to Palestine; . . . you are about to go to heaven."[28]

Saint John Damascene ✷ The priest Saint John of Damascus, who lived sometime between 650 and 750 — also writing in the East — forever closed the door on the theory that the Eucharist is only a symbol or a type. Writing in Greek, he says:

> The bread and wine are not a type [Gk. *tupos*] of the Body and Blood of Christ (may no one say that!); rather it is the very deified Body of the Lord. He himself said, "This is my Body," not a type of my Body, and, "This is my Blood," not a type of my Blood, but "my Blood." . . .
>
> . . . Let us approach with ardent desire and receive the Body of the Crucified with our hands held in the form of a cross; taking it to our eyes and lips and foreheads, let us partake of the Divine Coal . . . in order that we may be inflamed and divinized by our share in the divine fire. Isaiah saw [this] coal.[29]

Saint Hilary ✷ In the West Saint Hilary of Poitiers (circa 315-368) was one of the most dedicated opponents of the Arian heresy, which denied the divinity of Christ. He links belief in the Eucharist and divinity of Christ together because it is obviously impossible that anyone but God Himself could be the source of the Eucharist. A person transforming matter (bread and wine) in this way must have divine power, either personally or by divine delegation: "About the truth of his Flesh and Blood there is left no room for doubt. For by the Lord's own word and by our faith [we know] that it is truly flesh and truly blood. And when we have received and drunk these realities it comes about that we are in Christ and Christ in us. Is this not the truth? Let it happen that those who deny that Christ is God deny this also. He is in us through his Flesh, and we are in him, and that by which we are with him is in God."[30]

Saint Ambrose ✻ Saint Ambrose (340-397), the towering Archbishop of Milan, did much to define and stabilize the liturgy of the Church, especially the presentation of the sacraments. He very clearly indicates the belief of the early Church that the bread is transformed or transfigured — it is no longer bread but really the Body of Christ. He clearly states that because Christ has divine power, by reason of His blessing, "the nature of the elements" itself is changed.[31] In his book *De Fide* ("On the Faith") published around 380, commenting on John 6:55, he writes: " '. . . For my Flesh truly is food and my Blood truly is drink.' You hear of flesh, you hear of blood, and you are aware of the Sacraments of the Lord's death. . . . For as often as we receive the Sacraments, which, through the Mystery of the sacred prayer, are transfigured [*transfigurantur*] into Flesh and Blood, 'we announce the death of the Lord.' "[32]

Saint Augustine ✻ Saint Augustine (354-430), Bishop of Hippo, is considered by some to be the greatest of the Fathers, or at least the most influential of the Western Fathers. His impact is still felt profoundly today. Saint Augustine saw the Eucharist as the binding element of the Church, the cement, as it were, that holds the faithful together, or, to use his own words, it is the chain of love (*vinculum caritatis*). He also emphasizes the reality of the Eucharistic Presence of Christ because it makes the sacrifice of the Mass real, in which Christ is "immolated . . . every day."[33] He also presented the effects of the sacrament as very real, as it were, with a mystical realism: "Not only do we become Christians; we become Christ. . . ."[34]

It is important when one encounters the unflinching realism of Augustine's Eucharistic teaching to recall that prior to his conversion he had been involved in pseudo-mystical vagaries of the Manichees. Later he had been involved with the abstract and somewhat mystical speculations of the Neoplatonists. He found refuge from these vague systems in the Eucharist. No longer would he endure any shadowy projections of the human mind. For Augustine, Christ meant what He said and said what He meant. Monsignor O'Connor chooses the following two quotations, which powerfully illustrate Saint Augustine's belief in the reality of Christ's presence in the Eucharist in that he requires a personal act of adoration before anyone receives the sacrament:

> He took earth from earth, because flesh is from the earth, and he took Flesh of the flesh of Mary. He walked on earth in that same Flesh, and gave that same Flesh to us to be eaten for our salvation. Moreover no one eats that Flesh unless he has first adored it . . . and we sin by not adoring.[35]
>
> Who is the Bread of heaven except Christ? But in order that man might eat the bread of angels, the Lord of the angels became a man. If this had not happened, we would not have his Flesh: if we did not have his Flesh, we would not eat the Bread of the altar.[36]

Although it is not the focus of our discussion, we must mention that the doctrine of the Holy Eucharist is ultimately indistinguishable in Augustine from the Church's own concept of herself as established by Christ. One might easily make the following statement: No Church means no Eucharist. And no Eucharist means no Church. This doctrine is emphatically stated by Saint Augustine in *The City of God* (Book X, Chapter 6) although he repeated it in many other places: "This wholly redeemed city, the assembly and society of the saints, is offered to God as a universal sacrifice by the high priest who in the form of a slave went so far as to offer himself for us in his Passion, to make us the Body of so great a head. . . . Such is the sacrifice of Christians: 'we who are many are one Body in Christ.' The Church continues to reproduce this sacrifice in the sacrament of the altar so well-known to believers wherein it is evident to them that in what she offers she herself is offered."[37]

The teaching of Saint Augustine on the Holy Eucharist could be the subject of a very substantial book. We have only selected a few quotations to indicate Augustine's teaching on the topic we are considering, namely the Real Presence of Christ in the Eucharist. There is no question that Augustine saw the Eucharistic bread and wine as it lay on the altar as the real Body and Blood of Christ. He called for an act of external adoration to the consecrated elements that, as many of the other Fathers of the Church likewise indicated, had already been transformed from the bread and wine. Along with Saint John Chrysostom, we find in Augustine the beginnings of a recognition that believers should act when they are in proximity to the Eucharistic elements as if they were in the presence of Christ as He walked on the earth.

Saint Jerome ✱ Finally we come to Saint Jerome, the priest of Rome whose name is in the introduction of almost every Catholic and Protestant Bible. Saint Jerome (343-420), while certainly accepting that the Eucharist is really the Body of Christ, introduces a distinction that will be helpful to theology in later ages — the mode by which the Body exists. Jerome speculated that the mode of existence of the Body of the risen Christ was different from His pre-resurrection functioning. For example, He entered the Upper Room with the doors closed. Obviously there is also a difference between His mode of operation in Nazareth, and His mode of existence in the Eucharistic Bread. Jerome discusses this distinction, which may never be totally understood in theology, and perhaps must remain mysterious. The following quotation from his commentary on Ephesians 1:7 illustrates the problem: "Indeed, the Blood and Flesh of Christ are to be understood in two ways, either that spiritual and divine Flesh and Blood of which he himself said: 'My Flesh is real food, and my Blood is real drink' (Jn 6:56) and 'Unless you eat my Flesh and drink my Blood, you will not have eternal life'; or that Flesh which was crucified and that Blood which poured forth by the work of the soldier's lance. According to this distinction, a difference of flesh and blood is also to be understood in the case of the saints, such that one kind is the flesh that will see the salvation of God, another kind that which cannot inherit the Kingdom of God."[38]

Monsignor O'Connor's commentary on this quotation from Jerome is most helpful: "Jerome's remark has sometimes been taken as evidence that he did not defend the identity between the Eucharist and the body of Christ born of Mary. Such an assertion is wide of the mark, however. As noted, his observation is concerned with the nature of the change that takes place in a resurrected Body. In fact, his statement is an affirmation that the Eucharistic Body is the risen Body of Christ — a statement fully in harmony with that of

St. Ignatius of Antioch. Ignatius, however, simply asserted the identity between the pre- and post-Easter Body of the Lord; Jerome attempted to indicate that there is a difference. Later theology will be
able to express the difference as one of *modality*, not of identity."[39]

Summary: The Eucharist in the Early Church

This very brief review of the teaching of the Fathers Eastern
and Western (and many were omitted) should convince anyone that
the early Church did not see the bread and wine offered and blessed
at the Eucharist as simply a symbol. The word real, mysteriously
real, is shouted out by the Fathers and the faithful of the ancient
Church who were willing to die to keep the Eucharist from being
profaned by pagans. In fact, they hid the knowledge of this sacrament from those who did not believe. It is difficult to conceive how
those who know the writings of the Fathers from Ignatius in the
first century to Augustine (who, incidentally, successfully argued
to have Hebrews and Revelation included in the New Testament)
can deny that the Church ever thought of the celebration of the
Eucharist as a sort of religious play reminding people of the Last
Supper. Quite the opposite! As we have seen in this brief review, it
is incontrovertible that the ancient Church saw the celebration of
the Eucharist as a sacrifice, a real participation in the Paschal
Mystery of the Son of God, actually uniting the believer with His
holy life, death, and resurrection, and especially with His sacrifice
on the Cross. Only the baptized were allowed to enter into this
participation in the reality of Christ's worship, which is in fact the
life of the saints in heaven. To receive the Eucharist as a reality
and not merely as a symbol is inescapable. The words of Christ at
the Last Supper must be taken literally: "This is my Body; this is
my Blood."

ENDNOTES

1. Robert Jastrow, *God and the Astronomers*, 1978, pp. 114-116.
2. Quoted in *A Treasury of Quotations on Christian Themes*, ed. Carroll
   Simcox, 1975, p. 53.
3. *The Ascent of Mt. Carmel*, Bk. II, Ch. 3, in *The Collected Works of St.
   John of the Cross*, trans. K. Kavanaugh, OCD, and O. Rodriguez, OCD,
   1979, pp. 110-111.
4. Ven. John Henry Newman, *Discourses Addressed to Mixed Congrega-*

tions, Discourse XIII, "Mysteries of Nature and of Grace," 1899, pp. 274-275.

5. The educated reader wishing to explore the meaning of Christian mysteries at greater length may wish to delve more deeply into this aspect of the Christian faith. *The Mysteries of Christianity* by Matthias Joseph Scheeben, 1961, would be a very helpful study. Also, the mystery of the human life of the God-man is pondered very seriously by Romano Guardini in *The Humanity of Christ,* 1964.

6. Scheeben, p. 4.

7. Jastrow, p. 114.

8. *Psychology Today,* Vol. 17, No. 9, Sept. 1983, p. 25.

9. The number of people who are aware of the mysteries of God while studying the mysteries of science is far greater than assumed. The very distinguished scholar of science and religion Fr. Stanley Jaki, OSB, explored the relationship of science and religion in the Gifford Lectures at the University of Edinborough in 1975 and 1976. Published in 1978 under the title *The Road of Science and the Ways to God,* this outstanding work will reward the serious student amply for the labor necessary to read it.

10. On the Eucharistic theory of the Protestant reformer Ulrich Zwingli and the condemnation of Zwingli by the Council of Trent, see Msgr. James O'Connor, *The Hidden Manna: A Theology of the Eucharist,* 1988, pp. 141, 206ff.

11. Translation from *Saint Andrew Daily Missal: With Vespers for Sundays and Feasts,* ed. Dom Gaspar Lefebvre, OSB, 1943, pp. 771-773.

12. The reader may enjoy meditating upon a fine new edition of these texts, *Divinity I Adore Thee: The Hymns and Prayers of St. Thomas Aquinas,* trans. R. Anderson and J. Moser, 1993.

13. "Charles II of Spain," *Ave Maria,* Vol. 2, Dec. 22, 1866, pp. 805-806 (based on an account given by the Bollandists).

14. *The Hidden Manna: A Theology of the Eucharist,* 1988. In addition to this work and the new *Catechism of the Catholic Church,* Fr. Aidan Nichols's book, *The Holy Eucharist: From the New Testament to Pope John Paul II* (Oscott Series, No. 6), 1991, is also recommended to the reader seeking an in-depth presentation of the dogmatic theology of the Eucharist. For a more modern interpretation see Msgr. Robert Sokolowski, *Eucharistic Presence: A Study in the Theology of Disclosure,* 1993.

15. O'Connor, p. 16.

16. Ibid., p. 17.

17. Ibid.

18. Ibid., pp. 19-20.

19. Ibid., p. 20.

20. *Dialogue with Trypho the Jew,* quoted in ibid., p. 22.

21. *Adversus Haereses,* Bk. V, 2, 2-3, quoted in ibid., pp. 23-24. For

critical Latin text see *Irenée de Lyon: Contre les Hérésies, Livre V: Tome II: Texte et Traduction* (Vol. 153 of *Sources Chretiennes* series), pp. 28-32.

22. *Catechetical Lectures 19*, quoted in Nichols, p. 38.
23. *Catechetical Lectures 22*, quoted in ibid., p. 38.
24. *Catechetical Lectures 23*, quoted in ibid., pp. 38-39.
25. Ibid., p. 39.
26. *The Great Catechism*, Ch. 37, quoted in O'Connor, p. 35.
27. O'Connor, pp. 35-36.
28. *Homily 82 on the Gospel of Matthew*, quoted in ibid., p. 47.
29. *De Fide Orthodoxa*, quoted in ibid., pp. 78-79. Msgr. O'Connor mentions that, in some parts of the East, touching the forehead and eyes with the Host was apparently a custom before receiving Communion.
30. *De Trinitate*, 8, 13, and 14, quoted in ibid., p. 27. Msgr. O'Connor notes: "Reflections like those of St. Hilary on our divinization because of the Eucharist are also found in St. Cyril of Alexandria's *Commentary on the Gospel of John*, which was written around 428. Commenting on the text 'I in you, and you in me, that they may be perfected in truth,' he wrote: 'The Son as man is in us bodily, mixed and united with us through the mystic Eucharist' (*PG*, 74, 564). The whole of chap. II of Book XII of this commentary is an exposition of how the Eucharist makes the Church Christ's Body and makes us become one with the Father (*PG*, 74, 557-62)" (ibid., n. 45 on p. 27).
31. *De Mysteriis*, No. 52, quoted in ibid., p. 39.
32. *De Fide*, Bk. IV, Ch. 10, quoted in ibid., p. 41.
33. Letter 98 to Boniface, No. 9, quoted in ibid., pp. 52, 61.
34. *On John*, Tract 21, No. 8, quoted in ibid., p. 61.
35. *Ennarationes in Ps 98*, No. 9, quoted in ibid., p. 59.
36. Sermon 130, quoted in ibid., p. 59.
37. Quoted in *Catechism of the Catholic Church*, No. 1372, 1994, p. 346.
38. *Commentary on Ephesians*, Ch. 1, v. 7, quoted in O'Connor, pp. 45-46.
39. Ibid., p. 46.

Chapter 2

How Does It Happen?

The mind of the believer, deeply moved as it must be by the realization that the bread and wine have been truly changed into the Body and Blood of Christ, is likely to inquire how this happens. A great deal of time and energy has been spent over the centuries in trying to answer this question. The reader must realize that some of the discussion will appear to be airy speculation to those unfamiliar with theology. However, much of it is a very serious and noble attempt to keep the mystery of Christ from being misunderstood and the sacred species (a term often used for the precious Body and Blood of Christ in the Eucharist) from being misused.

We must now introduce a bit of theology. "Faith seeking understanding" describes the very best efforts to cope reasonably with the ultimately mysterious. Among all the scholars who since the Age of the Fathers have dedicated time and energy to the Eucharist, one man stands out as a most devoted, humble, and competent theologian — Saint Thomas Aquinas (1225-1274).

The entire theory of Saint Thomas on the Blessed Sacrament should be studied by anyone seriously interested in Eucharistic devotion. Like the Fathers on whom he built his theological teaching, Thomas examines every argument regarding this mystery — sacrament, sacrifice, presence, the unifying agent of the People of God, and reconciliation of sin, as well as preparation for eternal life. The new *Catechism of the Catholic Church* and the supplemental sourcebook for the latter published by Ignatius Press, along with the authors I have particularly relied upon (O'Connor and Nichols), are among a number of reliable and readable sources available on this subject.[1] Here we must try, somewhat artificially, to restrict our consideration of this sacrament as much as possible to the devotion to the Real Presence of Christ in the Eucharist, because this is the focal point of our book.

First of all, it needs to be said loud and clear that no explanation is going to answer all questions or even approach a complete rational explanation. Even those aspects of this or any other supernatural mystery that are capable of rational examination do not offer the possibility of complete comprehension. Saint Thomas wisely observes that our knowledge of God is always incomplete. How could it be otherwise, since God is infinite and we have to work so long to understand little things? In his commentary on the Creed, Saint Thomas mentions, with some humor, that he had heard of a philosopher who had lived in solitude for thirty years working to understand the nature of a bee. He never finished.[2] It's interesting to note that contemporary aeronautical engineers are still trying to understand this little creature. When you think of all the work that has been done and needs to be done on an atom or a DNA molecule, you should not be surprised to come to a completely unsolvable mystery in God.

Matthias Scheeben, that powerful critic of nineteenth-century theological rationalism, has placed any explanation of the Eucharist in its proper perspective:

> When set forth according to the norm of the Catholic faith, the Eucharist, like the Incarnation, is manifestly an astounding, supernatural work of God. It is a work hidden from the intellect, and is quite beyond our understanding. . . . Its mysterious character is so readily acknowledged that the Eucharist is often referred to simply as the mystery par excellence . . . [namely] that the substance of Christ's body and blood remains actually, truly, and essentially present as long as the appearances endure, yet in such a manner that it is present whole and indivisible under each species, as well as under any part thereof.
>
> The very wording of the dogma bears witness to its mysterious character. For the substantial presence of the body and blood

of Christ under alien species is plainly a fact at which we cannot arrive by reason alone, because we are naturally able to know substances only by their accidents and their outward appearance. According to the ordinary laws of thought, reason is quite justified in inferring a substance from the accidents that are naturally associated with it. Reason will not be led to affirm the presence of Christ's body by following its natural course; on the contrary, reason will pronounce without hesitation that it is not present. Faith is required, not only to assist reason by leading it further, but to bring its natural course to a halt. The fact of the mystery is utterly cut off from unaided reason, because it is a supernatural fact, one that is wrought not upon the surface of things, but in their innermost core.

The reality of the presence of Christ's body under the sacramental species is undiscernible and, in a higher sense, the nature of that presence is inconceivable. That is to say, its supernatural character places it beyond all natural concepts, and even beyond the natural conceptive power of the intellect.[3]

That said, let's proceed to what we can learn. When Saint Thomas approached the mystery of the Eucharist, he had the advantage of twelve hundred years of Christian thought since the Resurrection to rely on. He referred not only to the Gospels but to Saint Paul and all the Fathers of the Church. He also had the official teachings of the Church that had been formally defined in response to the controversies of a century or two before, particularly the partial challenge of Berengarius to the traditional teaching, and in response to the outright denial of the reality of the Real Presence by certain heretics such as the Waldensians and Cathari.[4]

What Thomas Learned and Taught

Saint Thomas also had a new tool to use — the word "transubstantiation." Contrary to popular misconception, he did not coin this word himself. Among others Pope Alexander III, whose own pontificate extended from 1159-1181, and who called the Third Lateran Council (1179), had used this term almost a century before.[5] The clear idea of a substance being changed goes back to the Fathers, and can be seen explicitly in the quotation that we cited before from Saint Gregory of Nyssa: ". . . the bread consecrated by the word of God has been changed [Gr. *metapoieisthai*] into the Body of God the Word."[6]

What Saint Thomas did was apply the new tools of rational analysis supplied by the recently translated Aristotelian texts that had arrived in Western Europe for the first time. In the third part of the *Summa Theologica* (Nos. 73-78) he poses this question: Is Christ's body in the sacrament "really and truly" (*secundum veritatem*) or is it there in a figurative way (*secundum figuram*)? It may be interesting to Evangelicals that he makes his choice of the "real" presence on the basis of the relationship of the Old and New Testaments. Briefly, the Old Testament sacrifices were a figure of the real saving sacrifice of the New Covenant. Christ who suffered was not a token or sign but rather the reality. Summarizing the thought of Saint Thomas, Father Aidan Nichols observes that this Eucharistic reality "befits the charity of Christ which led him to take a human body for our sakes at the Incarnation"[7]; thus Christ, our truest Friend, and whom we shall be with in eternity, "has not left us without his bodily presence."[8] Also, it is more fitting that Christ is with us not only in His Godhead but in His manhood as well. The Christ we believe in is God and man, and so we have with us on our journey not only the Word of God but also the human Jesus.

The following statement of Father Nichols serves us as a very good summary of this powerful idea. As we read it, we need to keep clearly in mind that a created substance does not exist on its own but by the continuous creative act of God. This continuous dependency of created substances is implicit in any understanding of Saint Thomas's thought on the Eucharist. All substances, whatever they are in this world, depend completely on the continuous creative act of God. Saint Francis of Assisi, who died the year after Saint Thomas's birth, joyfully sang "Amen" to this idea, which Thomas makes the foundation of his teaching. Father Nichols gives this illuminating summary:

> Thomas possesses a rich philosophical vocabulary for describing, or analysing, the concrete structure of reality, the way things are. Three of the most important key words are: *esse, substantia*

and *accidentia*. Accidents for mediaeval philosophy are not, evidently, what we mean in everyday speech today: events in the human world not willed by any human agent, like a child catching rabies, or King's Cross underground station catching fire. For Thomas, accidents are those aspects of reality which require for their existence a created ground which is other than themselves. Thus, while the redness of a red apple certainly exists, it only exists by inhering in the apple itself. Accidents are features of reality that have no visible means of support unless they find it in some other aspect of reality which has the ontological solidity that they lack. And this second aspect of reality Thomas calls *substance*. Substance is a concrete reality in so far as it needs no other created ground than itself. The desk on which I am writing is substantial because it is not parasitic on any other concrete reality for its existence. It does not inhere in anything, though something — for instance, oblong-shapedness, hardness, brownness — inheres in it. It is typical of substances, according to Thomas, that they enjoy a certain autonomy, independence, or self-sufficiency within the created order.[9]

Again we need to keep clearly in mind that created substances do not exist on their own. Remember that this dependency of created things is essential for understanding Thomas's thought: "Precisely by virtue of being created, the world, composed as it is of substances with their accidents, is a world which only endures because it constantly receives being. God who is infinite actuality . . . communicates being, the act of being, to creatures as the deepest foundation of their existence. So as to draw attention to the fact that substances with their accidents are dependent for their own ground on God, Thomas describes them as *entia*, 'be-ings,' from the verbal participle of *esse, ens*: finite participations in the infinite *esse* or act of being which God, as Creator, is."[10]

Having established in our own minds the continuous and complete dependence of all matter, of all things on God, at all times, for their existence, the stage is now set to look at this mystery. The bread and wine must substantively cease to exist at the consecration. The coexistence of the two substances, bread and the Body of Christ, is impossible. The concepts here are worth pondering to see how we get to the conclusion of Saint Thomas's explanation. Father Nichols continues: "He [Thomas] argues that Christ's body can only come to be in this sacrament by one of two ways. Either it is brought in from outside, or something already there is changed into it. But there can be no question of Christ's body moving through space: among many difficulties, this would entail that body ceasing to be in heaven. This leaves only the possibility that the substance of bread changes into it: and this explains why Christ said not 'Here is my body' but 'This is my body,' for the latter proposition would be false were the substance of bread still present. Moreover, the worship the Church gives this sacrament would be altogether misguided if the consecrated elements contained a created substance which ought not to receive adoration."[11]

It is important here to recall that Saint Thomas and many others have shown that this change is completely supernatural, mysterious, and effected only by the power of God. Thus, we arrive at the change of substances or *transubstantiation*, to use the word borrowed by Thomas from writers in the previous century.

It is required for Catholics to believe as an article of faith that the species of the Blessed Sacrament, after the consecration, is really the Body and Blood of Christ under the appearances of bread and wine. The following dogmatic statement of the Council of Trent summarizes this teaching very well: "Because Christ our Redeemer said that it was truly his body that he was offering under the species of bread, it has always been the conviction of the Church of God, and this holy Council now declares again, that by the consecration of the bread and wine there takes place a change of the whole substance of the bread into the substance of the body of Christ our Lord and of the whole substance of the wine into the substance of his blood. This change the holy Catholic Church has fittingly and properly called transubstantiation."[12]

From this citation we can see that the fact of the change of substance is a defined article of faith; and the use of the term transubstantiation to describe this process is approved. For the devout this whole discussion may seem a bit abstract, but these theological concepts are really necessary for the adoration of the Blessed Sacrament to be put on a solid footing. Saint Thomas's beautiful hymns and prayers for what was then the newly introduced Feast of Corpus Christi appropriately enough stress the Eucharist as the banquet of the soul, but they also indicate the presence of Christ in the Eucharist. His antiphon for Vespers on the Feast of Corpus Christi sums up this aspect of his teaching: "O sacred banquet in which Christ is received, the memory of his passion cultivated, the heart filled with grace, and the pledge of future glory given us!"[13]

Saint Thomas's hymn *Adoro Te Devote* summarizes beautifully his theology of the Holy Eucharist as sacrifice, sacrament, and presence. This splendid translation is by the Jesuit poet Gerard Manley Hopkins:

"Godhead Here In Hiding"[14]

Godhead here in hiding, Whom I do adore
Masked by these bare shadows, shape and nothing more,
See, Lord, at thy service low lies here a heart
Lost, all lost in wonder at the God thou art.

Seeing, touching, tasting are in thee deceived;
How says trusty hearing? that shall be believed;
What God's Son has told me, take for truth I do;
Truth himself speaks truly or there's nothing true.

On the cross thy godhead made no sign to men;
Here thy very manhood steals from human ken:
Both are my confession, both are my belief,
And I pray the prayer of the dying thief.

I am not like Thomas, wounds I cannot see,
But can plainly call thee Lord and God as he:
This faith each day deeper be my holding of,
Daily make me harder hope and dearer love.

O thou our reminder of Christ crucified,
Living Bread the life of us for whom he died,
Lend this life to me then: feed and feast my mind,
There be thou the sweetness man was meant to find.

Bring the tender tale true of the Pelican;[15]
Bathe me, Jesu Lord, in what thy bosom ran —
Blood that but one drop of has the world to win
All the world forgiveness of its world of sin.

Jesu whom I look at shrouded here below,
I beseech thee send me what I thirst for so.

Some day to gaze on thee face to face in light
And be blest for ever with thy glory's sight.

Saint Thomas Aquinas, like his teacher Saint Augustine, is a much maligned man. Because his powerful mind is able to far out-distance the intellectual strength of even the most educated read-ers, he is often caricatured as a cold intellectual and a pious ratio-nalist. Nothing could be further than the truth. His teaching is like a little square of bright light surrounded by the darkness of infinite mystery. He convincingly teaches us that Christ does not descend into the Eucharist but that the substance of the bread and wine changes while the appearances remain the same. This teaching is in fact slightly less mysterious for modern man because contempo-rary physics has explored some of the natural mysteries of the no-tion of physical substance — down to those mysterious subatomic particles that do not appear to agree with our conception of matter. If physical substances are so mysterious and appear to be largely fields of energy around nuclei that are even smaller, then the doc-trines of the Real Presence and transubstantiation don't appear so shocking to the human mind.

When we study matter in the light of contemporary physics, we find the same mysteries at the end of the microscope that we dis-cover at the end of the sky (as the astronomer Robert Jastrow has pointed out). In each case one catches a glimpse of a shadow of the infinite. Put in the context of the mysteries of contemporary phys-ics, the presence of Christ in the Eucharist and the phenomenon called transubstantiation do not seem quite so far-fetched. They are simply mysteries set among other mysteries. If all the energy found in a little pile of uranium can make a hydrogen explosion, and if the code of a whole life can be found in the minute details of the DNA molecule, we should not be completely surprised that the Eternal Son of God, a pure spirit, could leave us with so powerful and real a memorial of His time spent on earth as Son of man, a being of flesh and blood.

ENDNOTES

1. *Catechism of the Catholic Church*, 1994; *The Companion to the Cat-echism of the Catholic Church*, 1994.
2. Sermon Series on the Creed, in *The Three Greatest Prayers: Commen-*

taries on the Lord's Prayer, the Hail Mary, and the Apostles' Creed,
1990, p. 6.

3. Matthias Scheeben, *The Mysteries of Christianity*, 1961, pp. 469-470.

4. Fr. Aidan Nichols, OP, *The Holy Eucharist: From the New Testament to Pope John Paul II* (Oscott Series, No. 6), 1991, pp. 58-75.

5. Msgr. James T. O'Connor, *The Hidden Manna: A Theology of the Eucharist*, 1988, p. 182.

6. *The Great Catechism*, Ch. 37, quoted in ibid., p. 35.

7. Nichols, pp. 67-68.

8. Ibid., p. 68.

9. Ibid., p. 69 — see this entire section in Nichols summarizing the teaching of St. Thomas. For St. Thomas's own treatment of the subject, see *Summa Theologiae, Volume 58: The Eucharistic Presence*, ed. William Barden, OP, and *Summa Theologiae, Volume 59: Holy Communion (3a.79-83)*, ed. Thomas Gilby, OP, 1965 and 1975.

10. Nichols, pp. 69-70.

11. Ibid., pp. 70-71.

12. Council of Trent, Session XIII (Oct. 1551), Ch. IV, quoted in *Catechism of the Catholic Church*, No. 1376, p. 347.

13. *"O sacrum convivium,"* quoted in Nichols, p. 82.

14. "Rhythmus ad SS. Sacramentum," in *Poems of Gerard Manley Hopkins*, 3rd ed., 1948, No. 131, pp. 186-187.

15. The pelican feeding its young with its own blood became a symbol of the Eucharist. Although time has dispelled this mistaken idea about pelicans, the touching symbol still remains and is often seen in sacred art.

Chapter 3

The Reality of Christ's Presence

The sacraments are objective realities, really pledges given by Christ through His Church that the grace and mercy of God will flow upon us by a devout and believing fulfillment of the sacred sign. In recent decades theologians have emphasized the essential link between the seven sacraments and the Church herself, which can in a certain way be called the fundamental sacrament. This emphasis on the communal nature of sacraments is very useful as we shall see with regard to the celebration of the Eucharistic Presence, and corrects a well-intentioned but distorted view of the sacraments as sort of the individual's "direct line to God."[1]

The Latin word "*sacramentum*" simply means a pledge or promise to give something, an IOU given by God, not so different in this respect from the covenant promises given in the Old Testament to Israel. The Greek word most often used for a sacrament, "*mysterion*," stresses the invisible power of the sacramental sign; this term finds its root in the Greek verb "to close one's eyes." It stresses the invisible effects of the sacrament. Because they are external or perceptible promises of the immense reality of grace, of God's covenant of mercy with His children, sacraments are signs, but they are effective signs, not merely symbolic ones. They cause what they signify. God in His love binds Himself to His creatures.

A review of the theology of the seven sacraments, their essential relationship to the Paschal Mystery of Christ's atonement and second coming, their objective value (which puts them beyond the strength and weakness of those who use them), their New Testament origins, and their relationship to the whole Church community are fascinating subjects but beyond our purposes here. As we have already noted, an accurate and excellent summary of Catholic sacramental theology can be found in Part II of *The Catechism of the Catholic Church*. A thorough study of the sacraments and especially of the Eucharist is one of the fascinating adventures available to the thinking Christian. What is officially taught at the various levels of credence from dogma to opinion is intellectually captivating but complex. As Monsignor James O'Connor points out, even the Council of Trent, which defined much of the Catholic teaching on the Eucharist, properly left much undefined.[2]

While it is obvious to the informed reader, and for the record it should be noted, that there are a number of controversies raging in the Catholic Church and the whole Christian world about the sacraments and many other things, this book must restrict itself to those theories concerned with the Eucharistic devotion as much as possible. At times these controversies have been rooted in ecumenical aspirations or in an attempt to minimize the differences between different Christian Churches.[3]

Whatever may be said about this well-intentioned effort to find areas of agreement, it stands to reason that when it comes to Eucharistic devotion, ecumenically minded writers are going to have their difficulties and will often have a bias against this devotion that is generally not shared by non-Catholic Christians. Despite this, there is the remarkable fact that the preeminent Lutheran theologian Yngve Brilioth, in his monumental work *Eucharistic Faith and Practice*, shows profound respect for Eucharistic devotion as practiced by Catholics past and present.[4]

It is obvious that some members of the Anglican communion have managed to withstand the theological chaos and preserve Eucharistic devotion as it has come to flower with those referred to as "ritualists." Around 1990 I witnessed this myself at England's Shrine of Our Lady of Walsingham, where the Anglican Shrine leaves the Catholic completely in the shadows, sad to say, when it comes to Eucharistic devotion.

The Sacraments Are Real

Some sacraments are similar to each other, like Baptism and Confirmation, while some are quite different, such as the Anointing of the Sick and Matrimony, but all seven have several things in common. It is these common elements that have caused these distinct signs to be grouped together and designated by the same name and to be differentiated from other Christian signs (like the cross and the Bible).

For this reason there are certain key points of Christian tradition and Catholic sacramental theology that must be highlighted if we are to understand the devotion to the Eucharistic Presence. First of all, it is essential to note the objective reality of the sacraments, their radical independence of the dispositions of those who give them, and even of those who receive them without being able to respond, as is seen in the two teachings of the ancient Church about Baptism. Obviously an older child or adult receiving baptism should make a complete dedication to, and acceptance of, Christ as our Savior. The reception of any sacrament requires not only a commitment to Christ but a decision to follow His teachings. In the early Church, however, infants incapable of making this decision and retarded people were baptized.[5] Adults who were unconscious but whose intentions were known prior to illness were also baptized.[6] Thus the sacrament, although requiring a conversion and confession of faith, had its reality in something quite beyond the subjective dispositions of the individual. That something was the grace and life of the Messiah that He had come to bestow on the world, and has left us through the objective reality of the Church. He clearly taught this Himself: "I am the way, and the truth, and the life..." (Jn 14:6); "... I came that they may have life, and have it abundantly" (Jn 10:10).

The second fact is that the sacramental sign or promise did not depend on the disposition of the persons giving the sign but only on their authorization to give it.[7] This is very clear in the case of Baptism, which the early Church taught could, in some necessity, be given by an unbaptized person, either a catechumen (a person preparing for the sacrament of Baptism) or even a pagan who accepted the responsibility of doing what the God of the Christian wanted done. This rare but significant latter case might have occurred if an imprisoned Christian catechumen had only pagan cell mates before being led to the arena. This leads to the obvious question — Who really gives the sacrament? The answer is Christ Himself. In the Eucharist the priest who is the minister of the sacrament does not give his body (a revolting thought) but the Body of Christ. In Reconciliation the priest does not absolve sins on his own authority but by the power of the One who told the Apostles, "If you forgive the sins of any, they are forgiven . . ." (Jn 20:23). For this reason the early Church condemned the Donatists as heretics, because they taught that some serious sins on the part of the baptized required rebaptism, or on the part of a priest required his reordination.

So long as a sacrament is given by a person authorized to do so (and as we see in Baptism, this can be a very broad authorization), the reality is there. Saint Thomas Aquinas sums this up by teaching that "the sacrament is perfected not through the righteousness of the minister or the recipient of baptism, but rather through the power of God."[8] A sin of irreverence known as a *sacrilege* may occur when the person receiving the sacrament or even (in some cases) simply administering it is not basically converted to God in heart and mind. An example would be a person receiving the Eucharist in a state of serious sin, or a priest celebrating Mass in serious sin. In such a case the sacrament would be used unworthily. Saint Thomas Aquinas spoke of this tragic situation in *Lauda Sion*:

> The good receive, the evil receive:
> But to an unequal fate,
> One of life or of damnation.
> Death for the evil; life for the good.
> See what disparate results
> For what is equally received.[9]

Thus it is clear that the sacraments are real, not dependent on the personal or subjective attitudes of those who use them. Admittedly there are objects dependent for their usefulness on the subjective dispositions of the user — for example, religious art, symbols, and music. In the Christian tradition they are called sacramentals. What you put into them, you get out of them. But to repeat, sacraments are real and not subjective. This ancient teaching is far from the understanding of most Baptists and some other Protestants, who believe that the devotion of the minister is required, and that the individual must be able to make a profession of faith in all circumstances. For this reason many Baptists will rebaptize converts to their denomination, and do not permit the baptism of infants, despite the early Christian teachings on both of these practical issues.

The Need to Receive Christ with Mind and Heart

The other side of the reality of the sacraments is that for older children and adults the actual effectiveness of the sacraments depends on the degree of faith and devotion with which the sacred sign and the grace that it promises are received. The actual spiritual effects of the sacraments "depend on the disposition of the one who receives them."[10] In every sacrament it could be said that we meet or encounter Christ because we receive grace and mercy from Him. He baptizes, He absolves, He anoints, He unites. But the Eucharistic meeting is so intimate that we can say that we actually receive Him.

It is the constant teaching of the Church, for example, that the personal effects (or fruits) of receiving the Holy Eucharist are proportionate to the personal "dispositions" of the one who receives the Bread of Life. For example, two people, both of them in the state of grace (or friendship with God), receive Holy Communion at the same Mass. The first is a practicing Catholic layman who struggles along distracted, vacillating, at times fervent, and at times dissipating energies on many things, which if they are not worldly are at least of little spiritual value. The other is a woman who is energetically dedicated to the Christian life, to the honor of God, to the salvation of the world, and to her own spiritual progress. The first person receives the Body of Christ and returns from the altar a bit distracted. A moment of fervent prayer is followed by several minutes of distraction. Finally this man picks up a book and participates in the hymn being sung in an attempt to do something appropriate. But the mind slips back into distractions. At the end of the Mass he leaves the church somewhat encouraged, somewhat depressed, and looks around at the other distracted people. There is an old Italian proverb that aptly describes the feeling of encouragement such people experience as they join the other well-meaning but distracted parishioners for doughnuts and coffee: "A trouble shared is half a joy."

On the other hand, the woman who received Holy Communion was better prepared. She has been struggling all day with feelings of discouragement and hypersensitivity. This communicant has been hurt by others and knows that what she feels is half hypersensitivity, half self-love (that is, narcissism). But she has worked hard to prepare for Communion; she has made a meditation, and perhaps devoutly recited the prayers of the Liturgy. Christ coming to her in the Blessed Sacrament evokes powerful feelings of reverence and gratitude as well as contrition. After the reception of Communion, she takes her time to unite her day and her whole life with the sacrifice of Christ that the Liturgy has represented. Her powerful psychological response, integrated with the entire experience of thought and desire, of self-acceptance and self-respect, of penitence and resolution, of weakness and grace, is brought together by the belief that she has joined her Savior in this encompassing act of love, His agape. This experience is one of union in the sacrifice, of affirmation and strengthening in Holy Communion, of adoration of the Real Presence. This devout woman goes on her way after Mass much better prepared for another day of the Christian life than the man whom we just spoke of, although they both can be said to have received the Lord worthily.

The Reality of the Sacrifice

The reality of the sacrament of the Eucharist has three important dimensions: It is a sacrifice, a sacramental meal, and a presence. In this book we are concerned with the reality of the presence of Christ and with the appropriate response of the faithful and loving Christian to this Real Presence. Many will say that the presence is less important or only consequential to the sacrificial and sacramental aspects of the Eucharist. Their reasons will be theological as well as historical. It is obvious that the sacrificial and sacramental aspects are of supreme importance. But we shall see that they are deeply united with the reality of Christ's presence in His humanity as well as His divinity in the sacrament. What is offered in the Paschal sacrifice, what is received as the Bread of

Life, if it is not the presence of the One who said, "I am the bread of life" (Jn 6:48) and "I am with you always, to the close of the age" (Mt 28:20)? We cannot review at this time the whole theology of sacrifice and sacrament, but we need to consider carefully certain key elements if we are to understand why so many saints and so many struggling sinners have found the center of their lives to be in the Eucharistic Presence.

We have seen that ever since the time of Saint Paul and Saint Justin Martyr the Eucharist has been understood to be a presentation of the Saving Sacrifice of Christ the Victim and Eternal High Priest. In response to the denial of the Protestant reformers, the Council of Trent defined as an essential part of the Catholic faith the following teachings about the Eucharist as sacrifice:

> Therefore, inasmuch as in this divine sacrifice that is celebrated in the Mass the same Christ is contained and immolated in an unbloody manner who "offered himself in a bloody way once and for all" (cf. Heb 9:26) on the altar of the Cross, this holy synod teaches that this sacrifice is truly propitiatory (cf. Canon III) and that by means of it — if we draw near to God with a sincere heart and right faith, with fear and reverence, with sorrow and repentance — "we receive mercy and find grace at the appropriate time" (Heb 4:16). By the offering of this sacrifice the Lord is pleased and forgives crimes and even great sins, granting grace and the gift of penitence. For the victim is one and the same, the same who then offered himself on the Cross now offering by the ministry of priests, only the manner of offering being different. Indeed the fruits of this bloody oblation are abundantly received through this unbloody oblation. It does so in such a way that the unbloody oblation takes nothing away from the bloody oblation. Therefore it is properly offered, according to the Tradition of the Apostles, not only for the sins, satisfactions, and other necessities of the faithful who are living but also for the dead in Christ who are not yet fully purified (cf. Canon III).[11]

On the same occasion the Council of Trent also identified as heretical several propositions with regard to the Eucharist as a sacrifice, which should be noted:

Canon I: If anyone say that in the Mass there is not offered to God a true and proper sacrifice or that to be offered means no more than that Christ is given to us to eat, *anathema sit* [let him be condemned].

Canon II: If anyone say that, by these words, "Do this in memory of me" (Lk 22:19; 1 Cor 11:24), Christ did not institute the Apostles as priests or did not ordain that they and other priests offer his Body and Blood, *anathema sit*.[12]

Neither the Council of Trent nor the Church since that time has determined precisely how the Eucharistic Liturgy is a sacrifice. A number of very profound theories have been put forth that are often interrelated or reactive to each other. We do not have the time to review these theories, but we will summarize one of them — that of Matthias Scheeben and some German and French theologians of the late nineteenth century. They emphasized that the essence of the sacrifice is the offering rather than the destruction or immolation. Father Aidan Nichols writes of this opinion:

To find in immolation the pith and marrow of sacrifice is, they held, offensive to the goodness of the Father. In the Atonement it is not, strictly speaking, the Son's death which makes satisfaction for human sins and merits for us grace and glory, but the loving obedience expressed in the death. Such writers, and notably the late nineteenth-century Rhineland theologian Matthias Joseph Scheeben (1835-1888), held therefore that the only change in the bread and wine needed to make of them a sacrifice is the bringing to be of Christ's body and blood on the altar as an act of homage and honour, directed to the Father. Scheeben, whose theology is today sadly underrated, was especially anxious to emphasise the role, in the eucharistic action, of the Holy Spirit. For the economy of the Son, from Incarnation to Atonement, is dovetailed by that of the Spirit:

As Christ was conceived of the Holy Spirit, so in the Holy Spirit he offered himself to God undefiled on the Cross, and by the power of the same Holy Spirit he rose again to incorruptible life, in which he eternally displays and guards the value of his sacrificial death.

The Spirit's service of the mission of the Son continues in the eucharistic sacrifice.

> [In order] that this sacrifice [of Calvary], thus brought to pass in the Holy Spirit, may be embodied in the Church and the Church in it, the bread and wine are changed, by the power of the same Holy Spirit and in a renewal and continuation of the mystery of the Incarnation, into the body and blood of the Lamb already immolated and existing as an eternal, perfect holocaust.

And so, Scheeben concludes:

> In this way, Christ, as one who has already gone on ahead by reason of his death and resurrection, is offered to God from the midst of the Church as its sacrifice.[13]

The Eucharistic sacrifice on earth is the same sacrifice as Calvary and the same everlasting worship that Christ offers in eternal life. Saint Augustine, at the time of the death of his mother, Saint Monica, spoke of the Eucharist in a way that is neither an apology nor an argument, because it was the Tradition certainly accepted by the theologians of the Church at that time:

> For on that day when her death was so close, she was not concerned that her body should be sumptuously wrapped or embalmed with spices, nor with any thought of choosing a monument or even for burial in her own country. Of such things she gave us no command, but only desired to be remembered at Thy altar, which she had served without ever missing so much as a day, on which she knew that the holy Victim was offered, *by whom the handwriting is blotted out of the decree that was contrary to us*, by which offering too the enemy was overcome who, reckoning our sins and seeking what may be laid to our charge, found nothing in Him, in whom we are conquerors. Who shall restore to Him his innocent blood? Who shall give Him back the price by which He purchased us and so take us from Him? To this sacrament of our redemption Thy handmaid had bound her soul by the bond of faith.[14]

St. Aug. Confessions

Christ continuously surrenders Himself in heaven. Father Nichols cites the following passage from the Bavarian theologian Valentin Thalhofer (1825-1891):

In his soul, in his will, he retains the wholly willing and obedient renunciatory act of the surrender of his life on earth; and the willing act of his mediation on the Cross abides in him in the form of glory without strife or bitterness. . . . That the heavenly sacrifice also relates to the bodily nature of the Lord, that the permanence of the sacrifice of obedience in the soul of Christ must so be manifested somehow in his glorified bodily nature, can be understood of itself. Probably, the marks of the wounds which, according to Scripture and Tradition, Christ still bears in his body on high in heaven, are to be considered as the visible, bodily manifestation of the one abiding sacrifice in the soul. . . .

. . . [The act of eucharistic consecration] has the value and meaning of an act of sacrifice only because of its inner relation to that sacrificial death, which as a willing surrender of life it affirms anew, and continues, and recapitulates.[15]

Father Nichols parenthetically but insightfully points out that this view fits very well with the spirituality of the *Abandonment to Divine Providence* of Jean-Pierre de Caussade.[16] I know from my own struggles along the way that this rich and helpful spirituality of abandonment is one that is linked powerfully with the Eucharistic sacrifice. The following quotation from de Caussade's great eighteenth-century classic epitomizes the powerful link between the crucified Master and the struggling disciple: "If we wish to live according to the Gospel, we must abandon ourselves simply and completely to the action of God. Jesus Christ is its source. He 'is the same today as he was yesterday and as he will be forever' (Heb. 13:8). What he has done is finished, what remains to be done is being carried on every moment. Every saint shares in this divine life, and Jesus Christ, though always the same, is different in each one. The life of each saint is the life of Jesus Christ. It is a new gospel."[17]

In the twentieth century a similar understanding of the meaning of the sacrificial death of Christ and of the Eucharist as representing that complete act of self-giving has been developed by Hans Urs von Balthasar.[18] He develops beautifully the idea that the only way to interpret the life and especially the terrible death of the Lord is as one of obedient self-sacrifice. Von Balthasar sees the Liturgy of the Eucharist expressing this the same way that Christ did at the Last Supper in the distribution of His own Body and Blood, which had been surrendered to the Father:

> And when the primitive Church and Paul can, from the fact of Jesus' Resurrection, draw the conclusion that the Cross meant salvation for all (this remained unrecognized during the event itself) — "He was given up for our sins and raised for our justification" (Rom 4:25) — this truth, as a "sacred open secret," is already manifest in the gesture with which Jesus offers his Flesh and Blood at table as "given" and "poured out." . . . The passivity of the Passion, with its fetters, scourging, crucifixion and piercing, is the expression of a supremely active will to surrender which for that very reason transcends the limits of self-determination into the limitlessness of letting oneself be determined. On the other hand, such a will to surrender, which gives itself — in the eucharistic gesture of self-distribution — beyond all the bounds of human finitude. . . . Paul and John perceive this clearly in portraying the complete self-giving of Jesus to his own and to the world as the concretized self-giving of the Father, who, out of love for the world he created and in fidelity to his covenant with it, gives up what is most precious to him, his Son (Rom 8:32; Jn 3:16) . . . his Incarnation contains God's infinite will to give himself . . . insofar as it is God's personified gift to the world; and the realization of this self-giving at the Last Supper, the Passion and the Resurrection is nothing but the actualization of this self-giving that was always intended and really planned and initiated. . . . Jesus' eucharistic gesture of self-distribution to his Apostles, and through them to the world, is a definitive, eschatological and thus irreversible gesture. The Father's Word, made flesh, is definitively given and distributed by him and is never to be taken back.[19]

While it is not possible to do justice to von Balthasar's profound analysis, for our purposes it is sufficient to point out that for him the Mass is a sacrifice because it contains and proclaims the complete self-giving of the Son, and ultimately the overarching love of the Father. The proclamation of the death of the Lord until He comes must be sacrificial.

In all accepted theological theories about the Eucharistic sacrifice there is a single connecting element. The sacrifice is real because the bread and wine become the Body and Blood of Christ as He said they would at the Last Supper. He did not say, "This bread is my body"; rather He said, "This is my body."

Eucharistic sacrifice makes no sense unless Christ is really present as a man, as the Word made flesh, that is, with His Body and Blood, Soul and Divinity. The humanity of His person died on the cross, and so it is not His spirit as Word of God but rather His human reality as Son of man that is offered in the Mass. Since the Protestant reformers denied the Real Presence, they had to deny the sacrifice. The Eucharist became simply the Lord's Supper, a ritual passion play as it were, commemorating the death of Christ long ago. Of itself this sacred play even with Communion effected nothing for the believer other than a kind of edification, since salvation was an event completed in the past at the time of the conversion of the individual, rather than an ongoing vital relationship of development and struggle. By teaching this, the reformers rejected the whole postapostolic and patristic tradition, along with the theology of the Middle Ages that had come from it. They rejected everyone from Saint Ignatius of Antioch to Saint Augustine, as well as Saint Thomas and the Scholastics.

The following powerful sermon of Augustine (No. 329) sums up what the reformers lost and what the Catholic Church retains — namely, faith in the reality of Christ's presence in the Eucharist as His sacrifice:

> On the Cross, the Lord effected a great exchange; there the purse that contained the price of our redemption was opened. When his side was opened by the lance of the soldier, there flowed forth from it the price that redeemed the whole world. The faithful and the martyrs were bought by it, and the faith of the martyrs has been tested. Their blood is witness. They have given back what was paid for them, and fulfilled what St. John said, "As Christ laid down his life for us, so should we lay down our lives for the brethren." It is said elsewhere, "You have sat down at a great table. Diligently consider what is set before you because it is necessary

for you to prepare the same things." The great table is that at which the Lord of the table is himself the food. Now no one feeds the guests with his very self, but that is what the Lord Christ does. He is the One who invites, and he is the food and drink. Therefore the martyrs recognized what they ate and drank so that they might give back the same, viz. [their own lives].[20]

The Reality of Christ's Presence in Holy Communion

The word *communion* means the linking of two or more people in the same psychological reality. It may be the linking of people together in some heartfelt cause, or in the celebration of a loved one as with a birthday party, or in a grief shared as with a funeral. Communion can be said to exist on a deeply emotional and psychological level between spouses, friends, members of a family, or religious communities. There can be a kind of communion on the biological level, as we find with the mother and her unborn child. The word *communion* is generally reserved for positive relationships that go beyond the common needs and shared goals that characterize such institutions as trade unions or business corporations. Derived from the Latin *com* and *unio,* or *union together*, the term *communion* suggests a supportive and even loving relationship. A pack of thieves working closely together is a mob, not a communion; by contrast, the survivors of a concentration camp, meeting each other on the fiftieth anniversary of the end of World War II, reported that they experienced a communion forged by suffering and danger shared, even though they did not know each other earlier.

Religions often have expressions of communion, sacred unity, especially the monotheistic religions, in which one finds the communion of the children of a personal God, a heavenly Father. It is a part of religious history that Jesus of Nazareth placed communion at the center of the life of His new faith. Communion expressed the sharing of His good news, the Gospel. In a world of warring nations and combative tribes He sought to bring about a universal human communion with His prayer bidding all to call God "Our Father." It is no mere accident that on the grounds of the United Nations in New York City there is a statue of one of Christ's followers, the Augustinian friar José de la Victoria (1719-1798), who first wrote of a law of the nations. He was no doubt influenced by the work of the founder of his order, Saint Augustine's monumental classic, *The City of God.* No Father of the Church emphasizes the community aspect of the Eucharist more than Saint Augustine, for whom this sacrament is the *vinculum caritatis,* that is, the bond of unity in the Church.

Christ referred to the outcast as the least of His brothers (Mt 25:40). He said that whatever was done to them was done to Him, a very powerful expression of human communion. He taught that those who lived by the Word of God were brother and sister and mother to Him (Mt 12:50).

But Jesus of Nazareth brought this communion to a white-hot center of focus in the Eucharistic banquet, which is most properly known as Holy Communion. All Christians, whether they accept the Blessed Sacrament or not, see the bread and wine of communion as the bond of unity at least within their congregations, if not within the rest of the Christian world. There is no doubt that the nonsacramental exchange of bread and wine or even grape juice after the reading of the words of the Last Supper has formed a bond between many Christians who did not share with Catholic and Orthodox churches (and, to a lesser extent, with some Lutherans and Anglicans) the belief that these elements of the Eucharist are really the Body and Blood of Christ. I was deeply moved by this aspect of communion when I received the "Catholic Eucharist" at Taizé while Protestants received the "Protestant Eucharist" at the same communion service. This awkward yet devout communion service was held after the Mass, and it symbolized painfully — but clearly — the sad division in Christianity when the ancient faith in the reality of the Eucharist was lost.

In previous chapters we have reviewed the testimony and teaching of the Fathers and Doctors of the Church; however, it seems wise here to review modern Church teaching, since there appears to be some confusion and even muddling of the Catholic teaching on this most important subject.

Beginning again with the Council of Trent, we have the following decrees that all Catholics are bound to believe and confess. Deliberate denial of these teachings constitutes the serious sin of heresy for Catholics:

The holy synod teaches and openly and simply professes that, in the nourishing Sacrament of the holy Eucharist, after the Consecration of the bread and wine, Our Lord Jesus Christ, true God and man, is truly, really, and substantially contained under the species of those sensible realities (cf. Canon I). For it is not contradictory to say that our Savior himself always sits at the right hand of the Father in heaven, according to his natural mode of existing, and that, nevertheless, he is in many other places present to us sacramentally in his own substance, by a manner of existing that is possible to God, even though we can hardly express it in words, but that we, by an understanding illuminated by faith, are able to perceive and ought most firmly believe.

All our forefathers — as many of them as belonged to the true Church of Christ, and who have treated of this most holy Sacrament — have most clearly professed that our Redeemer instituted this admirable Sacrament at the Last Supper, when, after the blessing of the bread and wine, he testified in explicit and clear words that he gave them his own very Body and his own Blood.[21]

The Council of Trent also provides us with a clear and rather exhaustive list of the reasons why our Lord instituted the Eucharist as a sacrament, based on the words of Christ in the Gospel and the words of Saint Paul:

Therefore, our Savior, when about to depart out of this world to the Father, instituted this Sacrament, in which as it were he poured forth the riches of his divine love toward the human race, "making a memorial of his wonderful works" (Ps III:4). He commanded us in the reception of this Sacrament to venerate his memory (I Cor II:24) and to announce his death until he comes to judge the world (I Cor II:26). He willed also that this Sacrament should be received as the spiritual food of souls (Mt 26:26) by which those may be fed and strengthened who live with the life of him who said: "Whoever eats me shall live because of me" (Jn 6:58). He willed that it be an antidote by which we may be freed from daily faults and be preserved from mortal sins. He willed, furthermore, to have it be a pledge of our future glory and of everlasting happiness, and in this way be a symbol of that one Body of which he is the head (I Cor II:3) and to which he willed us to be joined as members united by the closest bonds of faith, hope, and charity, so that "we might all speak the same things, and there might be no schisms among us" (I Cor I:10).[22]

In more recent times, the Church has stressed that Christ is present to His people in many ways, but that none of these detract from the unique experience of the reception of Holy Communion and, in the aftermath of that reception, the adoration of the Real Presence. The following statement of the new *Catechism of the Catholic Church* summarizes this very well: " 'Christ Jesus, who died, yes, who was raised from the dead, who is at the right hand of God, who indeed intercedes for us,' is present in many ways to his Church: in his word, in his Church's prayer, 'where two or three are gathered in my name,' in the poor, the sick, and the imprisoned, in the sacraments of which he is the author, in the sacrifice of the Mass, and in the person of the minister. But 'he is present . . . most *especially in the Eucharistic species.*' "[23]

Recent Church documents have certainly stressed what might be called a principle of integration in sacramental theology, rather than stressing the unique significance of each sacrament. They have all been seen as strengthening our incorporation into the Mystical Body of Christ, and His life and presence that comes to us by this union, rather than minimizing the importance of any sacrament, it seems that this emphasis heightens the meaning of them all. The Real Presence of Christ in the Eucharist seen in this way is even more powerfully proclaimed, as Paul VI said in *Mysterium Fidei*: "This presence is called 'real' — by which is not intended to exclude the other types of presence as if they could not be 'real' too, but because it is presence in the fullest sense: that is to say, it is a substantial presence by which Christ, God and man, makes himself wholly and entirely present."[24]

In our coming chapter on opposition to Eucharistic worship, we will see that some have used this idea of integrating the sacraments into the whole mystery of Christ to minimize and sometimes to belittle Eucharistic worship. This was never the intention of the Church, as is clear from these words of Pope John Paul II in *Dominicae Cenae* ("Of the Supper of the Lord"): "The Church and the world have a great need for Eucharistic worship. Jesus awaits us in this sacrament of love. Let us not refuse the time to go to meet him in adoration, in contemplation full of faith, and open to making amends for the serious offenses and crimes of the world. Let our adoration never cease."[25]

In the world of tangible reality (which is, after all, how we measure the ultimate effects of theological teaching), one can see that it is precisely the same people that are deeply devoted to the liturgy as a prayerful expression of their unity with Christ who also adore His presence in the Eucharist. In an article in the *Canadian Catholic Review*, Leo Sands, CSB, makes the following statement, backing it up with the teaching of Pope Paul VI: "But as we probably have observed, those Catholics who pray before the Blessed Sacrament are often the same ones who are active participants at the Eucharist, particularly on weekdays. The two actions reinforce one another. This explains the repeated advocacy shortly after Vatican II of Eucharistic devotion, exposition, and Corpus Christi processions. Pope Paul VI spoke of 'the indescribable gift of the Eucharist the Church received from Christ as a pledge of his love . . . not only while the sacrifice is being offered . . . but as long as the Eucharist is kept in our churches and oratories, Christ is truly the Emmanuel, the God with us. . . . Day and night he is in our midst. . . . Anyone who approaches this August sacrament with special devotion . . . experiences how great is the value of communing with Christ . . . for there is nothing more effective for advancing on the road to holiness' " (*The Mystery of Faith* 1.67).[26]

The Bread of Life

As early as the fourth century, Saint Augustine encouraged people to receive Holy Communion every day: "Receive daily that it may profit you daily. . . . So live as to deserve to receive it [the sacrament] daily.[27] No doubt Augustine had learned this from his mother, who he tells us received Communion every day.[28]

Saint Thomas Aquinas had very practical ideas about the reception of Holy Communion based on the needs of the struggling Christian making the spiritual journey of life:

> Two considerations about the reception of this sacrament. The
> first regards the sacrament itself, the virtue of which is salutary

to man: consequently, it is profitable to receive daily, so as to gather its fruits daily. Hence Ambrose says, "if whenever Christ's blood is shed, it is shed for the forgiveness of sins, I, who sin often, should receive it often; I need a frequent remedy." The second (consideration) regards the recipient, who is required to approach this sacrament with great reverence and devotion. Consequently, if someone finds he has these dispositions every day, he does well to receive daily.

Augustine, after saying, "Receive daily that it may profit you daily," adds, "So live as to deserve to receive it daily." Since many are often impeded from such devotion, on account of indispositions of body and soul, it is not expedient for all to approach this sacrament daily, but as often as they find themselves properly prepared. So we are told, "Neither praise nor blame daily reception of the Eucharist."[29]

Saint Thomas makes an analogy between the food of nourishment and the feeding of the life of the soul. This is a perfectly appropriate analogy, for Christ Himself had used it when speaking of the Bread of Life that He said was His Body: "The body needs nourishment to restore what is lost daily through the action of natural heat. In the life of the soul, too, something is lost in us every day through venial sin which lessens the warmth of charity. But the Eucharist confers the virtue of charity, because it is the sacrament of love."[30]

The Bond of Unity

The reception of Communion was not only seen as nourishment and even medicine (because it takes away repented venial sins and faults) but also as the bond of unity in the Church. Modern writers stressing the ecclesial or communitarian aspects of the Eucharist often seem to be unaware that this was a very powerful theme in ancient times and in the medieval Church. Cardinal Henri de Lubac did a powerful study of precisely this aspect of the Eucharist in his work entitled *Corpus Mysticum: L'Eucharistie et l'Eglise au moyen age* ("The Mystical Body: The Eucharist and the Church in the Middle Ages"). He stressed that the sacrament was seen both as Eucharistic and personal on the one hand and ecclesial and communitarian on the other.[31]

One reason already alluded to for the Eucharist being a bond of unity is that it effectively removes class distinctions in the most authoritative way. All kneel in adoration before the presence of the universal Messiah and King. Already in the Gospel we see this in the case of the Roman centurion of Capernaum. His recognition of the authority of Christ would be remembered in the Mass till the end of the world: "Lord, I am not worthy to have you come under my roof; but only say the word, and my servant will be healed" (Mt 8:8). Only someone who has experienced the devout reception of the Eucharist at a Liturgy where the powerful and the weak of the world come together, as in a cathedral church or shrine, can know this leveling aspect of the presence of Jesus of Nazareth, carpenter and Messiah. It is a joyous leveling, not one inspired by law or constraint. It is a leveling of the heart.

Recently I was privileged to be one of a thousand priests who concelebrated and distributed the Bread of Life to the huge multitudes welcoming Pope John Paul II to New York's Central Park (October 7, 1995). Every ethnic group imaginable was there and all shared in the Banquet of the Lord. The rich, even the very rich, and the poor (including the homeless), scholars, and retarded people in wheelchairs were in the vast congregation of over one hundred thousand. All rejoiced mightily to gather in the mysterious presence of Christ, who came to each one individually. As we left in great crowds walking through the streets of Manhattan, each one going back to his or her own responsibilities, burdens, and modest joys, for a moment we knew that we were brothers and sisters in the same family. This process has been renewed continuously for two thousand years. Of course there are always people who don't get the point, as Saint Paul and Saint James observed in Gospel times:

> When you meet together, it is not the Lord's supper that you eat. For in eating, each one goes ahead with his own meal, and one is hungry and another is drunk. What! Do you not have houses to eat and drink in? Or do you despise the church of God and humiliate those who have nothing? What shall I say to you? Shall I commend you in this? No, I will not.
> — 1 Corinthians 11:20-22

My brethren, show no partiality as you hold the faith of our Lord Jesus Christ, the Lord of glory. For if a man with gold rings and in fine clothing comes into your assembly, and a poor man in shabby clothing also comes in, and you pay attention to the one who wears the fine clothing and say, "Have a seat here, please," while you say to the poor man, "Stand there," or, "Sit at my feet," have you not made distinctions among yourselves, and become judges with evil thoughts? Listen, my beloved brethren. Has not God chosen those who are poor in the world to be rich in faith and heirs of the kingdom which he has promised to those who love him? But you have dishonored the poor man. Is it not the rich who oppress you, is it not they who drag you into court? Is it not they who blaspheme that honorable name by which you are called?

— James 2:1-7

Even Jesus had to correct the disciples who wanted to be first. Nevertheless, the presence of Christ coming to all who are spiritually prepared by conversion of heart in every age preaches and evokes a response of universal human solidarity and brotherhood that no political or ideological system has ever been able to sustain. The power of this bonding and universalizing aspect of the Eucharist is inescapable precisely because the Christ received in the sacrament is one of us, an earthly carpenter and a heavenly King, a real presence in our world.

The Promise of Life After Death

The reception of the Holy Eucharist is also a promise and preparation for eternal life. The Church's celebration of the Real Presence of the human Christ in the sacrament in both East and West, in the Orthodox Churches as well as in the Catholic Church, is incomprehensible without the Resurrection. If Christ is not physically and bodily risen, the Eucharistic Liturgy becomes a kind of séance, the evocation of the spirit of a dead man. Many theologians see in the Eucharistic celebration and banquet the most powerful witness to the bodily resurrection of Christ, which is in turn our promise of eternal life. Surely it must be recognized that in the other monotheistic religions, or in the monotheistic interpretations of Buddhism and Hinduism (and this is not as unusual as Western people may think), the founders or sacred figures of these faiths held out the hope of survival of death. This is especially true in Judaism and Islam, since both proclaim that God is the God of Abraham, Isaac, and Jacob.

As Jesus pointed out, "not God of the dead, but of the living" (Mt 22:32). However, without any real religious parallel, the resurrection of Jesus of Nazareth as it is proclaimed in the whole New Testament is the return of the living man, not only a spirit: "But they were startled and frightened, and supposed that they saw a spirit. And he said to them, 'Why are you troubled, and why do questionings rise in your hearts? See my hands and my feet, that it is I myself; handle me, and see; for a spirit has not flesh and bones as you see that I have.' And when he had said this, he showed them his hands and his feet. And while they still disbelieved for joy, and wondered, he said to them, 'Have you anything here to eat?' They gave him a piece of broiled fish, and he took it and ate before them" (Lk 24:37-43).

It is the same living Person who, having returned from the dead, is received in the Eucharist. If only the divine Person of the Logos (or the Second Person of the Trinity) came to us in the Eucharist, this would not be a clear promise of our own bodily resurrection, although it could be an affirmation of the survival of the soul. As uncomfortable as it may make the "enlightened" Christians of our time, the teaching and promise of Christ about life after death is one that includes the whole person, body and soul linked forever, corporeally and spiritually if you will. It is one of the greater oddities of the present odd theological climate that the very same people who on the one hand emphasize the essential unity of body and soul to the point of denying the individual's survival of death on the other hand deny the physical reality of Christ's resurrection, and claim that His appearance was only spiritual and that His corpus remained in the ground. One way or the other it seems to this boy from Jersey City that they get "hoisted on their own petard."

It was a living man whom the disciples encountered and described. True, He lived a life like no other because He would not die again. But the Gospels emphasize His physicality, His wounds, His flesh and bones, His eating of the fish, and that He could be touched.

This is the Christ who mysteriously returns in the Eucharist, not simply a soul.

The Pilgrim's Bread

The intuition of the Church and the corporate realization of the meaning of the Real Presence of the human Christ in the Eucharist have caused her to link the reception of Holy Communion with the hour of death in Viaticum, that is, the pilgrim's Bread. Not only is this reception of the Eucharist a tremendous encouragement and reassurance to someone in danger of death and thinking of that mysterious passage (as anyone who has received Viaticum and survived can tell you), but the Blessed Sacrament is itself a mystical sign of the world to come.

Christ Himself at the Last Supper spoke mysteriously of the link between His sacramental act and the celebration of the Paschal Mystery in the world to come: "I tell you I shall not drink again of this fruit of the vine until that day when I drink it new with you in my Father's kingdom" (Mt 26:29; also see Lk 22:18 and Mk 14:25). Christians have never doubted that since Jesus had promised to come at the end of the ages (cf. Jn 14:28, Acts 1:11), and He had promised to go beyond death to prepare a place for us (cf. Jn 14:3), it was the resurrected Son of man and child of Mary who awaited them in eternal life. This is the radical meaning of His mysterious ascension. How can the Eucharist be a sign of eternal life and the world to come unless it is actually the mysterious and Real Presence of Christ in His Body and Blood who comes to us in Holy Communion?

The whole idea of the Eucharist is that it is a sign that at the end of the ages we shall with our body and soul be united with Christ who is really present to us now with His Body and Blood. "The death of the Lord" and His return are events that include body and spirit so that the Eucharist we celebrate is not simply spiritual but corporeal. For this reason Saint Paul states that in the Eucharist we "proclaim the Lord's death until he comes" (1 Cor 11:26).

The Mystery of Faith

Finally, an overlooked spiritual benefit of Holy Communion is that it confronts the believer with mystery. To look at the wafer and the sip of wine (fruits of the earth and work of human hands, and, I might add, machines) and to believe that because of the spoken words of a mortal man (even if ordained with apostolic succession) that this is the living Body of Christ, is a test of faith. Some people shy away from this test, but I say, "Great!" As we mentioned in the first chapter, the Eucharist is a mystery; but as far as we are concerned, it is only one of many mysteries that we confront if we open our eyes to what is happening around us.

Earthly mysteries — time, matter, the big bang, energy, gravity, life, thought, memory, decision, desire, human aspiration and relationships — are all around us (remember what Saint Thomas said about the philosopher and the bee). Revealed mysteries — creation, the fall, salvation, redemption, eternal life, the life of the Messiah, His miracles and resurrection — also surround us. If we have any intelligence at all, we must see that our human reason floats in seas of mystery. Some of the earthly mysteries are so vast that they might just as well be as unfathomable or infinite as the eternal ones are. The difference is that the natural ones are to some degree known through the senses, and the supernatural ones are known through revelation. Perhaps we will be able to understand the natural mysteries in eternal life if we care then at all about them. The supernatural ones will to some extent always elude us, because some of them are rooted in the infinite mystery of God.

Why then draw the line at the Eucharist? It remains a mystery to me how the Protestant reformers with their obvious faith in Christ ever drew the line at the Eucharist with its awesome scriptural roots, its splendid patristic foundations, and its wonderful effects in the lives of the saints. It is equally mysterious to me how some contemporary Catholics minimize, play down, or even distort beyond any real recognition the biblical and patristic faith of the Church in the reality of the Body and Blood, Soul and Divinity, of Christ in the mystical signs of the Eucharist, a knowledge available to all who turn their hearts and minds to Christ.

I brought Holy Communion as Viaticum to a repentant man who had in the past rejected Christ, hated the Church, involved himself in the gay scene with abandon and debauchery. According to his own account he had rejected his baptism and faith, hated and cursed the Church and all the Church stood for, and when the

Holy Spirit called to him shortly before the end, with tears of repentance and joyous gratitude, he embraced the death that sexual indulgence had caused. The Son of God (who had been made the Son of man in the womb of the Virgin Mother) came to him at the end of his wasted life and he embraced Christ. He acknowledged that the little wafer I put on his tongue as he lay dying was the same Jesus of Nazareth who summoned the good thief to paradise at the hour of death. It is a mystery to me that any person who claims that he or she accepts the Catholic faith and knows this does not fall down on his or her face before the Eucharist and cry out, "Jesus, Savior, have mercy on me a sinner."

The Reality of Christ's Presence Outside of the Liturgy

The familiar word "presence" actually refers to a complex phenomenon observable in all living things that enjoy some degree of awareness and consciousness. Even very simple animals react to one another, and may be said to have a sense of presence that is, however, not reflective. Human beings can think about the fact that they were and are aware of another living creature or fellow human being who responds to them.

On a much higher plane we restrict the idea of presence to human interactions; even pet lovers will be hesitant to say that they are, for example, in the presence of a cat. We certainly experience presence in a particular way with an infant, although the child is not reflective. Usually, we are most present to those who are present to us, who pay attention to us. Yet one can feel the presence in a person who is the center of attraction amidst a great crowd. If you were at a papal audience, you would have some sense of being present with the Pope, although he does not specifically know that you are there or who you are.

Presence has some rather mysterious elements to it. It has little to do with physical proximity. You may be actually touching the arm of a person sitting next to you on a bus and not even be aware if this passenger is a man or woman. You may be very close and yet not be present. On the other hand, you may speak to a friend ten thousand miles away on the telephone and nonetheless be present to that person through your responses via electrical impulses sent through the air. What is most mysterious is that you may find a letter from your grandmother who died years ago, and if you stop to reflect upon it you emotionally respond to memories, making it seem as if she were present. In a way she is.

What Do We Mean by the Presence of God?

When we speak of the presence of God, it is an act of faith in the omnipresence and omniscience of our Creator. Faith may make us aware of His presence, but often some scene of natural grandeur or the silence of some solitary place will draw our minds into a deeper experience of relationship and reverence with our Creator. Then the Psalmist's words will be so meaningful:

> Whither shall I go from thy Spirit?
> Or whither shall I flee from thy presence?
> If I ascend to heaven, thou art there!
> If I make my bed in Sheol, thou art there!
> If I take the wings of the morning
> and dwell in the uttermost parts of the sea,
> even there thy hand shall lead me,
> and thy right hand shall hold me.
> — Psalm 139:7-10

This experience of Divine Presence is an act of faith, which is to say it is also an act of decision or of the will. When we do not consciously make an act of faith, yet an awareness of the Divine Presence envelops us spontaneously, we have an example of one of the most profound religious experiences possible. One example of such an experience of the Divine Presence was the conversion of the French atheist and Communist André Frossard. While waiting for a friend, he had gone into the chapel of a cloistered convent as a "complacent atheist." Standing in the back of the chapel, he was literally overwhelmed by the presence of a God in whom he did not believe. His own words describe this experience of an unexpected presence that has been the source of many unexplainable conversions:

> The end of the chapel was rather brightly lit. The high altar
> was draped in white and covered with a great many plants and

candelabra and a variety of ornaments. Above it hung a large metal cross; at its centre there was a white disc, and three others that were slightly different were fixed to the extremities of the cross.

In the interest of art, I had previously visited churches but I had never before seen a host, much less a monstrance with a host in it. I was therefore quite unaware that before me was the Blessed Sacrament below which many candles were burning. . . .

I didn't see the point of all this, naturally, since I was not looking for it. Standing by the door, I looked out for my friend, but I was not able to identify him among the kneeling figures. . . . Then, for no particular reason, I fixed my eyes on the second candle on the left-hand side of the cross.

It was at this moment that, suddenly, the series of extraordinary events was set in motion whose extreme violence was about to dismantle the absurd creature that I had been until that moment and give birth to the dazzled child I had never been.

First, were the words: *spiritual life.*

They were not said to me nor did I form them in my mind; it was as though they were being spoken by someone close to me who was seeing something which I had not yet seen.

The last syllable had hardly brushed my conscious mind when an avalanche descended upon me. I am not saying that the heavens opened; they didn't open — they were hurled at me, they rose suddenly flashing silently from the depths of this innocent chapel in which they were mysteriously present.

How can I describe what took place in words which refuse to carry the sense, which indeed do worse, for they threaten to intercept what I have to say and in doing so to relegate my meaning to the land of fancy? Were a painter to be given the gift of seeing colours that are unknown to man what would he use to paint them with?

What can I say to describe that which I apprehended?

It was an indestructible crystal, totally transparent, luminous (to such a degree that any further intensity would have destroyed me), with a colour near to blue; a different world, whose brilliance and density made our world seem like the wraith of an unfulfilled dream. What I saw was reality; this was truth and I was seeing it from the dim shore on which I still stood. Now I knew that there is order in the universe and at its beginning, beyond the shining mists, the manifestation of God: a manifestation which is a presence, which is a person, the person whose existence I should have denied a moment ago, the presence of him whom the Christians call *Our Father*. And I knew that he was gentle, that his gentleness was unparalleled and that his was not the passive quality that is sometimes called by the name of gentleness, but an active shattering gentleness, far outstripping violence, able to smash the hardest stone and to smash something often harder than stone, the human heart.

This surging, overwhelming invasion brought with it a sense of joy comparable to that of a drowning man who is rescued at the last moment, but with this difference that it was at the moment in which I was being hauled to safety that I became aware of the mud in which, without noticing it, I had till then been stuck; and now I wondered how I had ever been able to breathe and to live in it.[32]

Commenting later on this experience, Frossard said that the fact that he emerged from the chapel a Catholic was similar to what his experience would have been if he had gone to the Paris Zoo and come out a giraffe. Ordinarily our experiences of God are not so startling or unexpected. Believing Christians usually need only make an act of faith that Christ is present.

We believe that He is the Word through which "all things were made" (Nicene Creed [ICEL translation]). And so to use the words of the Irish poet Joseph Mary Plunkett, we "see His blood upon the rose / And in the stars the glory of His eyes."[33] Yet Christians who undertake to serve the poor and needy occasionally have the profound and spontaneous experience of Christ's presence as they respond to His words in Matthew 25, ". . . I was hungry and you gave me food. . . . I was a stranger and you welcomed me . . ." (verse 35).

We also experience Christ's presence as an aspect of the omnipresence of God. Christians believe they can address prayers to Christ at any time or place because, to use the words of Saint Augustine, God "is ever mindful of us all" (*Confessions*, Book 9, Chapter 3). But again, to do this usually requires an act of faith. As the ancient prayer called "The Deer's Cry," or "St. Patrick's Breastplate," puts it so well, "Christ with me, Christ before me, Christ behind me, Christ in me, Christ beneath me, Christ above me. . . ."[34]

The Absence of God

A word must be said about the absence of God. This painful experience is often mentioned in the Jewish Scriptures. In the Book of Psalms we read, "But I, O Lord, cry to thee; in the morning my prayer comes before thee. O Lord, why dost thou cast me off? Why dost thou hide thy face from me? Afflicted and close to death from my youth up, I suffer thy terrors; I am helpless" (Ps 88:13-15).

Many Christian saints have written about the experience of God being "far away," especially in a time of suffering and darkness. The words of Saint Thérèse of Lisieux have a painful but familiar ring to so many on the spiritual journey. The remarkable quotation we are about to read is taken from the writings composed by Saint Thérèse a short time before her death on September 30, 1897, at the request of her prioress, Mother Marie de Gonzague. Saint Thérèse had suffered much in her very young life, and at the time of this writing was experiencing not only the effects of terminal tuberculosis, but also profound spiritual darkness:

I wish I could put down what I feel about it, but unfortunately that isn't possible; to appreciate the darkness of this tunnel, you have to have been through it. Perhaps, though, I might try to explain it by a comparison. You must imagine that I've been born in a country entirely overspread with a thick mist; I have never seen nature in her smiling mood, all bathed and transfigured in the sunlight. But I've heard of these wonderful experiences, ever since I was a child; and I know that the country in which I live is not my native country; *that lies elsewhere*, and it must always be the centre of my longings. Mightn't that, you suggest, be simply a fable, invented by some dweller in the mist? Oh no, the fact is certain; the King of that sunlit country has come and lived in the darkness, lived there for thirty-three years.

Poor darkness, that could not recognise him for what he was, the King of Light! But here am I, Lord, one of your own children, to whom your divine light has made itself known. . . .

Dear Mother, I seem to be writing just anyhow; here is my fairy-story about the country of darkness turning all of a sudden into a kind of prayer. I can't imagine how it can interest you, trying to master ideas so badly expressed and so confused as mine. But after all, Mother, I'm not writing for the sake of literary effect, I'm simply writing under obedience, and even if you find it tedious, you will at least realise that I've done my best. So I will make bold to take up my parable where I left off. What I was saying was that the sure prospect of escaping from this dark world of exile had been granted me from childhood upwards; and it wasn't simply that I accepted it on the authority of people who knew more of the matter than I did — I felt, in the very depths of my heart, aspirations which could only be satisfied by a world more beautiful than this. Just as Christopher Columbus divined, by instinct, the existence of a New World which nobody had hitherto dreamt of, so I had this feeling that a better country was to be, one day, my abiding home. And now, all of a sudden, the mists around me have become denser than ever; they sink deep into my soul and wrap it round so that I can't recover the dear image of my native country any more — everything has disappeared.

I get tired of the darkness all around me, and try to refresh my jaded spirits with the thoughts of that bright country where my hopes lie; and what happens? It is worse torment than ever; the darkness itself seems to borrow, from the sinners who live in it, the gift of speech. I hear its mocking accents: 'It's all a dream, this talk of a heavenly country, bathed in light, scented with delicious perfumes, and of a God who made it all, who is to be your possession in eternity! You really believe, do you, that the mist which hangs about you will clear away later on? All right, all right, go on longing for death! But death will make nonsense of your hopes; it will only mean a night darker than ever, the night of mere non-existence.' . . .

Dear Mother, does it sound as if I were exaggerating my symptoms? Of course, to judge by the sentiments I express in all the nice little poems I've made up during the last year, you might imagine that my soul was as full of consolations as it could hold;

that, for me, the veil which hides the unseen scarcely existed. And all the time it isn't just a veil, it's a great wall which reaches up to the sky and blots out the stars! No, when I write poems about the happiness of heaven and the eternal possession of God, it strikes no chord of happiness in my own heart — I'm simply talking about what I'd determined to believe. Sometimes, it's true, a tiny ray of light pierces through the darkness, and then, just for a moment, the ordeal is over; but immediately afterwards the memory of it brings me no happiness, it seems to make the darkness thicker than ever.[35]

Let me draw your attention to the fact that such an experience of isolation and loneliness is only possible because Saint Thérèse believed that God was present, and thus on rare occasions during her time of trial she experienced the Divine Presence as a "tiny ray of light." In a paradoxical way, it is only faith in God's presence that makes it possible to experience His absence.

The Experience of Presence

All of this should convince the reader that presence is a more complicated thing than initially assumed, especially an awareness of God's presence. Let's look for some answers to the question of what presence is in our own experience. The most obvious fact is that presence focuses our attention. Usually this focus is directed to a person or to a place. Since God is invisible, the religions of the world use natural objects, images, books, relics, or symbols to focus the attention of the seeker after God. It may be the great gilded boulder perched precariously on the edge of a cliff that Hindus visit, or for Buddhists the magnificent statue of the Buddha, or for Muslims the Dome of the Rock, or for Jews the western wall of the Temple, or simply, for a Christian, a well-worn Bible or an icon of Christ and our Lady. Presence needs some focus, because someone who is everywhere seems actually to be nowhere, and as we have seen, a presence that does not independently intrude upon our senses requires a decision, for otherwise we will not be aware of it.

To be aware of the presence of Christ, whether in a sacrament or not, we need a decision of the will to acknowledge this presence by faith. If we wish in some appropriate way to respond, we need the further decision to be attentive, reverent, and even adoring, with our attention powerfully focused. This is the decision to pray and to pray well. In his helpful book, *Sensing Your Hidden Presence*, Father Ignacio Larranaga analyzes the necessary and voluntary steps of the experience of the presence of God. He notes that for many the awareness of the presence of Christ is easier and more personally effective. While his entire book may be read with much profit, for our purposes the following citation on the awareness of the presence of Christ is quite sufficient:

> It is difficult for many people to place themselves in contact with the transcendant God. Nevertheless, these same people rapidly and easily enter into dialogue with the risen and present Jesus. This ease is all the more notable when they relate with Jesus in the Eucharist.
>
> While at prayer, they sense Jesus as Someone concrete and very near, like a close friend. They adore Him, praise Him, ask Him for forgiveness, strength or consolation; with Him and in Him they place their commitments and hardships; they are forgiven and they forgive others, and so the wounds of life are healed. There is no way to classify this prayer or even define it: figment of the imagination? A simple vision of faith? Although the greatest freedom is granted each individual, it is advisable, for the first steps, to have this familiar relationship with Jesus, in the simplicity of faith.
>
> On the other hand, there are those who, from the beginning, feel a dark and irresistible attraction to the Invisible, Eternal, and Omnipotent. No one knows whether this is a particular predisposition or a special grace.[36]

How We Respond to the Divine Presence of Christ

Throughout the ages man has sought to find, to name, and to experience his Creator. The most positive attitude we can take toward the universal phenomenon of religion is precisely this — it is a search by the creature for the Creator, the pursuit of the absolute, and in most cases a hungering by those who know they are wounded and incomplete for the absolute good. Monotheistic religions proclaim the belief that this mysterious creating force is "a person" who knows His creatures. Monotheistic believers fall before their Maker with a reverence so complete, so integrated, that we call it *adoration* in English, from the Latin words *ad orare* meaning "to pray to." A Greek word for the highest worship is *latria*, meaning complete and total reverence to be offered only to God.[37]

At least from the time of Abraham it has been clear that the worship described as adoration, or *latria*, is totally different from the honor shown to any remarkably blessed or dedicated person such as a prophet or saint. In Latin this latter kind of religious honor is called *dulia*, with its highest form, *hyperdulia*, reserved for the Virgin Mother of Christ. In no way does this honor approach the worship or adoration of God. It is important to note that even in its very early decades the Church offered the worship of *latria* — complete, unparalleled, and uninhibited worship — to Christ. We find this in the New Testament, for example, in the following magnificent quote from Saint Paul: ". . . at the name of Jesus every knee should bow, in heaven and on earth and under the earth . . ." (Phil 2:10). The adoration of Christ is also clearly brought out in the Book of Revelation:

> Grace to you and peace from him who is and who was and who is to come, and from the seven spirits who are before his throne, and from Jesus Christ the faithful witness, the first-born of the dead, and the ruler of kings on earth.
>
> To him who loves us and has freed us from our sins by his blood and made us a kingdom, priests to his God and Father, to him be glory and dominion for ever and ever. Amen. Behold, he is coming with the clouds, and every eye will see him, every one who pierced him; and all tribes of the earth will wail on account of him. Even so. Amen.
>
> "I am the Alpha and the Omega," says the Lord God, who is and who was and who is to come, the Almighty.
>
> — Revelation 1:4-8

Advancing from the first century to the second we find evidence of the worship of *latria*, or adoration, being offered to Christ in several authors, including Saint Ignatius of Antioch and Saint Justin

Martyr. On his way to martyrdom in Rome in the year 107, Ignatius wrote to the Church at Smyrna: "I give glory to Jesus Christ, the God who has imbued you with such wisdom. I am well aware that you have been made perfect in unwavering faith, like men nailed, in body and spirit, to the Cross of our Lord, Jesus Christ, and confirmed in love by the blood of Christ. In regard to our Lord, you are thoroughly convinced that He was of the race of David according to the flesh, and the Son of God by His will and power; that He was truly born of the Virgin and baptized by John in order that all due observance might be fulfilled by Him (Mt. 3:15); that in His body He was truly nailed to the Cross for our sake. . . ."[38]

Later in the second century, Justin Martyr apparently had a debate with a man he calls Trypho, one of the Jewish refugees from the war in Israel around the year 132. Afterward, perhaps as late as 160, Justin published this debate, apparently with much embellishment. It is a very useful document for understanding both the Judaism and the Christianity of the time. In a long section encompassing Chapters 48 to 108 Justin justifies the adoration of Christ and proves that He is the Messiah and Son of God. Commenting on the opening verses of Psalm 96, "O sing to the Lord a new song," Justin applies these verses to Christ as God, indicating that among the works of Christ He is Maker of heaven and earth: " 'Sing unto the Lord a new song; sing unto the Lord, all the earth: sing unto the Lord, and bless His name; show forth His salvation from day to day, His wonderful works among all people.' He bids the inhabitants of all the earth, who have known the mystery of this salvation, i.e., the suffering of Christ, by which He saved them, sing and give praises to God the Father of all things, and recognise that He is to be praised and feared, and that He is the Maker of heaven and earth, who effected this salvation in behalf of the human race, who also was crucified and was dead, and who was deemed worthy by Him (God) to reign over all the earth."[39]

It should come as no surprise that New Testament writers, as well as the Fathers immediately after the apostolic period, ascribed to Christ worship reserved to God, in view of the following texts related to the divinity of Christ. Admittedly the full importance of this mysterious fact that Jesus of Nazareth was the only-begotten Son of God was not made as clear as it could be until the great councils: Nicaea, Ephesus, and Chalcedon; nevertheless, members of the Church worshiped Christ as equal to the Father. With no great debate the Fathers of the Council of Nicaea (325) could proclaim that Jesus of Nazareth was "God from God, Light from Light, true God from true God, begotten, not made, one in Being with the Father" (Nicene Creed [ICEL translation]).

Even though the final codification of the New Testament would happen later at the end of the fourth century (in 398 at the Council of Carthage), the Gospel of John had been universally accepted since the second century. In that Gospel as well as in Saint Paul's letters the divinity of Christ was proclaimed. The skeptical environment of the nineteenth-century "Enlightenment" has had its own baneful return to life in the present materialistic age, when the foundation of belief in Christianity, faith in the divinity of its Founder, has been challenged again. Not only do some now question the ancient doctrine proclaimed by Nicaea, Ephesus, Chalcedon, and the other early councils, but they even question the scriptural origins of this belief. Naturally they oppose prayer to the risen Christ — if they believe in prayer at all.

My suspicion is that much of the skeptical irreverence shown to the Eucharistic Presence in our time is based on a gnawing doubt that one can pray to the risen Jesus at all. For a variety of reasons the virulence of this skepticism has begun to recede as the twentieth century draws to a close. Perhaps the reduction of this skepticism is partially attributable to the departure from the ranks of Christian theologians and students of those who nurtured profound doubts while still clinging to some religious practice. The high point of this skepticism came in the sixties and seventies, when belief in the transcendent mysteries of God was construed by many to be opposed to the social responsibility of Christians. Moreover, this rather dull skepticism has given way to what is worse, if possible — the ersatz mysticism of the New Age. The shadowy Christ of Rudolf Bultmann has been replaced by the Sophia-Christ of the shabby gnosticism of Shirley MacLaine and such people.

The Testimony of a Scholar

It is worthwhile for our purposes to look back and see that even in that skeptical atmosphere twenty-five years ago there were great biblical scholars whose own faith withstood the skepticism of the times. The following paragraphs are taken from a small but most significant book, *Belief in the New Testament*, by the eminent Catholic New Testament scholar Rudolf Schnackenburg, first published in 1973. It is significant for us to note that Father Schnackenburg did his most important writing on the Gospel of Saint John:

> John's Gospel, which has particularly occupied my thoughts in my theological work, clarifies for me in a particular way, which is at once time-conditioned and yet timeless, the unique significance of the person of Jesus for myself and for everyone. A lot would have to be said and clarified if I were not to be misunderstood. But I want just to take one sentence which I find particularly illuminating on the question of discipleship: 'I am the light of the world; anyone who follows me will not be walking in the dark; he will have the light of life' (8:12). This is not a magic Gnostic formula explaining human existence in mythical language, or a call to self-discovery, but an invitation to follow Jesus. Here again the earthly Jesus is prominent with his road to death on the Cross and his commandment to love which sums up everything that is demanded of me. But it has become a saying of the living, ever-present Lord who promises the light of life to whoever believes.
>
> As a young man I determined to accept this invitation of Jesus to be his disciple because it seemed to me to be the greatest thing I could live for. From that moment, despite all the historical changes and spiritual vicissitudes of my generation, I have not been mistaken. Indeed, all these upheavals, the sheer 'historicity' of everything human, the transitoriness of human ideologies, the short-lived vogue of even the most passionate popular movements have only led me to adhere more closely still to Jesus of Nazareth. He shows me what is most deeply human, the needs common to all men in their humanity, and the longing for the ultimate fulfilment of their being which cannot be stifled or silenced with material things. His life and work in history are programmatic and exemplary: a herald of limitless love and an advocate for the poor and despised, a helper of the weak, a man of understanding and forgiveness to sinners, a harsh critic of stony-hearted men who misuse their position, wealth and power, their intellectual and spiri-

tual authority, a man quick to detect untruthfulness and hypocrisy, a man of God for whom only God's standards are good enough: God is no respecter of persons, he looks not to what is exterior but to man's heart.

Even Jesus' life on earth seems to me exemplary: people's favour, the judgement of men, is irresolute and unreliable, success and external happiness are but temporary. No one can escape trial, suffering and death. Jesus too had to tread this path, and he accepted it with joy. Although rejected by man, he was acknowledged by God. The man who outwardly was a failure, who was executed on a cross, is justified by God, raised up and made 'Prince of Life.' This is not a myth, but the profoundest interpretation of human existence, which in the historical Jesus becomes for those who believe truth and reality, trust and hope.

So in my discipleship of Jesus I have not been disappointed.[40]

Along with the Johannine and Pauline writings, many other passages indirectly affirming the divinity of Christ are to be found in the Gospels. Ponder this one and ask yourself how you would have reacted to this itinerant preacher and to the question He poses. The scene is that of the paralyzed man being lowered through the opening in the roof because of the crowd:

> And when Jesus saw their faith, he said to the paralytic, "My son, your sins are forgiven." Now some of the scribes were sitting there, questioning in their hearts, "Why does this man speak thus? It is blasphemy! Who can forgive sins but God alone?" And immediately Jesus, perceiving in his spirit that they thus questioned within themselves, said to them, "Why do you question thus in your hearts? Which is easier, to say to the paralytic, 'Your sins are forgiven,' or to say, 'Rise, take up your pallet and walk'? But that you may know that the Son of man has authority on earth to forgive sins" — he said to the paralytic — "I say to you, rise, take up your pallet and go home." And he rose, and immediately took up the pallet and went out before them all; so that they were all amazed and glorified God, saying, "We never saw anything like this!"
>
> — Mark 2:5-12

I can tell you that if I had been there I would have had the most powerful suspicion that I was dealing with God Himself, although I would have been very mystified that the infinite God would stand in front of me and function with a human body and as a human being.

It might do many of us a great deal of good if we could imaginatively place ourselves in that little house with a hole in the roof, or if we could kneel with Thomas when he touched the wounds of his crucified and risen Master. Thomas was a Jew — consequently, he did not say lightly the words, "My Lord and My God!" (Jn 20:28). It was difficult for Jews even to deal with the idea of an incarnate God. Modern skepticism has latched on to this difficulty and used it to assert that the early followers of Jesus did not believe in His divinity. Schnackenburg takes up this issue:

> To proclaim to the Jewish people belief in a Messiah of this sort was far from being an easy matter. We know how Jesus' followers, themselves Jews by birth and mentality, proved their claim: it was because God raised the crucified Jesus from the dead and "made him both Lord and Christ" (Ac 2:36). They applied to him the words of Ps 110: "Yahweh's oracle to you, my Lord, 'Sit at my right hand and I will make your enemies a footstool for you' " (v. 1).
>
> This was how the early Jewish Christians tried to explain to "the whole house of Israel" how this man from Galilee, outwardly so little like a Messiah, was in fact, by God's hidden plan, the expected Saviour, the "Ruler" in a much deeper sense than the Jews had ever dreamed of. The carpenter's son who had been rejected by men was accepted and acknowledged by God and became for all who believe in him "the prince of life" (Ac 3:15).
>
> The first Christians then amplified their confession of Jesus as Messiah by adding new titles, one of the most important of which was "Son of God." In John's Gospel, Nathaniel exclaims: "Rabbi, you are the Son of God, you are the King of Israel" (1:49), and Martha confesses: "I believe that you are the Christ, the Son of God, the one who was to come into this world" (11:27). This is the creed of the Johannine community (cf. 20:31); the whole of John's Gospel is an attempt to demonstrate its reasonableness

and its cogency, and to convince his readers of it by the words and events of Jesus that he records.[41]

A Modern Objection

It is quite possible that a devotion to the now risen Christ present for the believer in the Eucharist could distract one from the responsibility of charity and justice that Christ's teaching demands in the Gospel. Perhaps this has sometimes occurred. But to deny the scriptural and psychological validity and appropriateness of such devotion is to throw the baby out with the bathwater and to make room for the pseudo-spirituality of conferring with crystals and massage retreats.

Schnackenburg, writing at the high moment of the social Gospel — a moment I was deeply involved in myself — had these sobering words to say about forgetting the living Christ while trying to enforce His call to justice:

> The massive reaction of today's youth against Christianity and the Church frightens and dismays me, although I have to admit that we have often given a false picture of Jesus' message, passed over too much of it in silence, and failed to put a lot into practice. This is especially true in the area of Christian social commitment. We have put too much emphasis on the "Christ-cult" — the honour paid to the ever-present Lord, and consequently neglected the wishes and demands of the historical Jesus. We have paid too much attention to an individualistic sort of piety and a triumphalistic image of the Church. We have a great deal to think through again and much to learn, we theologians perhaps most of all.
>
> Our teacher is still, as always, Jesus of Nazareth, unfathomable in his person, inexhaustible in his Gospel. We must inquire more and more deeply into the intentions of the historical Jesus, and meditate on their implications for mankind, in particular for society today. On the other hand, not a few people in our generation, even theologians, seem to me to fall into the other extreme, into one-sided views and even errors. Jesus did not advocate social reforms and structural changes exclusively or even insistently. He preached the New Man who is created in God's image, lives by his love and brings that love to men.

As Jesus' disciple, I am always a long way behind my Master; but he is still my Guide when I stray from the path and my helper when I flag. So Jesus of Nazareth for me is not only a light from the past but a present Lord who is always near and to whom I can look and pray. He is also the ground of my hope. I am certain that he will always move many hearts, including those of young people, with his message. That is my human hope for a reeling mankind dancing on the edge of the abyss. But my last hope, even if it is "against all hope," arises from my belief that God raised the crucified Jesus from the dead.[42]

We have also seen in Chapter 1 in the century after the end of the persecutions the two preeminent Fathers of the Church, one in the East, Saint John Chrysostom, and the other in the West, Saint Augustine. Both speak of Jesus Christ as personally present in the Eucharist. Chrysostom tells us to "touch Him," and Augustine tells us not to eat the flesh of Christ unless we have first adored Him, and that we sin by failing to adore.[43]

Both of these great Fathers, the pillars of the Church in East and West, stress the social responsibility to the poor and the needy, in fact, our duty to care for all members of Christ because of the Eucharist. Moreover, they teach that we are able to approach Christ in glory only because we serve Christ crucified in the suffering here on earth.

We have already summarized the teachings of the very early or postapostolic writers on the reality of the Eucharist as the Body and Blood of Christ (Chapter 1). They believed that Christ was present not only with His divinity but also His humanity, especially with His flesh and blood, and was mysteriously offered as a sacrifice to fulfill the prophecy of Malachi (1:10-12). Please review in Chapter 1 the words of Saint Justin Martyr written about 150.

In Chapter 5, which opens with the period after the last of the Fathers of the Church, beginning with the sixth century, we will see that the impulse to relate to the Eucharist as a Person continued to grow because of the Church's belief that this sacrament is the Body of Christ, not simply His spirit. Despite claims that the devotion to the Real Presence is medieval or even a Counter-Reformation idea (not that either of these claims would be anything to be ashamed of even if they were true), there was actually a growing devotion from the time of the Fathers, as we shall see in the next chapter.

We must put aside the historical development for the moment and continue our consideration of what "presence" means in terms of the Eucharist. The foundation of the adoration of the bread and wine transformed mysteriously into the Body and Blood of Christ, the living Christ with His humanity and divinity, is based on the simple fact of faith that a real transformation of the elements means that He really is there. Why not then react to Him as present even though He cannot be perceived by the senses? As Saint Thomas points out, the only sense that can be trusted in this case is hearing, and specifically, hearing the words, "This is my body — this is my blood." If one believes, why would one not react to the Eucharist as the presence of God, since God incarnate is sacramentally here? But He is here in His humanity as well as His divinity.

Two Important Considerations

One might object that we live always in the presence of God. In Him we live and move and have our being. So what's all the fuss? There are two important considerations brought out by this objection that in fact sums up a great deal of the present opposition to Eucharistic devotion.

First of all, although we do live in God's presence in the sense that He sustains all being, is it really true to say that we are present to Him? In a totally mysterious way "the hairs of your head are all numbered" (Mt 10:30), and not even a sparrow falls to earth without His knowing it (cf. Mt 10:29). But as Meister Eckhart, the strange medieval mystic, has pointed out, "God is near to us but we are far from him. God is within; we are without. God is at home; we are abroad."[44]

God is only present to us when we are aware of that presence and we respond to it. Presence above all things is a knowing response. God is present to us when we actually think of Him by praying to Him or meditating about Him. He can also be habitually present to us by a lasting, implicit, and effective intention to do His will and to lovingly serve Him. I have known a few very advanced souls on the spiritual journey in whom these two elements came together so that indeed God was always in their consciousness as they were always in His presence. I really don't think that anyone should speak or write about the spiritual journey until one has had the opportunity of thoughtfully observing such a subtle and incredible phenomenon.

Obviously a person approaching or receiving the Eucharist with devotion and reverence will have at least some awareness of the presence of the Son of God. This will easily expand to the Trinity because of the unity of the Divine Being. The devout communicant will spontaneously be aware of the heavenly Father and the Holy Spirit at the same time, and perhaps through that medium of the Divine Presence think even of our Lady and the souls of some of the celestial citizens, the angels and the saints. But — and this is a very important second condition — the serious and devout Christian receiving or approaching the Eucharist will also be aware through the teachings of faith of the presence of Jesus of Nazareth, not simply of the spirit of the Eternal Son. Christ is there mysteriously as He was in Galilee. Saint John Chrysostom taught sixteen hundred years ago, "How many there are who still say, 'I want to see his shape . . . his clothing, his sandals.' Behold, you do see him, you touch him, you eat him! . . . He gives himself to you . . . to be received within. . . ."[45]

A Powerful Conclusion

The presence of Christ in the Eucharist is different from all other meanings of the presence of God. It is human as well as divine, just as He became human and divine in the same single divine Person. In actuality, as far as we can conceive of these mysteries (and that's not very far), the Christ who is present is most aptly thought of as both offering and priest in the Eucharist. Again Saint John Chrysostom is helpful here, comparing the Eucharistic Presence to the presence of Christ in the manger when the Magi came to adore with awe: "For thou dost see Him not in a manger but on an altar, not with a woman holding Him but with a priest standing before Him, and the Spirit descending upon the offerings with great bounty. . . ."[46] Nor is this the only instance wherein Chrysostom speaks of Christ as being truly present on the altar in the Eucharist; in another homily he states: "Not in vain do we at the holy mysteries make mention of the departed, and draw near on their behalf, beseeching the Lamb who is lying on the altar, who took away the sin of the world."[47]

For this Christ the victim and the priest to be present to us (and not we to Him — that is God's work) we must make a decision to focus our attention on this invisible presence with faith, devotion, and (if we are capable) love. The Church has traditionally identified four kinds of prayer as most appropriate in the presence of the Eucharist, namely adoration and praise, thanksgiving, repentance, and trusting intercession. How can any sane person object to this kind of worship and devotion? No one would even question that this worship is or should be most properly offered at the Eucharistic sacrifice. Of course. But it is also obviously the most appropriate response to the reception of Holy Communion. Indeed the whole life of the devout Christian should be an extension of that meeting with Christ the priest, the victim, and the victor.

It is obvious that the worship of the Eucharist outside the Liturgy is an extension of the prayer begun at the altar. It is to be observed by anyone who takes the trouble to do so that those who most devoutly participate at the Liturgy are precisely the same people who place great importance upon the reverent adoration of the Eucharistic Presence after the Liturgy is completed. I myself have also observed that often those strangely opposed to Eucharistic devotion participate in the Liturgy more as a socioreligious event, emphasizing the social aspect of the Liturgy to such a disproportionate extent that the entire experience is made mundane or even irreverent.

This is to fall into the ever present danger of trivializing the mysteries of God, reducing the Liturgy of the Eucharist to one of several "religious services." The worst state of affairs arises when the attention of the congregation shifts from the mystical presence of Christ to the celebrant, and the Mass becomes an opportunity for a narcissistic display of technique, gesture, vesture, or even hairstyle. Like many of my readers I have witnessed the intrusive overexposure of the presence of the celebrant or other participants, resulting in the minimizing and trivialization of the Eucharistic mystery. Such distasteful and perhaps even sacrilegious displays suggest that the time for a true liturgical reform is again at hand.

ENDNOTES

1. Two notable works that emphasize this aspect of the sacraments are Fr. Louis Bouyer, *The Church, The Word and The Sacraments in Protestantism and Catholicism*, 1961, and Karl Rahner, *The Church and The Sacraments*, 1963.

2. Msgr. James T. O'Connor, *The Hidden Manna: A Theology of the Eucharist*, 1988, p. 235.

3. An example of this ecumenical approach, it seems, is the popular book *The Christian Sacraments of Initiation* by Kenan Osborne, OFM.

4. Yngve Brilioth, *Eucharistic Faith and Practice: Evangelical and Catholic*, 1965.

5. *Catechism of the Catholic Church*, 1994, Nos. 1252, 1282, pp. 319, 325; see also Acts 16:15, 16:33, 18:8, and 1 Cor 1:16 for examples of whole households being baptized.

6. See *The Confessions of St. Augustine*, Bk. 4, Ch. 4, trans. Frank J. Sheed, 1943, pp. 65-66.

7. *Catechism of the Catholic Church*, No. 1128, p. 292.

8. *Summa Theologica*, Pt. III, Q. 68, Art. 8, in *Summa Theologiae: Volume 57: Baptism and Confirmation (3a.66-72)*, ed. James J. Cunningham, OP, 1975, p. 105.

9. Quoted in O'Connor, p. 80.

10. *Catechism of the Catholic Church*, No. 1128, p. 292.

11. Council of Trent, Session 22 (Sept. 1562), "Decree on the Doctrine of the Sacrifice of the Mass," Ch. 2, quoted in O'Connor, pp. 233-234.

12. Ibid., p. 234.

13. Fr. Aidan Nichols, OP, *The Holy Eucharist: From the New Testament to Pope John Paul II* (Oscott Series, No. 6), 1991, pp. 95-96; passage from Scheeben quoted by Nichols can be found in Scheebens's *The Mysteries of Christianity*, 1961, p. 510.

14. *The Confessions of St. Augustine*, Bk. 9, Ch. 13, p. 207.

15. Nichols, pp. 96-97.

16. Ibid., p. 140.

17. Fr. Jean-Paul de Caussade, SJ, *Abandonment to Divine Providence*, trans. John Beevers, 1975, Ch. IV, No. 7, p. 84.

18. Hans Urs von Balthasar, *New Elucidations*, 1986.

19. Ibid., pp. 114-117.

20. Quoted in O'Connor, pp. 312-313 (original Latin text in *Patrologia Latina*, Vol. 38, cols. 1454-1455).

21. Council of Trent, Session XIII (Oct. 1551), Ch. 1, quoted in O'Connor, pp. 212-213.

22. Ibid., Ch. 2, pp. 213-214.

23. *Catechism of the Catholic Church*, No. 1373, p. 346.

24. *Mysterium Fidei*, No. 39, quoted in ibid., No. 1374, p. 346.

25. *Dominicae Cenae*, No. 3, quoted in ibid., No. 1380, p. 348.

26. "The Blessed Sacrament After Vatican II," *Canadian Catholic Review*, Vol. 12, Feb. 1994, p. 32.

27. *"Sermones Supposititios,"* Sermon 84, No. 3, as quoted by St. Thomas Aquinas and cited in Nichols, p. 80. This work is classed among the "supposed sermons" of St. Augustine (original Latin text in *Patrologia Latina*, Vol. 39, cols. 1908-1909).

28. *The Confessions of St. Augustine*, Bk. IX, Ch. 13, p. 207.

29. *Summa Theologica*, Pt. III, Q. 80, Art. 10, quoted in Nichols, pp. 79-80.

30. *Summa Theologica*, Pt. III, Q. 79, Art. 4, quoted in ibid., p. 82.

31. Nichols, pp. 83-84.

32. André Frossard, *I Have Met Him: God Exists*, 1971, pp. 116-119.

33. "I see His Blood upon the Rose," in *The Catholic Anthology: The World's Great Catholic Poetry*, ed. Thomas Walsh, 1942, p. 428.

34. Translation in Walsh, p. 19.

35. *Autobiography of St. Thérèse of Lisieux*, trans. Ronald Knox, 1958, Bk. III, Ch. 32, pp. 254-257.

36. Fr. Ignacio Larranaga, OFM Cap., *Sensing Your Hidden Presence: Toward Intimacy with God*, 1987, p. 122.

37. See *St. Augustine: The City of God: Books VIII-XVI* (The Fathers of the Church, Vol. 14), trans. Gerald G. Walsh, SJ, and Mother Grace Monahan, OSU, 1952, Bk. X, Ch. 1, p. 116.

38. Letter to the Smyrnaeans, Ch. 1, quoted in John R. Willis, *The Teachings of the Church Fathers*, 1966, p. 75. See this work by Willis as a comprehensive testimony to the patristic belief in the divinity of Christ.

39. *Dialogue with Trypho*, Ch. 74, in *The Ante-Nicene Fathers: Volume I: The Apostolic Fathers with Justin Martyr and Irenaeus*, ed. Alexander Roberts and James Donaldson, revised by A. Cleveland Coxe, 1973, p. 235.

40. Fr. Rudolph Schnackenburg, *Belief in the New Testament* (English trans.), 1974, pp. 115-116.

41. Ibid., pp. 14-15.

42. Ibid., pp. 117-118.

43. See Chrysostom, *Homily 82 on the Gospel of St. Matthew*, and Augustine, *Ennarationes in Ps. 98*, verse 9, quoted in O'Connor, pp. 47, 59.

44. Sermons, 6, "The Kingdom of God is at Hand," *in Meister Eckhart: A Modern Translation*, ed. Raymond B. Blakney, 1941, p. 132.

45. *Homily 82 on the Gospel of St. Matthew*, quoted in O'Connor, p. 47.

46. *Homily 24 in 1 Corinthians*, No. 5, quoted in Darwell Stone, *A History of the Doctrine of the Holy Eucharist*, 1909, Vol. I, p. 107.

47. *Homily 41 in 1 Corinthians*, No. 4, quoted in ibid., Vol. I, p. 107.

Chapter 4

A Sense of Presence

The Psychological Question

If our task is then to respond appropriately to faith's message that Christ, Son of God and Son of Mary, is present as our High Priest, as He is so gloriously described in the Epistle to the Hebrews, the question obviously presents itself : How do we do this? The answer is mainly provided by psychology and anthropology, rather than by theology. The focus of attention, the eliciting of proper sentiments and reactions, are after all part of the subject matter of religious psychology. There are several fascinating aspects to this answer.

We have already seen that more than anything else presence is a response — a focusing of attention, a summoning of feelings, emotions, or sentiments. How do we respond to that which we cannot perceive with our senses? Now we must explore a phenomenon by which we human beings are able to respond to that which is not really there, or, if it be there, is not perceivable by us. A sense of drama or a play provides a possibility of responding to that which is not there. We also respond to that which we do not perceive but which we know by some sensory process — for example, taking care to be covered when an X-ray machine is being used. If we had proper equipment we would be able to perceive the effects of the X rays sensibly.

Lacking that particular equipment, we rely on our intelligence and available information to help protect us from these dangerous but imperceptible rays. In the case of religious experience, we respond to the presence of God, a spiritual presence that is directly imperceptible. Finally, in the Holy Eucharist we have a religious experience of a physical presence that is imperceptible. It is not the ubiquitous and all-encompassing presence of God who in Christianity is recognized to be the Holy Trinity. Rather, the Christian faith tells us that it is the presence of Jesus of Nazareth with His Body and Blood. This is a unique event in the psychology of religion.

"Compositio Loci"

The technique by which we respond to the unseen, whether it be in drama or in religious experience, is classically known as *compositio loci*, or "putting oneself in the place." As a specifically religious response, this imaginative form of meditation or devotion was cherished and taught by two of the great spiritual figures of Western Christianity, Francis of Assisi and Ignatius Loyola. According to the way they and many other spiritual guides used this technique, *compositio loci* meant putting yourself in a place different from the one where you actually were. It may have been a time or place in the past, such as an incident in the life of Christ; or it may have been in the future, particularly in eternal life.

The faculty of imagination (a human capacity strangely underexplored in modern psychology) was brought into play, either by external objects that suggested an image to the mind or simply by the decision to produce an image out of memory by assembling the inner picture with bits and pieces that are recalled. Thus we see there are at least two distinct ways of putting yourself mentally in a place different from the one you are presently in. The first, using sensible objects, is more dramatic, and the second is more interior and intellectual. Usually they complement each other so that rarely do we see either of these techniques used exclusively without some aspects of the other. There is almost always some reliance on external stimuli, even if these are not so important.

We are going to focus our attention here on *compositio loci*, which uses external symbols called sensible props — usually visual or auditory. This is what is done in theater and is one of the most common features of human entertainment and cultural enrichment. Recall that you can profoundly react to a scene in a play or a film with deep emotions of joy, sorrow, or even horror, forgetting who and where you really are. You are drawn into a time long ago or a place far off, or even another part of the universe, as is done in science fiction. If it is effective theater, you are present there not only by imagination but by emotion and response.

You can gain some appreciation of this ability of composition of place to put you where you are not if you simply examine the effects of drama on your own mind. Even the most insensitive person may be mesmerized by a movie or feel deeply moved by what is in reality only a scene with actors. Any opera lover can tell you that the repetition of the story and plot does not take away from its ability to move one emotionally. A good storyteller or a poet can elicit the same response as a play or an opera, using words for props. A ballet can produce the same effect with music rather than words. And finally a mime can do this without any music or words at all. Faced with the presumed invisible presence of the divinity, the religions of the world, starting with the most simple and aboriginal societies, have used this technique of imagination and have developed sacred theater. It would be absurd to think that the Church with her faith in the invisible sacramental presence of Christ would not use these techniques.

The Reformation, which was more or less hostile to this form of religious experience (and initially even to meditation and contemplative prayer), replaced it with a stark, intellectual piety artificially cleansed of every use of the imagination. Preaching and hymn singing, and occasionally architecture, became the limited expressions of the imaginative and creative side of religion. I have often thought of what more the great Puritan poet John Milton could have done if he had not been so constricted by his religious beliefs.

"Theatro Sacro"

Most religions of the world and almost all of those from the past use the method of *compositio loci* at times. Occasionally it becomes the more refined *theatro sacro*. Great processions and liturgical representations of celestial or historical events are common, especially in Taoism and Hinduism; however, one has only to attend a

Passover Meal or the sunrise service of American Protestants to realize that *compositio loci* is still very much alive.[1]

The genius of *compositio loci* in Western Christianity is Saint Francis of Assisi, who popularized devotion to Christ Crucified and the use of realistic crucifixes — his order was later to take the lead in disseminating the devotion of the *Via Crucis*, the Stations of the Cross. Francis also popularized the Christmas crib that invites us to adore the Messiah in the company of the shepherds, the Magi, and even the angels. It is my conviction that it was the same poetic intuition that called Saint Francis to respond in a dramatic and deeply personal way to the presence of Christ in the Eucharist. The difference was that Christ's Body was truly *there* in the Eucharist, whereas in the Christmas crib it was not. As we shall see later on in the historical review, his profound genuflection with his face to the ground and his prayer *Adoramus Te* epitomized his ability to "see" and experience the presence of his beloved Savior in the sacramental signs of the Eucharist.

Although devotion to the Eucharistic Presence outside of Mass had begun to emerge in at least its seminal form by the tenth and eleventh centuries, it was Saint Francis and his disciples who made it one of the salient features of later medieval piety. As we shall see, Dominican, Augustinian, and most especially Franciscan friars, as well as the religious women and laity associated with these orders, were to popularize Eucharistic devotion in the second part of the thirteenth century, and laid the foundations for Eucharistic piety for ages to come. In popular devotions, in adoration outside the liturgy, in processions and many other acts of veneration, the presence of Christ was the focus of attention and called forth powerful responses, both individual and communal. Since the presence of Christ could not be seen and was not subject to any sense other than the hearing of Christ's words about the Eucharist read from the Scriptures, the friars used *compositio loci* with the props of *theatro sacro* to assist all in responding with reverence and joyful adoration.

The House of God

The veneration of the Eucharist in churches changed these buildings from essentially prayer halls and places of liturgical celebration to temples housing the Lord. With the coming of Gothic architecture, churches took on more and more the appearance of sacred places with shadowy walls and dazzling areas of falling sunlight amid the dark shadows. The use of candles, incense, and other sacred objects called for a response to the Divine Presence now certainly venerated as the very Body and Blood of the Savior. Magnificent cathedrals soared into the skies, and even parish churches and humble friaries became houses of God. The words of the Psalm — "O Lord, I love the habitation of thy house, and the place where thy glory dwells" (Ps 26:8) — became one of the most salient themes of the religious life of the vast majority of medieval people.

If you visit a great museum with a well-developed medieval section, you will get some glimpse of the vitality and fervor that nurtured the desire to find oneself with Christ in His house. The Cloisters Museum of the Metropolitan Museum of Art in New York gives most impressive examples of the piety of Catholic Europe in the later Middle Ages; it also speaks to what Saint Francis and other devout souls before him had unleashed in the hearts of the Christians of Western Europe. When examined from the perspective of psychology it is obvious that so much of their immense creative activity was fed by the human need to respond more faithfully, devoutly, and ever more eloquently to the presence of Christ. This is not to say that *compositio loci* had not been used earlier. The classical Romanesque churches of Europe are certainly palaces of the Great King. However, once the devotion to the Eucharist had become clear, the piety of the people focused on the church not as a great hall or basilica but as a temple containing the presence of God.

Impressive places of worship in all religious traditions called forth a sense of the presence of the divine. But the medieval churches and later the baroque and classical renaissance churches of Europe shouted out in works of stone and mortar, "He is here! He is here! Come and adore Him!"

The "Oratory of the Heart"

The other form of *compositio loci* depended much more on inner imagination and reasoning and less on external props. It was meditation with eyes closed and the senses withdrawn so as not to be distracted. Processions, incense, candles, and flowers might be seen as a bit of distraction. This more intellectual form of *compositio loci* was associated with renaissance piety and the Counter-Reformation, and is perhaps best represented by Saint Ignatius Loyola (1491-1556). In his renowned *Spiritual Exercises* he invites the devout soul to use imagination to place himself or herself in various biblical scenes. Much more complex ideas took the place of the simple experience of loving devotion before the crib, the cross, and the tabernacle. However, many of the psychological processes used in the earlier form were at work. Often, detailed pictures of biblical scenes in a book took the place of a pilgrimage on Christmas Eve out to a little shrine in a stable. Profound meditations on the Eucharist, the call of Christ, and the words of Scripture were memorized or read, and the silent adoration before the tabernacle became more important than the sometimes noisy processions.

These two different approaches to *compositio loci* complemented each other, and were rarely if ever competitive. The Jesuits had Christmas cribs in their churches and promoted the *Via Crucis*, while the friars taught people to meditate and make pictures in their minds. Such profound devotional prayers as the classic *Anima Christi* ("Soul of Christ") began with the Franciscan tradition and became most popular with Ignatius and his followers. Benedictines, representing in their tradition a piety less emotional and proletarian, responded to the times and along with Canons Regular of Saint Augustine produced some of the most remarkable examples of churches built for *compositio loci*. These include baroque abbeys and basilicas of Germany, Austria, Poland, Hungary, and in fact all of Eastern Europe (united with Rome). Throughout the vast territories governed by the Hapsburgs, reaching from Latin America through Spain and all the way to Eastern Europe, the devotion to the Eucharist provided a sense of unity as immensely different peoples and ethnic groups paused to worship the same Lord in the sacred precincts of the church. In the context of *compositio loci* the Eucharist, which presented the Paschal Mystery, became every man's journey to Jerusalem as it existed in New Testament times and everyone's glimpse of the eternal Jerusalem beyond the end of this life.

The Eastern Experience

It would be remiss not to mention the experience of the Eastern Churches. Except for those in union with Rome they do not have to this day a devotional life focused on the Eucharistic Presence of Christ apart from the liturgy. Although as in the ancient Church, the Holy Eucharist is reserved with dignity for the Communion of the sick and the dying, it is not usually the object of adoration. Unfortunately the example of the medieval saints and their profound devotion to Christ in the Eucharist could not be shared with Eastern Christianity because of the Great Schism. Nevertheless, in Eastern Christianity the use of icons, splendid and deeply religious paintings, in many respects provided for an experience of *compositio loci* similar to the Eucharistic piety in the West. And it would be altogether misleading to say that Eastern Churches do not accept and venerate the presence of Christ in the Eucharist. The powerful insight of Saint John Chrysostom given in a previous chapter is characteristic of this conviction. The ceremonies, rites, and sacramentals of the various Eastern Churches can only be understood psychologically as responses to the Divine Presence and especially to the presence of Christ in the Eucharist.

It is unwise for a Western writer, at least one who is not an oriental scholar, to say too much about Eastern Christianity. I use this term to describe a number of different traditions reaching from Greece and Russia all the way to India. But at least let me record my admiration for the liturgical reminders of the presence of Christ in the Eastern liturgies, especially the Byzantine Liturgy, with which I have been familiar for most of my life. Perhaps as the inevitable result of communications, as the treasures of Eastern and Western Christianity become more available to each other, the devotion to the presence of Christ apart from the liturgy may grow on its own in the East. I recall while visiting an Armenian apostolic church that when we came to the place of reservation of the Holy Eucharist I paused and knelt in adoration in the Presence of Our Savior. The Armenian priest stood quietly by, and when I arose he said, "We do not have the devotion of the Corpus Christi. It's too bad." I answered him that I was convinced that if this devotion were to be spread, the Eastern Churches would probably do a much better job of it than we are doing in the West at the present time. This statement was not idle flattery but a conviction based on observation of the devotion to the invisible presence of Christ hidden in the Eucharistic elements that I have perceived in the Eastern Churches, both the Orthodox and those united with Rome. Eastern liturgy uses the phenomenon of *compositio loci* to very prayerfully bring you not only to the Upper Room but also to the heavenly Jerusalem where the Paschal Mystery unfolds in eternity — for this reason it is called the Divine Liturgy.

The Essential Components of "Compositio Loci" in Eucharistic Devotion

Decision, imagination, intellectual and emotional response, and physical demeanor are all parts of the experience of *compositio loci*, whether it is simply an art form as in theater, or if it be in a religious rite (for example, Passover or Sunrise Service), or a sacrament where faith acknowledges the reality of that which is signified. Consequently, Eucharistic devotion requires first of all a decision to believe that which is not evident to the senses. When that belief is lacking, Eucharistic devotion becomes a meaningless formality or even a cynical fulfillment of a required task, like a soldier saluting an officer he does not respect. Because Eucharistic devotion is directed to a reality, it requires much more than the mere permission we give ourselves to be drawn into the action of a drama or even to participate in a group process such as a rally or sports event. Many religious services do not require a decision to surrender to the experience of *compositio loci*. Morning prayer or attention at a sermon does not require this; however, in simple private prayer the time taken to put oneself "in the presence of the invisible God" will make the prayer much more meaningful.

Eucharistic devotion moves one step further, because its focus is not the omnipresence of God but the personal and corporeal presence of the Word made flesh and blood. In a way it's the difference between praying to God in a field or on a bus on the one hand, and knocking at the door in Nazareth on the other. Faith brings us even further into the presence of Jesus of Nazareth, who is the incarnate Word of God now leading the whole celestial universe of angels and saints, as well as those mortals still on their journey in the everlasting worship of the Trinity. That Eternal High Priest is the One whom the believer meets in the presence of the Eucharist if the attention is properly focused and the heart is lifted up.

Obviously — as happens in the experience of theater — imagination, intelligence, and emotion must be willed into action. This act of the will may not be obvious as one enters a church or a theater, but the results will be clearly seen if this is not done. Many who work in theatrical production, from directors to stagehands, do not make the act of the will to participate in the drama, for otherwise they would be distracted from their duties. But real actors must do both. They must keep an eye on being in the theater, but if they fail to enter into the situation by *compositio loci* their acting will be mechanical and unconvincing. The same can be observed when one watches participants in the Mass. Often the devout in the pews move into the Mass, but the sacristans and master of ceremonies can only respond by being reverent and attentive. They do not really move in. Hopefully the celebrant does both. It is a real effort to keep an eye on the congregation, and at the same time to lead them into the real Paschal Mystery, which transcends all thought or feeling.

Here is where the devotion to the Eucharistic Presence outside of Mass is a great, yes, superlative spiritual help. During Eucharistic adoration there is no need at all to keep an eye on how things are going at the Liturgy. One can choose with will, mind, heart, and body to respond to the truth of faith: "I am with you. . . . This is my Body, this is my Blood. . . . Come to me." It defies imagination how anyone can be opposed to such a loving, healing encounter with Christ. Sadly some might not believe in the Eucharist. This may not be their fault. But believing in the Eucharistic Presence and not responding, or teaching others not to respond, is beyond the grasp of my mind.

The Attack on Eucharistic Devotion

In many schools, seminaries, and parishes there has been a deliberate attempt to minimize or even eradicate Eucharistic devotion. I could write a sad and sorry book filled with absurd and even scandalous attempts at this. More than one seminarian requesting a monthly Eucharistic day of recollection has been asked, "Do you worship potato chips or a chunk of bread?" Apart from the obvious heresy of such statements, there is a profound insensitivity to the religious sensibilities of others. However, besides these horror stories there is something more insidious and ultimately more dangerous, and that is the tendency to minimize all signs of reverence for the Blessed Sacrament. For example, one of the most common responses to the Eucharistic Presence in the Western Church from the time of Saint Francis has been kneeling or genuflection. Augustine, eight centuries before Saint Francis, had warned of the sinfulness of approaching the sacrament without an act of reverence. Somehow this reverence has been lost just as it appears to have been lost in the period shortly before the Reformation. It is interesting to note that "The Oratory of Divine Love," the lay reform movement begun by Saint Catherine of Genoa in the last decades before the Reformation, required its members specifically to be reverent in church as part of their reform.[2]

In the history of thirteenth-century Eucharistic devotion given in Chapter 9, there are many examples of bishops calling for reform in the reverence shown the Eucharist, both as regards external behavior and the location of the tabernacle. To minimize or eradicate external signs of reverence such as genuflections, kneeling, and bows, as well as to place the sacrament in some out-of-the-way place in unimpressive containers, is to detract from the experience of *compositio loci.* It may not lead to a denial of the Eucharist, but it certainly detracts from the devotion that could strengthen, encourage, enlighten, and enrich the struggling Christian — presuming of course that encountering Christ on some level is what this person wishes to do.

To participate creatively even as a spectator at a drama or concert, you need to put yourself into a frame of mind to enter into the created situation. The opera has its overture and the film its dramatic introduction. Props of all kinds and even the architectural design of the theater — sometimes quite magnificent — are employed to serve this purpose. Consequently, to approach responsively the invisible presence of the Savior, signs and visible things are also necessary. The location of the tabernacle, the prominence and dignity of the place — all are explicitly called for in the rubrics. As regards the location of the tabernacle, the new *Code of Canon Law* (1983) requires that the "tabernacle in which the blessed Eucharist is reserved should be sited in a distinguished place in the church or oratory, a place which is conspicuous, suitably adorned and conducive to prayer."[3] Equally explicit in this regard is the 1980 Vatican instruction *Inaestabile donum*, which states that the "*tabernacle* in which the Eucharist is kept can be located on an altar, or away from it, in a spot in the church which is very prominent, truly noble and duly decorated, or in a chapel suitable for private prayer and for adoration by the faithful."[4]

In an obvious reference to the ideas we have been discussing in relation to *compositio loci*, the fourth edition of the "General Instruction of the Roman Missal," issued by the Holy See in March of 1975 and incorporated into the 1985 revised English-language edition of the *Sacramentary*, specifies that "the places and requisites for worship should be truly worthy and beautiful, signs and symbols of heavenly realities."[5] The instruction goes on to state: "At all times, therefore, the Church seeks out the service of the arts and welcomes the artistic expressions of all peoples and regions. The Church is intent on keeping the works of art and the treasures handed down from the past and, when necessary, on adapting them to new needs. It strives as well to promote new works of art that appeal to the contemporary mentality." Continuing, the instruction points out: "In commissioning artists and choosing works of art that are to become part of a church, the highest artistic standard is therefore to be set, in order that art may aid faith and devotion and be true to the reality it is to symbolize and the purpose it is to serve."[6]

As for the specifics regarding the reservation of the Eucharist, the instruction states: "Every encouragement should be given to the practice of eucharistic reservation in a chapel suited to the faithful's private adoration and prayer. If this is impossible because of the structure of the church, the sacrament should be reserved at an altar or elsewhere, in keeping with local custom, and in a part of the church that is worthy and properly adorned."[7]

It is obvious from this instruction that no one should have any doubt that the Catholic Church remains committed to the use of beautiful visual objects as well as to music to create an atmosphere suggesting the Divine Presence. There has been, in recent years, a trend toward minimalization or the desacralization of Eucharistic worship. The celebration of Mass at a coffee table with ordinary eating utensils and without any vestments is obviously far from the mark of either the tradition or the intention of the Church. These peculiarities are so strange that one could not even fairly compare them to the stark worship of the Protestant churches surrounding their Holy Communion. At least in the latter situation the accouterments used are dignified and raise the entire experience above the level of lunch or a cocktail party. At some peculiar moment in the history of the Catholic Church in the United States and other countries, the idea of making the Mass as pedestrian as possible came in after the Second Vatican Council. One wonders what the thinking behind such liturgical peculiarities really was. Was it an attempt to celebrate the Divine Presence — or was it perhaps to deny it and merely focus on the human presence that one experiences when gathering with a group of friends for lunch? To escape the latter conclusion one would have to prove that there was not implied in such undignified procedures a denial of the transcendent significance of both the Eucharistic celebration of the Paschal Mystery and of the presence of Christ in the Holy Eucharist.

Ongoing Reform

In citing the instruction from the *Roman Missal* it is not my purpose to engage in a debate on the finer points of liturgical propriety. In fact I often find much of these discussions arbitrary, tedious, and lacking in focus. Frequently the theme of such debates is what is old, what is new, what was done then, or what should be done now or in the future. I'm a preacher and psychologist, and my interest is in what helps people in their spiritual journey, in their inner identity as Catholic Christians. My point is that the common human technique (*compositio loci*) used to help an individual to relate to what is not physically palpable must be put into use at any religious ceremony that goes beyond the level of a pious pep rally. The ceremonies of the Church and her liturgy should go far beyond group sessions, public-relations events, and luncheon meetings. However well intentioned these attempts may have been, the liturgy and the ceremonies directly related to it (including solemn exposition of the Blessed Sacrament and devotion to the Eucharistic Presence) should call upon all of human potentials, not just intelligence and voice, especially when these two are being used with such meager results.

The whole tradition of the Church in East and West bears witness to an age-old integrated psychological response of all the powers of the individual. The experience of sacred *compositio loci* (as distinct from a purely dramatic presentation) is of utmost importance, since it brings the totality of human potentials into play. Not only reason but imagination, not only dedication but desire, not only thought but will, not only head but heart and body are to be used. The Psalms used as liturgical prayers only make sense in this way. What could be duller and more formalistic than a purely intellectual reading of the Psalms? What could be more inappropriate than an abstract acknowledgment that the Eucharist is the real Body of Christ with no response of reverence and awe?

If one accepts the premise that the preconciliar liturgy needed reform, then one should be able to live with the possibility that the present drab situation may also need reform. A great place to start would be the very obvious and very widespread desire of many clergy and multitudes of the faithful for a more meaningful, psychologically integrated, and personally expressive devotion to the sacramental presence of Christ that comes to us as a continuation of the celebration of the Paschal Mystery in the Eucharistic sacrifice. Anyone who travels around the English-speaking world and is willing to listen to very large numbers of devout Catholics knows that there is, at this point, a growing tide of discontent about liturgical practice. The very people who support the Church most generously and stand by it most loyally complain with bitterness about the lack of any sense of reverence, or any acknowledgment of the transcendence of God and of the presence of Christ in the Eucharist or, in fact, in any other way. Banality, utilitarianism, clerical narcissism, skepticism about the holiest truths of the Gospel of the Catholic faith, and just plain ugliness are observable on many sides. Leadership will often express impatience or disdain for those who voice their complaints, brushing off their concerns as the gripes of the "little people." It might be time to listen to the little people if for no other reason than that they pay the bills and appear to provide most of the vocations.

ENDNOTES

1. P. Bishop and M. Darton, *Encyclopedia of World Faiths*, 1987, pp. 177-183.

2. Text in John C. Olin, *The Catholic Reformation: Savonarola to Ignatius Loyola*, 1992, pp. 22-24.

3. Canon 938, No. 2, in *The Code of Canon Law, in English Translation*, ed. Canon Law Society of Great Britain and Ireland, 1983, p. 170.

4. Sacred Congregation for the Sacraments and Divine Worship, *Inaestabile donum*, April 3, 1980, No. 24, in *Vatican Council II: More Postconciliar Documents* (Vatican Collection, Vol. II), ed. Austin Flannery, OP, 1982, p. 98.

5. "General Instruction of the Roman Missal," No. 253, in *The Roman Missal: The Sacramentary*, 1985, p. 43 (of General Instruction section).

6. Ibid., No. 254, p. 43 (of General Instruction section).

7. Ibid., No. 276, p. 45 (of General Instruction section).

Chapter 5

A Presence to Be Adored

The obvious occasion for Saint Thomas Aquinas's theological study of the Eucharist was the clash between theologians, some Catholic, some heretical, over the meaning of Scripture and the teaching of the Fathers on the Blessed Sacrament. Saint Thomas's profound study did not come out of a vacuum but was deeply influenced by the events that preceded it. In the second part of this book these historical events are described in detail, but we will summarize them here as well as we can with a thumbnail sketch of how devotion to the presence of Christ in the Eucharist developed, so as to demonstrate the historical validity of this time-honored practice. Not only is it a remarkable history, but one that glows with events founded on the personal sanctity and spirituality of an impressive number of people over several centuries.

The early incidents of Eucharistic devotion are fragmentary and occurred in different parts of Europe at a time when communications were extremely primitive. We who live in a time when all parts of the world can contact each other in a few minutes do not realize that communication from one end of medieval Europe to the other took many months. In terms of contacts with each other, cities on the continent, to our way of thinking, were worlds apart. Evidence that perpetual adoration of the Blessed Sacrament in the Cathedral of Lugo, Spain, may have arisen as early as the sixth century will come as a rude awakening. In Chapter 8 we find startling evidence that a portable tabernacle described as containing "the relics of holy God" was a focus of veneration as early as the seventh century in Lugo's sister Diocese of Braga. The Eucharist had been reserved from the time of the Fathers so that the sacrament could be given to the dying. Although by no means conclusive, evidence does exist to support at least the possibility that even in the late patristic and early medieval era devout souls had been quietly and apparently with little knowledge of each other drawn to pray to Christ present in the Eucharist. Saint Guthrac (died 714) spent his last hours on earth in what may have constituted adoration and supplication before the Eucharist in the English Abbey of Croyland (see Chapter 8).

In some places by the tenth century the Eucharist had been moved out of the sacristy and into the church, and was placed in a vessel that would eventually become the tabernacle. As we move into the medieval period, Eucharistic devotion begins to become a more important part of Catholic life, as we will see in Chapter 9.

The Two Middle Ages

As the first millennium of Christianity drew to a close and the barbarian invasions with the destruction of the Roman Empire became a distant memory, devout people moved from the struggle simply to preserve the teachings of the Bible and of the Fathers of the Church to a gradual new development. This springtime of human history is now called the Middle Ages, a period that differs from the preceding Dark Ages in a variety of ways. People now had time to think, to study, and even for a few, to study diligently for a whole lifetime. Almost all of this new culture and development expressed itself in religious ways; art, drama, music, architecture, and theology flowed into the larger and growing river of the Middle Ages that history has divided into two successive phases not very clearly distinct. The dividing point is seen as the early part of the thirteenth century, and in fact, the life of Saint Francis of Assisi may be considered a bridge between the "two Middle Ages."

The two preeminent orders of this time were the Benedictines and the Canons Regular of Saint Augustine, both of whom had kept culture alive during the Dark Ages. Although people do not associate Eucharistic devotion particularly with the Benedictine Order, these monks in fact provide an extremely interesting link between the first millennium and the Middle Ages. For example, the medieval Benedictine practice of solemn Eucharistic processions in which the Eucharist was carried to sick monks, as well as the use of candles and the special rules of the Cluniac Benedictine reform, all show a gradual development of the awareness that the Eucharist should be treated like the physical presence of the resurrected Lord. Although, as we have seen, Eucharistic devotions may have already been going on in Lugo, Spain, for several centuries, we find that a very early liturgical Eucharistic procession was held by Lanfranc of Pavia, former Benedictine Abbot of Bec and Norman Archbishop of Canterbury, at the end of the eleventh century. The description of this procession, in which are recorded the first liturgical genuflections before the Eucharist, is given in Chapter 8 of this volume (pages 200-202). It is a popular misconception that Benedictine piety was not Eucharistic. Despite this assumption, it is interesting to note that one of the earliest examples of perpetual adoration apart from the Cathedral of Lugo was established in 1230 at the Cistercian Monastery of Santa Maria d'Alcobaça in Portugal. Besides Lanfranc, another great Benedictine, Saint Ulrich, Bishop of Augsburg (893-973), is known to have officiated at a solemn Eucharistic devotion that began on Good Friday and concluded on Easter Sunday. This included processions, candles, and incense.[1]

One of the most interesting developments in Eucharistic piety took place during the twelfth century, wherein we find evidence strongly suggesting the emergence of prayer over a period of time before the Blessed Sacrament in places other than Lugo. Our history (Chapter 8) mentions that in the year 1177 the Croatian city of Zara was granted a papal privilege permitting a forty hours' vigil — probably Eucharistic — during Holy Week. This vigil lasted from the evening of Holy Thursday until Holy Saturday afternoon. Moreover, the twelfth-century English Cistercian Walthen of Melrose is reported to have prayed before an altar where the Blessed Sacrament was reserved. Even more impressive is the witness of Saint Thomas Becket, Archbishop of Canterbury (died 1170), who mentions that he had prayed for his king, Henry II, before the "majesty of the Body of Christ." Finally, the Cistercian theologian Baldwin of Ford (died 1190) was to speak of the continual Eucharistic Presence of Christ as the fulfillment of the Lord's promise to be always with us.[2] Although the promise of Christ to be with the Church may be interpreted in other ways, it is certainly most tangibly and dramatically fulfilled in the Eucharistic Presence.

Holy Week became a special time for Eucharistic devotion — people obviously wanted to be close to the living Christ in commemorating His Paschal Mystery. Ceremonies, some beautiful and some theologically awkward, became popular at this time. Some, like the "entombment" of the Eucharist on Good Friday, would strike us as peculiar. But perhaps they are no more peculiar than Saint Paul's description of the boisterous parish suppers that at his time were held in conjunction with the celebration of the Eucharist.

Saint Norbert, Archbishop of Magdeburg and a Canon Regular of Saint Augustine, was one of the leaders in the reform of religious life and of the Church in France and Germany during the twelfth century. So great a devotion did he have to the Eucharist that to this day the founder of the Premonstratensians is pictured holding the Blessed Sacrament in his hands during debates with heretics who denied its reality.

A visit to the Cloisters Museum in New York City or any great medieval gallery with a treasury will amply demonstrate how over the course of the Middle Ages an increasing number of beautiful objects of art were produced dedicated to liturgical services and the reservation of the Eucharist. Obviously more and more people were coming to think of the Eucharist as the personal presence of Jesus Christ.

At this time a very quiet and secluded group of people, often overlooked in ecclesiastical history, were adding their part to Eucharistic devotion. These were the anchorites and anchoresses (hermits and hermitesses) who inhabited cells in ecclesiastical buildings and even parish churches. These devout souls, the most famous of whom is the fourteenth-century mystic Julian of Norwich, often earned their daily bread by keeping watch over the churches at night and keeping the candles burning. They also performed the devout function of praying in the church for long periods of time. Usually they lived in a cell attached to the church, and when it was opened to the public they remained in seclusion.

There is ample evidence of Eucharistic devotion developing among these forgotten members of the ecclesiastical scene in the Middle Ages. It was some of these hermits who requested permission to keep the Eucharist reserved in their cells from the Good Friday Liturgy until Easter Sunday morning. There they could watch with Christ in the tomb. Actually, this period of watching during the Easter Triduum, lasting about forty hours, would eventually become the foundation of a special Eucharistic devotion in the sixteenth century that to this day we refer to as the "Forty Hours devotion."

Saint Francis — The Bridge Between Two Ages

As we have seen, there is good reason to think of the early (or first) Middle Ages passing over to a more sophisticated and cultur- ally self-conscious stage around the death of Saint Francis (1226). Despite the Poverello's dislike for formal studies and any kind of reflective analysis of things, his own disciples, including Bonaventure, Alexander of Hales, and Duns Scotus, were to be- come an important part of a much more intellectual and self-reflec- tive second Middle Ages, joining especially with the Dominicans and other friars in the intellectual ferment of the times. Whereas the Benedictines and Canons Regular had kept culture alive dur- ing the Dark Ages and early Middle Ages, the focus would now move to universities, and towering figures like Albert the Great and Thomas Aquinas would take over the intellectual scene.

As the first Middle Ages came to an end, Eucharistic devotion would achieve a permanent, clear, and universal acceptance be- cause of the efforts of such friars as Saint Francis, Saint Anthony of Padua, and Saint Thomas Aquinas. The nuns associated with these orders of friars would also be especially noted for their devotion to the Eucharistic Presence. Preeminent among these was Saint Clare of Assisi, who is often shown holding a ciborium or, anachronistically, a monstrance. This depiction relates to an episode in which Saint Clare is said to have fended off an attack of Saracen mercenaries using the Blessed Sacrament as her only defense.

Saint Francis and the Eucharist

The special place of Saint Francis in Eucharistic devotion needs to be examined because we have seen that his intuition demon- strated the psychological features of devotion to the Real Presence.

His use of *compositio loci* has already been noted as an important intuition in the development of Eucharistic devotion. Saint Francis was not a theologian at all, but his experience profoundly affected the theology of the second Middle Ages. The Franciscan vision — rich with poetry and warm affection, filled with intriguing psychological experience and with a self-awareness, yet transformed by humility, with desires raised out of the closed circuit of narcissism — touched almost all reflective minds in Western Europe.

The profound self-awareness and insight we observe earlier in Saint Augustine, Saint Gregory of Nyssa, and Saint Basil the Great, which was subsequently lost during much of the Dark Ages, now found innumerable echoes in the religious experience of men and women like Saint Francis. Augustine's profound personalism, as well as his self-awareness and insight, had seemed less important than his theology to a Church trying to rebuild after the collapse of the Roman Empire and the barbarian invasions; but as the descendants of these same barbarians became more and more civilized, they gradually found time and leisure to ask the old Augustinian questions — Who am I? What kind of man am I? Who are you, O Lord? How do you know me? How do I come to you, all my joy and my fulfillment, the insatiable desire of my restless heart?

During the eleventh and twelfth centuries these questions grew louder and louder. Crucifixes filled with personal feeling replaced the jeweled crosses that resembled the royal standards of the Roman Empire. The image of the *Pantocrator* (or All-Powerful Christ of Glory) was replaced by the suffering Messiah and even the *Bambino Gesu*. Saint Bernard of Clairvaux, who had died thirty-six years before the birth of Saint Francis, could write in his splendid expression of Christian religious experience, the hymn *Jesu Dulcis Memoria*, the following words:

> Jesu, the very thought of Thee
> With sweetness fills my breast;
> But sweeter far Thy face to see,
> And in Thy presence rest.[3]

From the different developments we have sketched above, it should be no surprise that the thirteenth century became the time of great Eucharistic devotion. It is significant that this century began with the inauguration of the "major elevation" during Mass (that is, the raising of the Host above the head of the celebrating priest immediately following the words of consecration). This elevation first appeared in Paris during or shortly after the episcopate of Bishop Eudes de Sully, who died in 1208, when Saint Francis was just moving toward his conversion. The Eucharistic tide was beginning to swell as the first Middle Ages drew to a close. In our review of *compositio loci* we saw that Saint Francis was a genius of this devotion, and we discussed his approach to Eucharistic Presence. Just a few of the details of what he did should be recorded here.

In his deathbed *Testament* Saint Francis wrote, "And God inspired me with such faith in his churches that I used to pray with all simplicity, saying, 'We adore you, Lord Jesus Christ, here and in all your churches in the whole world, and we bless you, because by your holy cross you have redeemed the world.' "[4]

In the context of Saint Francis' life it is perfectly obvious that this related to the presence of the Eucharist in the Church. In his letter to all the clerical members of the order he demands that when they find the Blessed Sacrament reserved in unsuitable places or carried about irreverently they should see to it that the Eucharist be brought to a place properly prepared where it could be kept safe.[5] In his letter to a chapter meeting of his order written late in his life, he states, "I beg you to show the greatest possible reverence and honour for the most holy Body and Blood of our Lord Jesus Christ through *whom all things, whether on the earth or in the heavens,* have been brought to peace and reconciled with Almighty God."[6] In his letter to all the superiors of the Friars Minor, he orders that when the Blessed Sacrament is carried, people should kneel and pray to "our Lord and God, living and true," and begs the friars to petition with all humility the parish priests to have "the greatest possible reverence for the Body and Blood of our Lord Jesus Christ."[7] Saint Francis particularly loved France because he found there a great devotion to the Eucharist; moreover, according to one of his early biographers, "He wished at one time to send his brothers through the world with precious pyxes, so that wherever they should see the price of our redemption [the Eucharist] kept in an unbecoming manner, they should place it in the very best place."[8] As Francis stated in his Testament, "Above everything else, I want this most holy Sacrament to be honoured and venerated and reserved in places which are richly ornamented."[9]

After the death of Saint Francis in 1226, many Franciscan bishops and friars came out with documents calling for the devout reservation of the Eucharist and the veneration of the Body of Christ in this sacrament. These writings are amply described in Chapter 9 of this book. In his chronicle of his own Franciscan Order, Salimbene of Adam (1221-circa 1288) gives three reasons for the devout reservation of the Eucharist. The first is the ancient reason — the ability to give Viaticum to the sick; the second is for the veneration and adoration of the faithful; and the third is to proclaim and embody the fulfillment of Christ's promise to remain with the Church to the end of the world. These reasons have remained the stable motivations till the present day, although popular piety may have reversed the order of importance.

Probably the reason for the very strong Franciscan emphasis on the Eucharist is that it was in touch with popular piety. The Franciscan Order had grown spectacularly, even in the time of Saint Francis, to include several thousand men and women. It continued to grow quickly as the thirteenth century went on. The friars were in touch with the most vibrant grassroots needs of the peoples of Europe; from Italy to England, from Spain to Germany, the friars preached and gave examples of devotion to Christ focusing on the Eucharist. This warm, personal, shall we say, psychologically oriented devotion was part and parcel of the new self-awareness of mankind coming to flower in the second Middle Ages. One might almost say that modern interest in human psychology and our twentieth-century preoccupation with our own wants, needs, loves, and hates had their roots in European civilization during this time. Part of that growth in individual awareness certainly was the devotion to a personal presence of Christ in the Eucharist.

In the historical section of this book one can read of the significant involvement of Franciscans, especially bishops, in the devotion to the Eucharist. The life of Saint Anthony of Padua, second only to Saint Francis in his popularity, contains a legend that illustrates the saint's devotion to the Eucharistic Presence of Christ.[10]

As a result of the traditional linking of Saint Anthony to the Eucharist, the Blessed Sacrament is always exposed for adoration at his tomb in a rather elaborate altar with a permanent marble monstrance.

Thirteenth-Century Women and the Eucharist

Devotion to the Eucharist since the thirteenth century has had a particular appeal to women. We've already seen that Saint Clare of Assisi has been marked by tradition as one of the great devotees of the Eucharistic Presence. Another group of women in northern Europe had particularly important roles to play. Many of these women belonged to a group called the Beguines; they were similar to what we would presently call members of a secular institute. Although they lived in community and followed the vows, they did not make a permanent commitment. In contrast to all the nuns of the time they were not cloistered but took care of the sick and the disabled in their homes.

Although the Beguines eventually were the object of a great deal of suspicion, a number of their members were recognized as people of great holiness, and were devoted to the Eucharist. Blessed Mary of Oignies (died 1213) would spend the entire vigil of a feast day "in the presence of Christ" (in the church). The Venerable Ida of Louvain, who died in 1300, a Beguine who eventually became a Cistercian nun, would utter in the presence of the reserved Sacrament a beautiful Eucharistic prayer that is given in Chapter 9 of this text.[11] A rule composed before 1220 for English anchoresses, women religious in certain respects similar to but distinct from the Beguines, gives a description of how such devout women would worship Christ in the Eucharist.[12]

The Fascinating History of the Feast of Corpus Christi

It is unfortunate that one of the most fascinating and mysterious historical events in medieval Christianity has never been made the subject of a great drama or a film. It is the story of the Augustinian nun Blessed Juliana of Cornillon (1192-1258) — an astonishing account of immense courage and devotion regarding one of the sadly forgotten great women of Church history. Juliana was left an orphan at the age of five and raised by Augustinian nuns in their convent on the edge of the Belgian city of Liège. She confided to her superior certain extraordinary visions that she had had in the year 1208, practically the same time that Saint Francis was beginning his community. She reported a mysterious vision of a full moon darkened in one spot and the message that there was a feast missing in the liturgical calendar, namely a great celebration in honor of the Body of Christ.

Twenty years after the initial vision she divulged what she had seen to the Archdeacon of Liège, Jacques Pantaléon. This extraordinary man was rather advanced in years and probably knew Juliana because he was in charge of diocesan charities. Juliana soon became the prioress of her community but was eventually thrown into the street for her efforts at reform in her convent. After Juliana's death Pantaléon was appointed Archbishop of Jerusalem and was sent by the Pope to settle matters in the Crusader kingdom, where there was a good deal of turbulence. By the time Pantaléon arrived back in Rome, Pope Alexander IV had died and the eight cardinals unexpectedly elected this elderly Belgian as Pope Urban IV. Among the important things he did in his rather brief pontificate was to establish and decree the Feast of Corpus Christi. He also had the immense wisdom to ask the brilliant young Dominican theologian of the time, Thomas Aquinas, to compose the Mass and Office for this feast. Thomas's great work has been called the literary masterpiece of the Catholic liturgy. It includes a large number of Eucharistic hymns that are sung to this day. It is one of the many disasters of modern liturgical history that this masterpiece was somewhat defaced with the new presentation of the office. In place of some of Thomas's magnificent hymns creations of lesser value have for the moment been inserted. Pope Urban himself did not live to see the widespread acceptance of his decree establishing the Feast of Corpus Christi. A new decree by Clement V (1305-1314) mandated the universal observance, and in 1319 the Franciscans became the first religious order to stipulate the universal observance of the Feast of Corpus Christi in their legislation.

The Two Centuries of Development

As the devotion to the Eucharist spread across Europe, the fourteenth and fifteenth centuries saw remarkable developments. In order to understand Eucharistic devotion one must see that these developments had two distinct forms, which we discussed in the previous chapter. One was the devotion to the Eucharist as a silent personal Friend, before whom any Christian soul could kneel and pour out his or her heart in adoration and supplication. In sharp contrast to this was the public veneration that began to be shown to the Eucharist, modeled more than anything else on the regal procession that was called the "royal progress." The meaning of such events is rather lost on people who live in our democratic times. Obviously people related to the Eucharistic Presence as that of the King of Kings, and strove to show to Christ their King honors that were even greater than those bestowed upon secular rulers who were often despised. When a monarch or member of the royal family would arrive in a particular place, he or she would usually hold court or receive visitors and settle things in some noble situation — a great hall or perhaps a throne erected outside with a canopy and appropriate furnishings. The people of the late Middle Ages and Renaissance strove to show similar honors to Christ.

During the fourteenth century, monstrances in their earliest forms began to be seen everywhere, although the very first monstrances were introduced even earlier, evinced by the oldest known depiction of such a vessel, shown in the hands of Saint Clare, in a Franciscan manuscript dated between 1250 and 1275.[13] Great Eucharistic processions were held on Palm Sunday and during Holy Week from Holy Thursday to Holy Saturday, and were repeated on the Feast of Corpus Christi, which was observed on the Thursday after Trinity Sunday. During Corpus Christi all of the signs of a "royal progress" were displayed to salute the presence of Christ in the Blessed Sacrament. From St. Peter's in Rome to the alpine chapels of northern Europe, to little parish churches in Spain and England, people attempted to bring out their greatest finery; buildings would be decorated along the road that the procession would take. Clergy and laity, along with the local officials and even military units, would participate in the Eucharistic procession. The ever present trade guilds would vie with each other to be represented appropriately by banners or even the best samples of their handiwork.

Yet despite all of this grandeur and pomp the most important part of Eucharistic devotion remained the quiet visit of the devout soul or even the sinner who entered into the sacramental presence of Christ. A new church furnishing (no longer used) called the "sacrament-house" began to appear, especially in northern Europe. To our way of thinking these were actually Eucharistic shrines often containing in a single unit candleholders and a place for the reservation of the Blessed Sacrament, either on public view or hidden in a tabernacle. These again reflected an appreciation of the Eucharist as the Divine Presence but seen in a more intimate way than in the great Eucharistic processions. Ultimately, the most moving and touching pictures of Eucharistic devotion from this time are the quiet saints and holy people who spent long hours in vigils. Practically every religious community has in its annals stories of saints and blesseds who passed many hours, often at night, praying before the Eucharist. There are remarkable accounts like that of Saint Paschal Baylon (1540-1592), who even as a toddler was once discovered by his anxious parents on the altar steps of their parish church gazing upon the tabernacle, a foreshadowing of the hours he would later spend as a Franciscan prostrate before the reserved Sacrament.[14]

The fourteenth century was a time of incredible turmoil and cruelty in European history, and the fifteenth century a time of extreme chaos and confusion leading up to both national and religious wars. During all of this the great and the small, the saints and the sinners, found a center for their piety and devotion before the silent tabernacle, or sacrament-house. In particular the Eucharist exposed to public view became an important part of Catholic piety. This exposition permitted people to gaze on the Eucharist for long periods of time. In fact this devotion enlisted a universal anthropological symbol, the mandala, a geometric configuration focusing one's attention on the center. This figure that we recognize as the monstrance is used in different world religions to assist people in meditation. One sees mandalas in both Hinduism and Buddhism. Somehow this pattern, which has profound psychological and anthropological roots, became a natural addition to the Eucharistic devotion. Tabernacles and particularly monstrances became more symmetrical, and the latter drew the individual's eyes and mind to the exposed Blessed Sacrament — the visible sign of the presence of Jesus in the world, who is the ultimate source of all order in creation.

The Century of the Forty Hours

Most Catholics think of the sixteenth century as a time of immense religious conflict out of which grew the powerful currents of the Catholic Counter-Reformation. An army of saints comes from this period. Preeminent among them are Saint Ignatius Loyola, Saint Teresa of Ávila, Saint John of the Cross, Saint Charles Borromeo, Saint Philip Neri, Saint Lawrence of Brindisi (superior general of the Capuchins), and Saint Anthony Mary Zaccaria (founder of the Barnabites). The Catholic Church in this age needed a revival, and although we are not aware of it as we should be, the devotion to the Eucharist provided the focus for this need. One of the things that separated Protestants from Catholics during this time was the belief that the Eucharist was really the Body of Christ and worthy of adoration. Catholic populations also needed instruction for the revival of their faith. All of this came together in a devotion called the "Forty Hours."

Whenever this devotion was held, commemorating the time Christ spent in the tomb, an entire village, town, or parish of a large city would be plunged into intense religious activity. Sermons would be preached almost continuously in the presence of the Blessed Sacrament, which was at times carried through the streets in solemn procession with altars erected at various spots. The entire population was encouraged to go to confession and receive Holy Communion. Often commercial business ground to a halt, except that which was necessary to care for the needs of the pilgrims from other places who came to attend the devotions. Different kinds of food would be available, and a festive atmosphere was created. Nonetheless, because of the penitential preaching of the friars or the Clerks Regular, there was a very serious tone to the entire event. Sometimes the friars would preach crowned with thorns. Unrepentant sinners would be publicly called to repentance. And when everything was over, a monument would be erected to remind the people of what was both a religious revival and a public religious celebration. Eventually the parish mission or revival would grow out of this experience, but when it was done in conjunction with the "Forty Hours" it had a magnificence and almost theatrical splendor that attracted the simplest and humblest of souls, as well as the wealthy and prestigious members of the local community.

The Centuries of the Baroque

The seventeenth and eighteenth centuries — the age of baroque art, architecture, and music — offered to the Catholics of Europe a marvelous opportunity to celebrate the kingship of Christ. From the hidden chapels of the Catholic recusants in England to the white churches of Austria and the religious palaces of Slavic Europe, all the way to the shrines of Italy and Spain, the baroque era offered a unique opportunity to celebrate the glories of Christ. At the same time it must be admitted that unfortunately the loss of the Latin language as a general medium of communication among the peoples of Europe tended to put the celebration of the Eucharistic sacrifice into the background. This was not the fault of Eucharistic devotion outside of Mass but rather the result of a regrettable deemphasis of the meaning of the Mass because of linguistic difficulties. The Mass remained, as it always will be, the center of Catholic worship but not necessarily the center of pious attention.

The Century of Sacrilege and Reparation

The nineteenth century took much of its shape from the French Revolution that immediately preceded it. The revolutions that spread through Europe were often an occasion for the desecration and confiscation of churches. Persecutions, especially in Spain and France, were accompanied by blasphemy and especially hatred of the Eucharist. Sacred vessels were stolen and melted down, altars smashed, clergy and religious killed or sent into exile. A fascinating response came from the Catholic community — the popular devotion of reparation — founded explicitly upon the revelations of the Sacred Heart of Jesus to Saint Margaret Mary Alacoque, a French cloistered nun living two centuries before.

One preeminent example of this piety that focused on the Eucharistic Presence will serve to illustrate the spirituality of repentance — the building of the Basilica of the Sacred Heart on Montmartre high above the city of Paris. The purpose of this national shrine was to express a nationwide act of penance and make prayerful reparation for the horrors of the French Revolution and its various continuations. Since the Basilica opened in the 1870s, perpetual adoration of the Eucharist has continued, being maintained even during the allied bombing of Paris. The spirit of reparation has never died out and is enjoying a revival now as the twenty-first century approaches. Not only at Montmartre, but in great basilicas, parish churches, and convent chapels throughout the world, innumerable devout souls offer acts of devotion and penance to Christ in the Eucharist. Inasmuch as the revelations of Saint Margaret Mary occurred in her convent chapel in close proximity to the tabernacle, the two devotions of the Holy Eucharist and the Sacred Heart have remained intimately linked ever since.

The Century of Reform and Confusion

In the twentieth century the reform called the "Liturgical Movement" appropriately sought to return the Mass to its position of preeminence over all forms of Catholic life. Unfortunately, in doing so, many lost sight of the meaning of devotion to the presence of the Eucharistic Christ outside of the liturgy or, rather, as an extension of it. At the same time there was a rejection of all the ideas of the baroque and the neoclassical in art, architecture, and music. The artistic forms in the second part of the twentieth century have been completely at odds with the formulations of the baroque. The baroque was lavish — the twentieth century is minimalist. The baroque sought to raise you to heaven; unfortunately twentieth-century art generally drags you down to the dust. One might wonder what the great baroque artists and architects would think walking through the Tate Gallery in London or the Museum of Modern Art in New York and seeing a pile of varnished potatoes or painted garbage boxes presented as works of art. Whatever one wants to say about either of these two expressions — the baroque and the modern — they are obviously at great odds with each other. In music one might say that the baroque attempted to lift you up to the skies, while much contemporary music attempts to pull you down under the earth. When the modern is beautiful it makes a strong appeal to the plain and the natural. This perhaps has played a part in the revival of the popularity of Saint Francis.

The rejection of baroque artistic forms added to the decline of pageantry in Eucharistic piety. However, it is necessary to recall when discussing the decline of the neoclassical and baroque that the private, personal devotion to the Eucharist continued among the faithful. Whether the vessel for the Blessed Sacrament was a medieval reliquary or an ornamental golden tabernacle that one sees in Rome looking much like a jewel box, devout Christians of all ranks paused to pray in the presence of the Eucharistic Lord and to humble their hearts and minds before this mysterious presence. Even in our time of ceramic chalices and wooden tabernacles there are great numbers of people who preserve a love for the Eucharistic Presence despite their being far removed from the influence of the medieval, classical, or baroque.

The Eucharist and the Emergence of the Modern Person

The men and women of modern European civilization rose out of a period of immense conflict and revolution, actually out of an incredible storm. Although at times these conflicts were harmful to the Church, nevertheless there emerged from these circumstances a new kind of Christian in the twentieth century. This person belonged to the very large group of what we call middle-class people. Universal education, the opportunity for travel, and cultural enrichment have spread through society by electronic means — and all of these have produced a society of people who are no longer burdened with the struggle to earn their daily bread. Few now work sixty or seventy hours a week to simply survive. In fact it is often the more educated who work long hours, while the average citizen is only employed for forty hours a week. While it is tragic that this potential for a truly enlightened human life has backfired into the present anticulture, nevertheless the obvious fact is that very large numbers of men and women now on earth have a more active awareness of their inner lives, their needs and gifts, their psychological aspirations. It has become, for good or ill, an age of popular psychology. This gradual change from a largely peasant population to a middle-class society is reflected in all aspects of religious life and even in the forms of liturgical piety and Eucharistic devotion.

The eighteenth century began to see larger numbers of people drawn to quiet adoration of the Eucharist. Priests like Saint Alphonsus Liguori, women religious, lay brothers who formerly had not been able to read or write, working people, shopkeepers, inventors, and scientists became aware that Christ awaited them in the tabernacle. The visits developed from the simple adoration of the previous ages into opportunities for profound introspection and self-examination. In a word, they became more psychological.

One of the most interesting aspects of this development was the number of converts brought to the Catholic Church by Eucharistic devotion. Two remarkable examples are Saint Elizabeth Ann Seton and the Venerable John Henry Newman, both converts from the Anglican Church and both devotees of the Eucharist. In Chapter 12 their reactions to learning about Catholic Eucharistic piety are described.

At the same time in Italy, people like Saint Alphonsus Liguori carried on the tradition of Saint Charles Borromeo and placed a strong emphasis on the Eucharist as a place for the individual to know and love Christ. France, which as we have seen has always been associated with Eucharistic piety, produced a whole school seeking the renewal of the priesthood through the Eucharist, typified by Saint Vincent de Paul and Saint John Eudes in the seventeenth century and continuing thereafter into the eighteenth century. A most unusual example of Eucharistic piety is Saint Benedict Joseph Labre, the homeless and apparently mentally disturbed beggar who spent long hours of his life rapt in silent ecstasy before the Eucharist in Rome, even in the sacrament-chapel of St. Peter's.

In the nineteenth century, France, recovering from the French Revolution, produced such outstanding Eucharistic saints as John Marie Vianney, Peter Julian Eymard, and Thérèse of Lisieux, all of whose lives centered on the presence of Christ. It can be honestly said that in the eighteenth and nineteenth centuries no Catholic saint could be found who did not place Eucharistic piety at the center of his or her life. In the beginnings of the Liturgical Movement, especially with the Benedictine Dom Prosper Guéranger, Abbot of Solesmes, a strong emphasis on Eucharistic piety as well as on the liturgy of the Mass and the reception of the Holy Eucharist was observable.

The twentieth century presents many interesting contrasts. It began with a great Eucharistic Pope, Saint Pius X, and the elaboration of great liturgical reform by the Benedictine monks. Up until the Second World War there was a strong conjoining of private Eucharistic piety with the liturgical reforms. After the war, many of the liturgists of that time criticized what they saw as an excessive attention paid to the Eucharistic Presence rather than to the Mass. They were displeased with the outpourings of public sentiment in solemn Corpus Christi processions, particularly the presence of civil authorities or even military personnel. They were not at all moved by the somewhat baroque decorations that had come to surround the presence of Christ in the Eucharist — a dozen candles, flowers, etc. They reacted along with almost everyone else against the baroque in all of its forms.

A simplicity of liturgical vesture became a theme of the Liturgical Movement. In music, art, and architecture simple lines were favored. Many people seemed to be unaware that some of the simplicity and minimalism was not only aimed at the baroque but directed against any sense of the transcendent in human thinking. The minimalist architecture of the German Bauhaus movement was transported into churches and shrines. Probably those who had initially conceived these designs would be astonished that they were so easily incorporated into Christian religious expression. Certainly some of the simplicity also arose from the new kinds of construction materials that were mass-produced and required greater simplicity of design.

Not only were new buildings simple, but they were often ugly. A deconstructionist trend moved from the attraction of the simple to the glorification of the damaged. Found objects, partly disfigured by time, often spoke of the ancient and the mysterious. But as artists began to glorify the ugly, like comic-book pictures and soup cans, this spirit entered into the life and expression of the Church. The simple, the folkloric, even the improvised could always speak of God as it does so beautifully in the scenes of the life of Saint Francis. But the hideous began to make its way into church under the banner of deconstruction. A pilgrimage of horror could be conducted through several abbeys and chapels of great religious houses in America. I remember my consternation when I finally got to an abbey church originally designed by Pugin and made famous by Thomas Merton, only to find that it now looked for all the world like an airplane hangar. An informed and cultured friend who accompanied me could say only, "An enemy hath done this." Sadly, liturgy, like everything else, began to be ugly.

Finally, as we have seen, there was a growing skepticism, often unspoken, about the reality of Christ's presence. As a result of the demythologizing efforts of some Scripture scholars, the figure of Christ became more and more remote. Christ was no longer someone you poured out your heart to but someone you thought about. People no longer concentrated on what Christ had accomplished and done in His short earthly life but rather on what He had not done, not meant, not said, and not even known. Despite the efforts of the last five Popes to preserve in the midst of all this a respect and love for Eucharistic devotion, many diocesan officials and religious superiors carried on what some have called open war against Eucharistic devotion. Ignoring the encouragement of the Popes, Eucharistic processions were considered passé and even forbidden. The tabernacles were relegated to obscure corners of the church or even to other buildings. When architectural changes were made in churches, the Eucharist was positioned in such a way that no one could even kneel before it. One has only to visit some contemporary churches and even cathedrals to observe the fact that only a very small number of people are even able to pause to pray before the tabernacle. In one seminary I found the tabernacle absurdly perched on the third-story gallery, much like a fire escape. As this place was in the care of Franciscans I was surprised that the Poverello was not seen at night weeping in the chapel.

The Blue Vase Experiment

The negative reaction of multitudes of the faithful to the moving of the tabernacle to the side or even out of the church proper was of considerable significance to any psychologist of religion. Church architects and liturgists might have acted with much greater sensitivity if they had had any kind of notion of the effect of the changes they made casually and often insensitively. Studies have been done in the psychology of religion that could have guided these efforts. One of the most important is called the "Experiment of the Blue Vase." Arthur J. Deikman, an experimental psychologist who has done fascinating work on the psychology of meditation and mysticism, used a simple room containing a small blue vase to study the responses of college students who gazed at this object with simple meditative techniques. After several sessions the blue vase was moved in the room, and finally in the thirteenth and final session entirely removed. All subjects reported that they found meditation with focusing on the vase "pleasurable, valuable and rewarding." When it was moved or removed, all the subjects "reacted as if they had lost something they were very attached to."[15]

Obviously the subjects attached no theological importance to the vase. Nevertheless, its presence had helped them to focus their attention as they tried to experience "contemplative meditation," a kind of imageless thought that Deikman associated with, among others, the fourteenth-century Catholic mystic Walter Hilton. Although it was not his purpose to show that the vase was a positive help and its removal a loss, he noted that the sense of loss was a significant result with all experimental subjects.

Such a scientific observation should demonstrate two things: first, that there is a solid psychological foundation for the experience of Eucharistic devotion; second, that the reaction to the sudden architectural interruption of the circumstances of Eucharistic reservation would be negative. When you add the fact that we are not speaking of a simple artifact like a vase but an object of powerful faith and devotion, it should be no surprise that extraordinarily negative reactions have occurred. The experiment also suggests that the lost Eucharist will again be restored to its proper place of importance, permitting the powerful focus of attention and devotion in prayer.

The Young and the Eucharist

In the next chapter we will turn our attention to objections to Eucharistic piety, but this chapter should not come to a close without mentioning the fact that among very many young people, teenagers to those in their early thirties, there is an observable renewal of interest in the Eucharist both in Europe and in the United States. Many of these young people have been exposed to so much wretched religious education that they are almost totally unaware of the Catholic teaching on the Eucharist. Nonetheless, when told of this teaching, within a matter of an hour they are brought to a fervent devotion to the presence of Christ in the Eucharist and a renewed interest in the Mass as an act of profound religious significance representing the suffering, sacrificial death, and glorious resurrection of Jesus Christ. The Community of Franciscans of the Renewal, of which I am a member, has been associated for several years with a movement called Youth 2000. This movement, founded by devout lay people, is centered on a weekend lay event that is actually the Forty Hours devotion for the young. Using a large pyramid that supports a monstrance and many vigil lights, the exposed Blessed Sacrament becomes the focus of a series of sermons, prayer experiences, and instructions. The only interruptions are liturgies oriented for youth. The ambience, outside the church building proper, makes an almost continuous experience of adoration possible, much like the town square or field where the "Forty Hours" was conducted centuries ago. One cannot readily overstate the enthusiastic reception of the sacraments of the Holy Eucharist and of Reconciliation that commonly takes place on these weekends.

One could very easily sustain the hypothesis at the present time that we are on the verge of a new revival of devotion to the presence of Christ in the Eucharist. This revival will hopefully link together a greater appreciation for the liturgy as the Holy Sacrifice of Christ with a profound respect for the Holy Eucharist as a personal presence and as a spiritual banquet strengthening the Christian for the challenges of an unbelieving world. Nothing would be more helpful for the reform and renewal of the Church.

ENDNOTES

1. See the full description of this practice in Ch. 8, pp. 198-199.
2. For more specific information on the cases of Walthen of Melrose, St. Thomas Becket, and Baldwin of Ford, see Ch. 8, pp. 203, 204-205.
3. First verse from translation in Fr. Matthew Britt, OSB, *The Hymns of the Breviary and Missal*, 1922, p. 109 (Hymn 43).
4. "The Testament of St. Francis," in *St. Francis of Assisi: Writings and Early Biographies: English Omnibus of the Sources for the Life of St. Francis*, ed. Marion A. Habig, 1973, p. 67.
5. "Letter to All Clerics," in ibid., p. 101.
6. "Letter to a General Chapter," in ibid., p. 104.
7. "Letter to All Superiors of the Friars Minor," in ibid., p. 113.
8. Thomas of Celano, Bk. II, Ch. 152, No. 201, in ibid., p. 523.
9. "The Testament of St. Francis," in ibid., p. 67.
10. See Ch. 9, pp. 221-222, of this volume.

11. See pp. 223-224.
12. See p. 224.
13. S.J.P. Van Dijk, OFM, and J. Hazelden Walker, *The Myth of the Aumbry: Notes on Medieval Reservation Practice and Eucharistic Devotion*, 1957, plate facing title page; Archdale King, *Eucharistic reservation in the Western Church*, 1965, p. 136.
14. Fr. Oswald Staniforth, OSFC, *The Saint of the Eucharist: Saint Paschal Baylon*, 1908, p. 5; Msgr. Paul Guerin, *Les Petits Bollandistes: Vies des Saints: Tome Cinquieme: Du 24 Avril au 18 Mai*, 1872-1874, p. 619.
15. A.J. Deikman, "Experimental Meditation," in *Altered States of Consciousness*, ed. Charles Tart, 1972, p. 210.

Chapter 6

Objections to Eucharistic Devotion and Replies

The second half of the twentieth century has seen a consistent discomfort with Eucharistic devotion on the part of some Catholic intellectuals, writers, and liturgists. To be fair we must not confuse this discomfort, even when it leads to a rejection of Eucharistic piety, with the hatred of the Eucharist that often accompanies persecution of the Church. Many objections come from those who love the Church, and some even come from those who favor Eucharistic piety but are uncomfortable with some aspects of its expression. It is not at all our purpose to lump together those who express this discomfort, or even those raising theological objections, with those who hate the Eucharist. It would be both silly and calumnious to do this. Therefore, in choosing writers with various objections I have tried to cite modern opinions moderately expressed, and I have passed over those that are caustic and insensitive to the deepest devotional expressions of others. But we must for the sake of completeness at least mention violent hostility to the Eucharist.

The Hatred of the Eucharist
When the Church is attacked, it stands to reason that its attackers will vilify its most sacred symbols. When one attacks the Catholic Church, two special targets are obvious: the devotions to the Eucharistic Presence and the devotions to the Mother of God.

At times this hatred will be to such excess that one may even be excused for suspecting diabolical influence. I have seen militant pro-abortion pickets carrying blasphemous signs mocking the Virgin Mary, and I witnessed a member of Act Up desecrate a Host I had unknowingly distributed to him in St. Patrick's Cathedral. Of course Catholics respond to the desecration of their most sacred and beloved signs of God's loving providence with horror. Having lived through these desecrations, I have found that the best response is one of sorrow and sadness. God in His infinite majesty is beyond being attacked directly. Sadly we all live with and take much too lightly the obvious sufferings of Christ in the poor that we see every day. God is mocked and Christ is crucified all around us in His least brethren, and at best we arrive late with Joseph of Arimathea to take Him down from the cross. Those who vilify the Eucharist should elicit from us sorrowful prayers for their conversion rather than our rage, for they do not know what they are doing. I was made deeply aware of the propriety of this response at the interrupted Sunday Mass in St. Patrick's Cathedral, when the powerful response of Cardinal O'Connor was eloquently one of great sorrow and sadness.

In modern times the Bolsheviks and Nazis showed a special hatred for the Eucharist. History has passed a terrible judgment on both of these movements. But to the devout who read the accounts of their blasphemies I ask, "Did not the Messiah have to suffer these things?" He had to join His beloved and suffering children because He had to remind us that what we do to them we do to Him. The Nazis attacked the Corpus Christi processions from the beginning and eventually outlawed them completely.[1] In Spain the desecration of churches by Communist forces included an almost insane violence against the Blessed Sacrament.

Objections Based on Theological and Liturgical Considerations

In reviewing contemporary objections to Eucharistic devotion it seems best to divide them into those that are based on liturgical studies and theology, those that are based on history, and finally those that are really objections to religious devotion. There may be all of these elements in any one given statement of objection. We will try to avoid more abstruse objections and restrict ourselves to those that are popularly expressed, often by members of the clergy or religious.

It is important to note that I am not addressing objections that are blatantly heretical. Without a doubt, some of the objectors to Eucharistic devotion simply do not believe in the Real Presence, or in the Eucharist as anything other than a visible sign of unity, really a sacramental like palms and holy water. The earlier chapters of this book are aimed quite directly at a number of currents observable in theological circles, and even in religious education, that are implicitly denials of the Catholic faith. But here I am addressing objections of believing Catholics who accept the dogmatic teachings of the Church but differ on what is an appropriate response to Christ's Eucharistic Presence.

The principal theological objection seems to be that devotion to the Eucharistic Presence, especially outside of Mass, detracts from the preeminent importance of the Eucharist as both sacrifice and sacrament. Many of the pioneers in the liturgical reform voiced this objection. Such great liturgical writers as Father Louis Bouyer and Father Hans Ansgar Reinhold, among others, wrote that the emphasis of popular piety was out of focus.[2] They never suggested that Eucharistic devotion should be done away with entirely but rather that it needed to be refined. Many of these writers especially objected to elaborate Corpus Christi processions in which some who seldom attended Mass took prominent positions, and at which national and political figures with national insignia marched along with the armed forces. While these events may have been powerful and beneficial expressions of human solidarity and, at the time, even of social justice, nonetheless the emphasis had shifted from the primary purposes of the sacrament, namely union with the Paschal Mystery of Christ in the liturgy and participation in the Paschal Banquet.

There has been less serious objection to the private and personal devotion to the Eucharist on theological grounds. How can anyone object to meditation and contemplative prayer simply because the focus of the individual is on Christ as He is present in the Blessed Sacrament? One might question either the faith or the emotional balance of anyone who wants to stop a devout soul from sitting with Mary at the feet of the Savior. The objection that the Eucharist is simply a food and that food is not to be admired invites one to respond in an equally silly way by suggesting that the objectors never make this statement to Italians, Frenchmen, Spaniards, Greeks, Chinese, or Japanese people, all of whom think that food needs to be attractive and admired. (Ask a silly question and you get a silly answer!)

Defenders of Eucharistic Devotion — Rahner, Daly, von Balthasar, Paul VI

In contrast to those who have theological reservations about Eucharistic devotion either public or private, there are a number of serious and respected authors who in the postconciliar period have defended the validity and propriety of Eucharistic devotion. Perhaps the most notable of these is Karl Rahner. Repeatedly, this renowned theologian, who is more often admired by the liberal side of the Church, powerfully defended Eucharistic devotion with no compromises. Rahner was very strong especially in the defense of the Corpus Christi processions that are so solemnly celebrated in his native Black Forest. In the following lines from an essay on Corpus Christi, this generally sedate theologian strikes a deeply emotional and devotional note:

> The Church today carries its sacrament in festive procession through all the fields of human reality. Joyfully singing hymns it walks through the streets of the world and shows to this world with an almost frightening exuberance and exultation its most intimate possession, the blessed presence of its Lord. . . .
>
> . . . While he accompanies us now in the sacrament (as he does every day in the grace of his spirit) those who walk invoke him who suffered under Pontius Pilate, died and was buried, descended into hell. But this is said of him who is the eternal Word of the Father, who is wisdom, light and strength, life and resurrection. When the sign of the ultimate and most terrible death is raised in blessing over those who are on their knees, it means that in the sign of death which blesses mortal men on their way to death, life is present, not death, the life which made of death itself the victory of life. And so, once a year for us Christians our road

becomes a *via triumphalis* and we walk behind one who, bearing life in himself, became our life by sharing our death. He goes on ahead. His sacrament announces his death. And also ours. Since he goes on before us, he does not delude us with any stupefying trivialities. He says, you share my fate which you proclaim in this sacrament; you share its hardship, difficulty and inexorability. And by this solemn procession, we proclaim that his fate is ours too. And in its entirety, of which it is written, "I died and behold I am alive for evermore, and I have the keys of death and Hades" (Rev 1:18).

We cannot grasp all at once the immeasurable significance of a procession like this with him who died and who lives. Who could comprehend God and the world, life and death, time and eternity united as they are in this festival?[3]

In a superb article, "Eucharistic Devotion," Cardinal Cahal Daly, Primate of Ireland, backs up Rahner's defense of Eucharistic devotion as an extension of the mystery of Christ in the Mass: "The Eucharistic procession is a particularly dramatic recall of the biblical truth of the abiding presence of God among his pilgrim people on their march through life and through history. It is a vivid demonstration of our will to 'eucharistify' and Christify our daily lives and work, our place of business, work and pleasure, our cities and our fields."[4]

Rahner was even more determined in his defense of private Eucharistic devotion, going so far as to question the motives of those who disparage this kind of prayer. In the following text he brings out several theological points manifesting his unequivocal view that a visit to the Blessed Sacrament constitutes the placing of oneself in the objective presence of the Messiah. There is no question that he believes a visit brings the individual to the Savior:

. . . we now have the content and precise meaning of a "visit." It, too, is man's presence before the objective sacramental sign of Jesus' sacrificial death for our salvation; it is a subjective prolongation of Mass and a beginning of one's next Communion. Hence everything that was said on the subject of thanksgiving applies to it, and everything that there is to say on the real meaning of preparation for Communion. It makes sense that they should take place before the objective sign of the cause and appropriation of salvation, the true body and blood of the Lord; in the presence of the Lord, present in his concrete bodiliness as sacrificial food for me in particular. Reservation of the Sacrament is reservation of the Lord made present in the Mass *as such*, and of the food to be eaten *as such*.[5]

Rahner suspected that the opposition directed against prayer to Christ in the reserved Sacrament was in fact the opposition of "activists" to contemplative prayer in general:

> But it is possible to suspect that the specific concrete problems and difficulties brought up against "visits" (i.e., prayer "before" the reserved Sacrament of the Altar) are often apt to be, at bottom, problems and difficulties directed against private, prolonged, contemplative prayer in general; that the objections raised against visits as such are for the most part only a sort of ideological cover, supplied in retrospect, for a general withdrawal from the severe demands of meditation. Does one in fact know many cases of people who are really given to the practice of prolonged contemplative prayer and who also experience difficulties on the subject of visits? The question must at least be raised, with the man who is "anti-visit," of whether his objections are not in reality the protests of an activist against being called on to bring himself constantly into the presence of God, in quiet, calm, silent abandonment, and to endure the correction and purification of the silence of God.[6]

Karl Rahner never lost his profound love for Eucharistic devotion. In his final writings he was as devoted as he was in his earlier years, and warned that Eucharistic devotion should not be lost to the Church: ". . . this worshipping of Jesus in the sacrament must not disappear. Its history may have started from almost unnoticeable beginnings. However, in salvation history and in the history of the Church something cannot disappear simply because it started almost without being noticed. No, as Catholics we wish, individually and together, to look to the sign of the presence of the one who has loved us and has offered himself up for us. It should not be unusual for us to kneel at times in private prayer before the Lord who has saved us."[7]

Although he did not write as frequently or as extensively on Eucharistic devotion, Hans Urs von Balthasar supported this practice as strongly as Rahner. He saw the Eucharist and the designation of "Corpus Christi" as a powerful statement of the realism of the Christological teaching of the Church. In this way von Balthasar saw Eucharistic devotion as an antidote to the vague liberal acceptance of Jesus of Nazareth that he saw entering into the Catholic Church from liberal Protestantism. In a pointed statement he brings up the following during a radio sermon: "All this forms a unity, and no stone can be pulled from this wall without causing the whole edifice to collapse. If Jesus Christ is not the incarnate Word of Yahweh but merely, for instance, the last of the prophets or the purely human vice-regent of God, Corpus Christi, the Feast of the Lord's Body, the Feast of the Eucharist, has no meaning whatsoever. If that were the case, we could certainly be edified by his words and deeds, but what good would his Flesh and Blood be to us?"[8]

The realism of Scripture echoed in the Christological dogmas of the early Church is powerfully expressed in the devotion to the sacramental Body of Christ. Perhaps this is why at the present time large numbers of informed young Catholics, including many seminarians, are intuitively drawn to Eucharistic piety of which they were never informed or only heard about in disparaging ways. Von Balthasar is merciless, as he should be, in pushing the Eucharistic realism of Saint Paul as an antidote to vague theological liberalism:

> The Bible displays an amazing and shocking realism, both as regards the divine Sonship of Jesus and as regards his Eucharist. Paul pushes this realism to its ultimate conclusion when insisting that the Corinthians examine themselves to see whether they understand what "eating and drinking" mean here. For if they fail to discern the Body and Blood of Christ, they could "eat and drink judgment upon themselves" (I Cor 11:29), and the Apostle believes that things that have happened in the community go to show that this is in fact the case.

This is a divine kind of realism: in his Corpus Christi gift God is much more real, much more concrete, than we can imagine. It is a pneumatic realism, for God's Holy Spirit, in his nature and his workings and his creativity, is much more real, much more concrete, than our spirit. Thus the two truths can stand side by side, equally valid: "Unless you eat the Flesh of the Son of Man and drink his Blood, you have no life in you," and "It is the Spirit that gives life; the flesh is of no avail." The bodily Lord is also, equally, the spiritual Lord. Only in this way is he the concreteness of the God who is truth. . . .

If we accept that the formula so often used by Paul, "in Christ Jesus," is not a mere pious phrase but, as he himself understands it, expresses the profoundest reality of our Faith, would it be possible to live together merely in the Spirit of Jesus and communicate in this Spirit without at the same time participating together in his body? This is utterly inconceivable if we take the Incarnation of the Word of God seriously. If it were only a question of Jesus' Spirit, the latter would soon fade to a vague "attitude," "approach" or "way of thinking," as happens in all liberal Christianity; and this "attitude," in turn, would quickly become a merely human attitude, with Jesus as an ethical model. No. The true and living Christ is the risen Christ, who, as before, is both body and Spirit. He fills the Church (and through her, the universe) equally powerfully through his corporality and through his Spirit. Only if we take Corpus Christi seriously can we speak of the Church as the mystical body of Christ and of a "cosmic Christ," of whom the Letter to the Colossians says that "in him the whole fullness of Deity dwells bodily" and that "in him all things were created, in heaven and on earth . . . all things were created through him and for him."[9]

Thus Eucharistic devotion is an antidote to the shallow Christological thinking about some vague and marginal Galilean prophet that is served up so fruitlessly as a pale substitute for the Incarnate Son of God.

Some of those who have no trouble with the realism of the Church's faith in Christ have nevertheless expressed difficulties with Eucharistic devotion apart from Mass. In his encyclical

Mysterium Fidei (September 3, 1965), Pope Paul VI authoritatively made it very clear that Eucharistic devotion did not present an essential theological problem in relation to the Mass. Like Rahner and many others, he saw this devotion as a prayerful continuation of the participation in the liturgy and the reception of Holy Communion. For those who believe that the Church has changed her teaching on Eucharistic devotion, the following quotation is of utmost importance: "The Catholic Church has always offered and still offers the cult of Latria to the Sacrament of the Eucharist, not only during Mass, but also outside of it, reserving Consecrated Hosts with the utmost care, exposing them to solemn veneration, and carrying them processionally to the joy of great crowds of the faithful."[10]

Sadly, this powerful encyclical of Pope Paul VI seems to have been completely forgotten by many people working in liturgical offices and publishing. It is as if it never existed. To remedy this situation Pope John Paul II, in his apostolic letter *Dominicae Cenae* (February 24, 1980), reiterated exactly the same teaching as Paul VI: "The Church and the world have a great need of Eucharistic worship. Jesus waits for us in this Sacrament of love. Let us be generous with our time in going to meet him in adoration and in contemplation that is full of faith and ready to make reparation for the great faults and crimes of the world. May our adoration never cease."[11]

These two powerful documents should be studied carefully by all concerned with the liturgical life of the Church precisely because seminarians, lay students, and members of the faithful are often told with absolutely no foundation at all that Eucharistic adoration is no longer a relevant part of Catholic life. In vague terms they are told that this practice is against the spirit of Vatican II and that it has gone completely out of vogue because it was theologically inappropriate.

The Other Side

In sharp contrast to these statements of Pope Paul VI, Pope John Paul II, Karl Rahner, Cardinal Daly, and many others are the observations of Ralph Keifer in his book on the Eucharist, *Blest and Broken*, one of the volumes in the *Message of the Sacraments* series edited by Monika Hellwig. Keifer's chapter on Eucharistic devotions, which expresses a painful alienation from much of the Catholic tradition, perhaps inspires sympathy more than anything else. Although the author shows little patience with those who find traditional Catholicism meaningful, his own self-disclosure demonstrates a sincerity that impels us to listen to him and to a number of other Catholics who are at odds with their own past. In reading the following I think that it is fair to characterize this approach as more immanentist than transcendental, more toward finding God in us rather than us in God:

> In a liturgy where Christ is understood as present first of all within the world and the assembly, and present on the altar because of that presence first in the church, the event of consecration is simply an unfolding of that presence from within, and is less dramatically marked. . . . The high drama of the new eucharistic rite comes, less at the elevation of the host and chalice at the consecration, which is very modest, than at the doxology, where, identifying ourselves with Christ ("through Him, with Him, in Him, in the unity of the Holy Spirit"), we present ourselves united to Christ to the Father. This speaks eloquently for a Christ within the community, and for a eucharistic celebration that speaks, not for a God who intervenes from without, but who is present with his people in all their time of sorrow and joy.
>
> In view of this, to the extent that people enter into a contemporary religious consciousness, former practices such as Benediction may not only be obsolete but also profoundly alienating if they are promoted for a people who have ceased to need them.[12]

I will return later to some of Keifer's other observations. Here it is sufficient to point out that his answer to the problem is quite at odds with Catholic theology and even with eminent Catholic writers of our time, some of whom we have cited. While he is impatient with traditional forms of Eucharistic devotion and a bit authoritarian at that, he is not as hostile as some tend to be.

Keifer's approach seems to lose track of the fact that revelation is a break into the cosmos rather than something immanent in it. Such thinking has been quite popular in theological circles and especially in seminary training in the last twenty years. It is an observable fact, much to the chagrin of some, that the contemporary crop of young people interested in their faith reject such an anti-transcendent approach. For this reason they are profoundly attracted to Eucharistic piety even without encouragement.

Eucharistic Adoration Brings the Controversy over the Transcendent into Focus

It is a truism that out of controversies in the Church new emphasis and fresh vitality often emerge. This may be what is actually happening at the present time with prolonged or even perpetual Eucharistic adoration. In 1988 the distinguished liturgical scholar Father Kilian McDonnell, OSB, of St. John's University, Collegeville, Minnesota, attended a meeting of the International Brotherhood of Covenant Communities at Paray-le-Monial in France. Like many American liturgists Father McDonnell admits to having placed Eucharistic devotion far in the back of his conscious mind. Like others, he thought it to be competitive with the Mass and a form of medieval piety that had outlived its usefulness. But Father McDonnell was deeply impressed by the Eucharistic devotion and general liturgical sense of the thousands of young people who were gathered there. The Eucharist was reserved in a monstrance for public veneration in a quiet area off to the side during the entire time of the meeting. Initially Father McDonnell was somewhat nonplussed. Yet like others cited above, he has come to reappraise the practice, especially the new emphasis that Eucharistic adoration outside of Mass is a prolongation of the experience of the liturgy and a preparation for the next liturgy that one is to attend. There is no devotee of the Eucharistic Presence who would object to such a theological framework. Father McDonnell's reflections appeared in the February 25, 1989, issue of *America* magazine:

> Paray-le-Monial taught me this new framework for thinking about exposition. Adoration is carried over from the pre-Vatican II devotional practice. Alongside of adoration, however, there is also a strong accent on praise, mostly silent praise. That little tent in the field lent itself to the Psalms of cosmic praise. . . .
>
> This new liturgical and biblical situation can give day-long

exposition in a parish a new character. There the eucharistic presence will derive from the Mass and lead back to it. If the pastor makes clear the place exposition has in the hierarchy of eucharistic truths, why should that practice be looked down upon?[13]

It is important to observe that Father McDonnell in his article mentions that he has discussed this whole matter of the renewal of Eucharistic adoration with two other distinguished liturgists from his abbey, Father Godfrey Diekmann, OSB, and Father Michael Marx, OSB, both former editors of the journal *Worship*. Father Diekmann observed, "Eucharistic exposition and adoration are nothing else than the action of the Mass held in contemplation."[14] Father Michael Marx agreed so much with Father McDonnell's observations that he suggested he publish them — hence the article in *America* magazine.

Despite this well-publicized retraction by well-known liturgists, six years later a priest who appears to be interested and informed on liturgical matters, Father Roger O'Brien, pastor of St. Luke's parish in Seattle, Washington, wrote to the *Catholic Northwest Progress* objecting to an article on perpetual adoration in the October 12, 1995, edition of that paper. Father O'Brien takes a very negative view of the idea of perpetual adoration in a parish:

> . . . church directives, reflecting the mind of Vatican II, have been crafted in the hope the Eucharist would not be reduced to an object that functions as a sign of a static presence, a "being there," rather than a challenging invitation to active relationship implied in taking, eating, and drinking — and in doing Eucharist as God's people committed to charity, justice, and peace-making.
>
> Such directives have sought to prevent the degeneration of eucharistic devotion (our history is replete with such tendencies, from the eleventh century on) into an individualistic piety, lacking in scriptural foundation, that isolates Eucharist from community, and from liturgy itself.[15]

Father O'Brien questions whether the newspaper has a "preconciliar agenda." I cite Father O'Brien's article because, in general, it is a reasonably well-balanced objection brought by the other side. It represents a kind of thinking that at this point, I believe, has become dated itself. I wonder if he has read Father McDonnell's article, which was written six years before. Anyone in touch with the piety of young people at this time knows that they deeply yearn for a personal contact with Christ, and that they have absolutely no objection to seeing this contact in the Eucharist as a continuation of the liturgy and as a preparation for the next liturgy. They also do not reject the communitarian and social aspect of the Eucharist. As a matter of fact, by processions, Eucharistic prayer meetings, vigils, and experiences like Youth 2000, they rejoice in the Eucharist as a magnet to draw them together for praise, thanksgiving, and community. I'm afraid I must observe that Father O'Brien's letter, though reasonably well-balanced, suggests an attitude that is already becoming obsolete and a period piece. Eucharistic devotion, as Father Kilian McDonnell discovered at Paray-le-Monial, is moving back into being a significant part of Catholic life.

The New Church

Perhaps the most serious challenge to Eucharistic piety in recent years has come from an assumption rather than from any particular objection. This is the rather vague but widespread hunch on the part of fairly large numbers of educated people that the Church is about to evolve from its basic theological structure, and that it is about to become a new Church, or as some say, a *Novum.* This assumption is rarely made explicit, and few are really willing to take it to its logical conclusion, which seems to be the actual end of historical and theological Catholicism. Because this view is seldom made explicit it is difficult to pin many people down. Some writers like Hans Küng and Richard McBrien seem to be getting there, but they appear to stop in their tracks at the edge of the cliff. Some of the radical feminist writers, on the other hand, do go over the edge and openly demand a church that by any laws of logic would be Catholic in name only, without real sacraments, and even devoid of any acknowledgment of divine revelation as it has been defined by the whole Judeo-Christian tradition. Almost without exception people of this mind are opposed to Eucharistic adoration for all sorts of reasons.

One group must be identified, and that is those who simply

deny any enduring dogmatic structure of the Church. Frequently they call the enduring nature of dogma into question, and usually this is done in such a way that it is not explicitly heretical. This group is very influential, and their effect is seen in Catholic education and in the decisions of local diocesan officials. An example of this kind of thinking is the popular book *Doors to the Sacred* by Joseph Martos. Without ever directly challenging the dogmas of the Church he calls them into question, and presents his view as part of the historical tide of the Church, claiming as his allies theologians who would most certainly have rejected his conclusions — in this case the Benedictine monks who began the liturgical reform movement of the nineteenth and twentieth centuries:

> Although the Catholic church officially still recognizes the doctrines of the Council of Trent as its own, Catholicism in general is quietly laying them aside. Its theologians no longer speak about the mass as a sacrifice, its preachers and catechists no longer urge special devotion to the blessed sacrament, and its congregations no longer attend the Latin mass that the Tridentine dogmas defended and explained. The term *transubstantiation*, once found in every Catholic catechism, is virtually unknown to younger Catholics, and even the word mass, though still in popular use, is disappearing from the Catholic theological vocabulary.
>
> The immediate cause of this shift was the change in Catholic worship that resulted from the Second Vatican Council, but the beginnings of the shift were already being felt decades before in the liturgical movement. Initially this movement toward liturgical renewal was neither an organized movement nor an attempt at genuine renewal. Rather it began as an attempt at "restoration," an effort to restore to the Roman mass some of the things it seemed to have before the Council of Trent. And in the beginning it affected only the monks in a few European monasteries.[16]

If we were to accept this evolutionary point of view, then every dogma from the Incarnation on could be called into question without directly risking the charge of heresy. It is often a matter of interpretation of words — disguised words. Martos is perhaps a bit more honest and says that the dogmas are just going to be forgotten. I think this is a terribly naïve assumption, since libraries exist and people will always be able to see what was said in the past. Moreover, Martos's assumptions made in the early 1980s about developments going in a straight line are now obviously wrong. The increased devotion to the Eucharistic Presence and the publication of the *Catechism of the Catholic Church* indicate that he and many others misread the signs of the times.

That there was a concerted effort to wipe out Eucharistic devotion can be seen simply by reviewing the popular religious-education textbooks that swept through the Church in the English-speaking world. In the two decades after Vatican II, there was an obvious ignoring or downplaying of Catholic dogmas, including the divinity of Christ, Benediction, and other Eucharistic devotions in religious-education texts, except those that were known for their orthodoxy. Eucharistic devotions were often disapproved of or even forbidden by diocesan religious-education offices. The alarming situation described in a fairly recent *New York Times/CBS News Poll* (April 1994), indicating that less than half of Catholics who attend Mass believe that the Eucharist is really the Body and Blood of Christ, should not come as a surprise to anyone. Saint Paul's words are pertinent: "And how are they to believe in him of whom they have never heard? And how are they to hear without a preacher?" (Rom 10:14). Many younger Catholics, including seminarians, have never been to Benediction or any other Eucharistic devotion.

In some quarters there has been a strong reaction to this concerted effort to rid the Church of the presence of Christ. Writing after a "Summer School on the Eucharist" held at Maynooth, Ireland, Father Raymond Moloney, SJ, went so far as to say: "This decline in Benediction was a subject for general regret in the workshops. Many of the older generation probably do not realize just how completely the experience of Benediction is a closed book for many of our young people. Indeed among some of the participants there was quite an anger expressed against the clergy for letting this decline come about."[17]

Among theological objections there is a particular bias against the doctrine of transubstantiation, and this objection spills over into hostility to Eucharistic devotion in general. Much of this opposition seems to come from simply denying any validity to medieval thought at all. A good deal of the opposition has a smart-aleck ring to it. One writer who seems to have no problem in taking on the greatest Doctors of the Church is P.J. Fitzpatrick. After admitting that the accepted theology of the Church on the Real Presence (he calls this "the Galilean presence") is simply the most vivid and basic presence, like the one the disciples experienced, he then attempts to demolish it and put up his own theory in its place. The following question from his book *In Breaking of Bread: The Eucharist and Ritual* (1993) will give a sense of this critique:

> Eucharistic devotions do not remedy the incoherence of the Galilean presence, they simply give ritual expression to it. And in so expressing it, they cannot but reveal the very mixed heritage that lies behind eucharistic belief. It is enough by now to recall briefly from earlier pages just how mixed it is: the incoherence of transubstantiation; its expression in terms of primitive natural science; the forcing of the terminology used into dimensional categories, with the unwanted consequences thereof; the presence of speculations in Aquinas and others that need violence doing to them if they are not to be read as camouflaged cannibalism; the grossness in miracle stories, legends, professions of faith and phrases in the *Missale Romanum*; most of all, because most pertinent to matters like eucharistic processions, the separation of the consecrated elements from the eucharistic rite, and their treatment as a commodity only accidentally linked with their being shared in the rite. I have conceded ("contended" might be the word for some readers) that professions of belief like that found at Trent can be accepted if we adjust the unit of significance. That is, we can take them simply as witnesses to belief that Christ's eucharistic presence is a reality not reducible to a loving memory, or to a human giving, or to anything whatever achievable by or depending u on our means alone. But the whole point of adjusting the unit of significance is to deny an independent meaning to details — and it is just such details that are crystallized in ceremonies like those I have mentioned.[18]

A really unfortunate but regretfully significant exploration of the Eucharistic Presence appeared in the January 27, 1995, edition of *Commonweal* magazine. The issue began on a really encouraging note from the editor: "Nothing is more important to the health and future of the church than an authentic understanding of the Eucharist."[19] While some of the articles had merit, P.J. Fitzpatrick was back with his broadside attack on the Catholic tradition. He is, to use his own term, still after the Galilean presence. He inaccurately calls transubstantiation a mystery, something that Saint Thomas would not do. The Eucharist is a mystery. Transubstantiation is a theological term that has been declared to be most apt by the Church.[20] Nonetheless, Fitzpatrick writes: "Of course the Eucharist is a mystery, and if transubstantiation did no more than acknowledge the mystery I would not object. But it does far more. It takes terms devised to express change, and it puts them together in a way that makes no sense. Because it does this, it offers an appearance of sense that turns a mystery into a misleading riddle."[21]

Fitzpatrick does at least mention that the Eucharist is a mystery, and rejects any account that reduces it to a human memorial or an expression of fellowship. He misrepresents in a highly objectionable way a citation from Cardinal John Henry Newman, who admits in regard to transubstantiation that he cannot tell "how it is." The answer that Fitzpatrick seems determined to offer is to accuse others of such stature as Aquinas and Newman of giving faulty answers. While he admits that the ultimate nature of matter is still not understood by science, he maintains that his explanation goes along with science. One could argue that the latest physical theories on the nature of material substance fit even better with the doctrine of transubstantiation than the medieval understanding of matter.

With all of his cynical disregard for the Catholic tradition, Fitzpatrick admits the power of the Eucharistic devotion that expressed this tradition. The following citation from *In Breaking of Bread* says this rather well:

> The attraction does indeed have to do with the confusion, but it is also an attraction both understandable and not unworthy of its setting. The attraction lies in associating the eucharistic presence with a presence of Christ, imperceptible indeed, but resem-

bling the way in which he was present to those with whom he walked and talked in Galilee. It is this 'Galilean presence' which is cultically pictured in the Old Mass, and brought into even greater prominence by the physical structures directed towards exposition of the consecrated host. And that such a presence should be attractive needs no proof. We have seen something of how the human quest for God manifests itself. Belief in the incarnation combines this quest with the vividness and tangibility of an encounter with another human being. 'That which was from the beginning, which we have heard, which we have seen with our eyes, which we have looked upon, and our hands have handled. . .' — the opening words of the First Epistle of John enshrine the grace of that encounter in Galilee, the unique grace that lives on in the memory of the writer. The presence I call Galilean is quite simply the most vivid and basic presence we have yet encountered; it was in such a presence that the disciples came to know and to love their Master; what more understandable than to think in terms of such a presence, when we think of our eucharistic sharing in the Lord's body and blood?

Indeed, I would go further. I claimed as a merit for my Way of Ritual that it had an uneasiness and incompleteness about it; I now make the claim again. I cannot offer anything as attractive as the Galilean presence, no account can that takes the notion of sign seriously.[22]

The whole objection of Fitzpatrick is really quite extraordinary. According to Fitzpatrick, Saint Thomas Aquinas (and a host of others who agree with him) "makes no sense," and Aquinas's theory can be read as "camouflaged cannibalism." In its place we are to put Fitzpatrick's "Way of Ritual."

Cult and Controversy

As we have mentioned already, one of the bases for attacks on devotion to the Eucharistic Presence is upon historical grounds — namely, that these devotions were medieval and that they did not go back to the very early Church, or even reflect the patristic thinking on the Eucharist. This argument has almost never been made on its own but rather in conjunction with theological considerations and dissatisfaction with the Mass as it was celebrated before Vatican II. We have already seen that the essential ingredient of Eucharistic devotion — the recognition of the presence of Christ as Jesus of Nazareth and not simply the ubiquitous presence of the Word — can be traced to the Fathers of the Church. It is even erroneous to speak as if it were a certainty that this devotion did not begin until the Middle Ages, in view of the evidence that we have given of its possible origins in the sixth century.

A very influential and erudite book that was written in a popular style, *Cult and Controversy: The Worship of the Eucharist Outside Mass* (1982), did much to undermine Eucharistic devotion after the Second Vatican Council. Written by Nathan Mitchell, then a monk of St. Meinrad Abbey, it did not use the polemics and sarcasm of P.J. Fitzpatrick, and seemed to offer no new theory of the Eucharist but simply suggested a return to ancient ideas, customs, and usages of this sacrament. The author felt that these were more in keeping with the needs of modern man.

There are, however, some very strange gaps in Mitchell's historic study. When one considers the importance of Saint Francis and the early Franciscans in popularizing Eucharistic devotion, it is amazing that neither his name nor the name of his order appears in the index of this book. It is all the more puzzling, since the sources Mitchell used often mention the impact of the Franciscans on Eucharistic piety. There are other significant omissions — for example, there is no mention of the possible sixth-century beginnings of Eucharistic devotion in Lugo, Spain.

Mitchell does not dismiss the medieval times as barbaric or uncultured. Unlike Fitzpatrick, he sees the theological efforts of this time as an attempt to bring the beginnings of scientific inquiry to bear on the usages and symbols of the ancient Church. Although he often reduces Eucharistic devotion to folk religion, he does not dismiss it as such: "Our brief analysis of folk religion and personal presence can help us assess more adequately the role of eucharistic devotions in Christian life. These devotions seem to stress two things: first, there is a legitimate human need, recognizable in all forms of folk religion, to adapt symbols to the concrete immediacies of daily life, especially in situations where the Great Tradition offers no compelling solution; secondly, Christians have sensed,

almost from the beginning, that there is a unique connection between the Lord's presence and the eucharistic elements . . . the
very transmission of the eucharistic traditions in the New Testament texts seems to point toward an early linkage between the
presence of Christ and the bread and wine of the Supper."[23]

Despite this recognition of the legitimacy of Eucharistic devotion, Mitchell ultimately reduces it to a form of religious immaturity or spiritual childishness. Borrowing from concepts of the renowned developmental theorist Erik Erikson, Mitchell makes a case
that reliance on visual and auditory symbols and on the experiences of security, familiarity, and mutuality that they bring is part
of early psychological development, but that if one were to cling to
these experiences one would be blocked from achieving generativity,
which is the highest level of human development. Mitchell is correct in recognizing generativity as the highest level of development
in Erickson's original sequence, a desirable value in religious life
and experience: "At the generative level of ritual expression, people
are ready to take on the larger responsibilities of adult life, e.g., the
intimacy shared by husband and wife expands to generate new life
and personality in a child; the minister's personal intimacy with
the Lord expands to embrace others by serving their needs and
answering their call for help."[24]

But then Mitchell proceeds to a rather naïve application of
Erikson's theory, which although obviously sincere and enthusiastic is extremely uncritical and shows a lack of that caution which
anyone ought to use when relating psychological theory to human
custom, culture, and especially revealed religion and faith. In effect what Mitchell does is reduce Eucharistic piety as it was known
in the Church to a cultural expression of emotional immaturity.
Many of Mitchell's readers at that heady time (the early 1980s) were
only too happy to find reason for dismissing the piety with which
they had been raised. They probably were totally unaware that
Erikson, writing for a secular audience, defended vowed religious
chastity as one of the highest forms of generativity.[25]

Since many recognized that indeed there were people who did
use Eucharistic piety during and outside of Mass as an escape
from some of the more disturbing and unpleasant requirements of
the Gospel, like the care of the poor and the sick, Mitchell's argu-

ments appeared all too cogent. He did not throw out Eucharistic devotion but relegated it to an embarrassing second-class position. Mature and altruistic Christians who had arrived at a higher level of development, generativity, no longer had need for these expressions. Mitchell has a remarkable way of using other people's ideas out of context, and of using one idea or concept while ignoring completely the other important things they said. Considering what Karl Rahner had written about Eucharistic devotion, it is rather distressing to see him cited on the other side by Mitchell: "Karl Rahner's comments about the 'liturgy of the world,' already mentioned in Chapter Seven, are apropos here as well. Christian worship is not an oasis of intimacy in an otherwise harsh and wicked world. It is a sacramental symbol that points toward the world as the place where God constantly celebrates, and causes to be celebrated, that vast liturgy of human life 'breathing of death and sacrifice.' Sacramental symbols are neither a temple that enclose the holy nor a group-therapy session on identity and intimacy. Rather, they 'constitute the manifestation of the holiness and the redeemed state of the secular dimension of human life and of the world.' "[26]

Not only does Mitchell ignore what Rahner had already written, but he now amazingly ignores the fact that some of the Church's greatest apostles of charity and social reform, holy people as well with a profound sense of the beauty of God and of the world, have been deeply devoted to the kind of Eucharistic devotion that he describes as immature or ungenerative. Saint Francis, Saint Vincent de Paul, the great religious Mothers Seton, Cabrini, Drexel, and, in our own time, Teresa of Calcutta — these are all recognized as people of great creativity and generativity, and are known to have cherished Eucharistic piety. Is it too much to suggest that there is a flaw here in Mitchell's broad generalizations? I think of Mother Mary Joseph Rogers, who founded the Maryknoll Sisters, a generative Christian if there ever was one. It was she who started the custom of perpetual adoration of the Eucharist at the Maryknoll Motherhouse, which continued until the mid-eighties, when the sisters caught up with Mitchell's criticism of Eucharistic devotion and discontinued the practice. Some communities must have taken the words of Mitchell (such as the following) too seriously to get them to give up their cherished Eucharistic devotion: "But mature adult development in faith as in the rest of human life demands that we integrate this legitimate need for security, familiarity and mutuality into generative modes of symbolic expression and ritual behavior. This means that one must mature beyond the point where worship is perceived merely as private prayer in a communal setting or as personal intimacy with God. Generativity requires that in celebrating the liturgy we also embrace the larger mission of the church: the mission to become bread broken in service for a hungering world."[27]

At this moment of Church history — when so much of great value has been lost — one can lament that such seemingly innocent observations were accepted uncritically, and then became so very destructive to the religious lives of so many.

The Liturgy of the World

Many deeply devout believers in the Church's teaching on the Eucharist have perceived the link between the Eucharist and the cosmos, seeing this sacrament as a sanctifying and sacralizing Presence flowing from the Incarnation of the Word of God. The problem is that Nathan Mitchell and others like him have been moving toward a position that, unintentionally or otherwise, muddles the whole traditional understanding of the Eucharist so that it is no longer seen as the saving presence of Christ in the cosmos wounded by sin but rather a means of discovering a kind of Divine Presence already in nature. There is indeed such a Divine Presence — "In him we live and move and have our being" (Acts 17:28).

It was Saint Paul who, having powerfully preached the unique transcendent and saving power of Christ Jesus, Son of a woman and Son of God, likewise said that from the visible things in the world we can also come to know the invisible things of God: "Ever since the creation of the world his invisible nature, namely, his eternal power and deity, has been clearly perceived in the things that have been made" (Rom 1:20). Many Catholics, enthusiastic for an authentic Catholic liturgical life, seek Christ's same presence extended in time and space but beginning with the Paschal Mystery — the whole historical Christ. Today's "New Age Catholics" do quite the opposite. They capitalize on some awareness of the presence of the divinity in the cosmos and pretend that this is the presence of Christ. One tries charitably to assume that this is done because they have forgotten or perhaps never known the experience of Christ Jesus as a real Person in their lives.

Nathan Mitchell sadly seems to be one of these people. He has reemerged as the associate director for research at the Center for Pastoral Liturgy at Notre Dame. In the same issue of *Commonweal* entitled "Eucharistic Presence" (January 27, 1995), we find a long article by Mitchell — "Who Is at the Table? Reclaiming Real Presence" — which basically trivializes the sacraments of the Church.[28] Claiming to represent Karl Rahner, Mitchell sees the sacraments of the Church as "humble landmarks, 'small signs'" that the entire world is God's. He even enlists Saint Thomas Aquinas to support his view. This article is a strange blend of insights and obfuscations, of quotes taken out of context and totally new (and exotic) ideas presented as logical extensions of the Catholic tradition. He dismisses the renewed interest in traditional Eucharistic devotion as a "resacralizing reaction." But in its place he puts the following description of the "Real Presence of Christ":

> The primary liturgy through which Christians experience the Real Presence of God in Christ is nothing more or less than "the liturgy of the world." It is to this liturgy, "smelling of death and sacrifice," that all the church's ritual actions return. There, God is met in the confused impurity of the human condition — in the weight of mineral; the light of honey; the sound of the words "night" and "good-by"; the heaping abundance of wheat, ivory, and tears; lifted objects of leather, wood, and food; faded photos that gather our lives like walls; the red noise of bones; the thunder of flesh; the smack of kisses, gasps, and sobs; the roar of water passing across bone; muffled snow; garlic and sapphires in the mud. There, God is met as One who *suffers with us*, as One who forgives a thief on the cross. All this is what the liturgy of the world celebrates; all this is what the liturgy of the church points to. We arrive at mystery, at Real Presence, at God, only by embracing the human with all its poignancy and terror.[29]

I suspect that your reaction to this quotation may be similar to my own. The long sentence ending with "garlic and sapphires in the mud" is to me a pretentious mishmash, an incomprehensible attempt at poetry (making for a pathetic imitation of T.S. Eliot),[30] although admittedly felt sincerely by the writer. I have no experience of water passing over bones or of sapphires in the mud, or garlic either. I am ultimately puzzled and appalled by the applying of these things to the Eucharist. After the poetry we move into the soft sell. This is a way to save the Real Presence, I am assured. Then we move to the hard sell. "We can only do this. We can recognize this only if we do that. . . . It is our responsibility." I am more than amused. I am offended. Back to the seventies with their smoke screens and phony agendas. "*We* must do this, recognize that, accept the other, so that *we* can save the Church." The first question is: Who does "*we*" refer to? Not me! In the seventies a lot of people took this seriously, and we are all now sitting in the ruins. The people who got us into this mess are back to tell us that we must follow them another time. Surely they are sincere, but the above passage suggests that they also are, in fact, deluded.

Years ago Nathan Mitchell was someone who was able to catch the trend of the moment and use his considerable talent in developing the ideas that people caught in the same trend wanted to hear. In this article he still plays to his fans, who by this time are a bit superannuated: "One cannot help feeling that the call to resacralize worship is sometimes a 'code' for recreating a culture in which aging white males of European origin call all the shots, make all the rules, and determine all the parameters of legitimate discussion. The sacral, transcendent character of Christian worship does not, after all, rest upon an arbitrary ensemble of acts and artifacts (incense, orphreys, genuflections, plainchant). It arises from the ability to perceive 'heaven in ordinarie.' "[31]

In a warm but typical fruit salad of quotes taken out of context, throwing together brilliant and wacky ideas, Mitchell blames the Church for a distorted view of the body and proceeds to make the immanent rather than the transcendent approach the only really acceptable one. Strange ideas are mixed with apparently orthodox formulas in such a way as to confuse someone who has only a partially informed faith. Sample the following: "The body of Christ offered to Christians in consecrated bread and wine is not some*thing* but some*one*. In the Eucharist, Christ is present not as an 'object' to be admired but as a person (a 'subject') to be encountered. Thomas Aquinas understood this well, and so insisted that the ultimate intent (the *res*) of celebrating Eucharist is not to produce the sacred species for purposes of reservation or adoration, but to create that united body of Christ which is the church."[32]

Mitchell in this article seems to borrow ideas from that amorphous but noisy phenomenon called the New Age. It is difficult to ever pin this label on anyone who does not expressly claim it, but the new Mitchell seems to be at least moving in that direction. Convinced no doubt that the new approach is more psychologically mature and generative, he will probably be back for a second round, having rejoined the liturgical *avant-garde* at Notre Dame. This venue has produced more than one great liturgical light who ended up being an absolute enemy of the Church. I hope this does not happen to him. Despite all the noise and smoke I suspect he does have some real affection for the Church, and even for the presence of Christ. I think he even sees Eucharistic devotion as still helpful to us poor peasants. But with friends like this, do we even need enemies?

The Eucharistic adventures of the deep-dyed New Age Catholics go beyond the scope of this book, insofar as we have said we would not discuss opposition to Eucharistic devotion that had an unequivocally heretical foundation. The reader should be aware that these enemies are around. In order not to formally lose their Church membership, they largely content themselves with mocking Eucharistic devotion as "potato-chip worship" or "playing with your food." Cardinal Newman, in his *Idea of a University*, directly warned those who make their own minds "the measure of all things" and refuse to listen to the "Prophets and Apostles, to whom the sights and sounds of Heaven were immediately conveyed":

> It is not that you will at once reject Catholicism, but you will measure and proportion it by an earthly standard. You will throw its highest and most momentous disclosures into the background, you will deny its principles, explain away its doctrines, rearrange its precepts, and make light of its practices even while you profess it. . . .

... Let this spirit be freely evolved out of that philosophical condition of mind ... and it is impossible but, first indifference, then laxity of belief, then even heresy will be the successive results.[33]

The Saddest Objection of All

While some of the objections we have discussed are either arrogant, silly, or exotic, there is one objection that is very sad indeed. There are a number of people who, styling themselves Catholic intellectuals, really object to Eucharistic piety precisely because it does what it is supposed to do — it makes us more aware of Christ's fulfillment of His promise to be with us till the end of the world. We have already seen Karl Rahner's warning about such objections. While it is true that almost all great spiritual writers tell us there will be times when God seems far away, when we will even feel rejected by Him, they identify these experiences as times of necessary and purifying suffering; they are not the status quo, so to speak. If God always seems far away, and the person is always isolated from Him, it may be that something is wrong with the person or his approach to God.

Saint John of the Cross tells us that for the believer this dark night of the soul is brighter than the day. Such diverse modern spiritual classics as the *Autobiography of St. Thérèse of Lisieux* and *Markings*, the spiritual diary of Dag Hammarskjöld, suggest that spiritual darkness is not the same as the experience of alienation that a sincere person with an adequate faith may encounter. This is particularly clear in *Markings*, which relates how Hammarskjöld moved from an incomplete faith to a powerful knowledge of God.[34] The assumption that a head full of theological knowledge or even a high IQ leads to spiritual maturity is an absurd but persistent superstition of the intellectually well-endowed.

If there is one thing I have learned in twenty-five years as a psychologist and teacher of behavioral sciences, it is that there is probably an inverse or negative correlation between what bright people know about psychodynamics and their actual psychological maturity. I once worked in a psychiatric hospital where a number of the well-trained staff marveled at the maturity and wisdom of the old black lady who served lunch to them. The same is obvious in the spiritual life. We have it on the very best authority that our Father in heaven does not reveal things to the wise and prudent but to little ones (Lk 10:21). Christ also warns us not to despise little ones (Mt 18:10).

We promised to return to the objections of Ralph Keifer when we reviewed his critique of Eucharistic piety earlier in this chapter.[35] The following text really speaks loudly and sadly for itself. Since Keifer makes himself a spokesman for these alienated "intellectuals," we must return to his objections:

> For many people, one of the most disconcerting features of the Christian spiritual life has become the convention of speaking of God, Jesus Christ, or the Holy Spirit primarily as though they were persons who are somehow to be intimately known as lover, companion, friend, or parent. Sometimes, the uncritical and reflective use of this sort of language can be one of the most significant barriers to growth in the life of the Spirit. There are many people who assume that they either do not or cannot pray authentically because they do not find themselves experiencing a "personal" presence of God, i.e., a sense of a divine Other present as friend, lover, companion, or parent. Since they so view themselves as flawed believers, such people are, at the very least, deprived of something of the joy and freedom of the children of God. Where this felt lack is also accompanied by a seriousness about the things of the Spirit, the result can verge on torment. . . .
>
> In the experience of this writer, at least, this problem of Christian "personalism" is *not* a problem for the naïve, the simple, or the theologically uneducated. Intuitively and unreflectively, they seem to be able to deal with various languages of piety with the appropriate accuracy and the right sort of tentativeness. This is why the worst sort of fundamentalist jargon or devotionalistic saccharine can sound wholly authentic on the lips of some people. They seem to possess a certain untroubled "savvy" about when such language is appropriate and when it is not. On the other hand, I have found that it is the brighter sort of seminarian, or the university graduate, who can be utterly thrown by the assumption that a serious person of faith and prayer should experience God literally as lover, companion, friend, or parent.[36]

While I leave it to the readers to evaluate these objections for themselves, I need to point out that the anger and prejudice reflected in these sad observations is typical of a man who opposes Eucharistic devotion and whom the author identifies as the "brighter sort of seminarian, or the university graduate." This kind of thinking runs head-on into some very wise warnings from that "brighter sort of apostle," Saint Paul. In his first letter to the Corinthians he observes:

> For it is written, "I will destroy the wisdom of the wise, and the cleverness of the clever I will thwart." Where is the wise man? Where is the scribe? Where is the debater of this age? Has not God made foolish the wisdom of the world? For since, in the wisdom of God, the world did not know God through wisdom, it pleased God through the folly of what we preach to save those who believe. . . . For the foolishness of God is wiser than men, and the weakness of God is stronger than men.
>
> For consider your call, brethren; not many of you were wise according to worldly standards, not many were powerful, not many were of noble birth; but God chose what is foolish in the world to shame the wise, God chose what is weak in the world to shame the strong, God chose what is low and despised in the world, even things that are not, to bring to nothing things that are, so that no human being might boast in the presence of God. He is the source of your life in Christ Jesus, whom God made our wisdom, our righteousness and sanctification and redemption; therefore, as it is written, "Let him who boasts, boast of the Lord."
>
> — 1 Corinthians 1:19-21, 25-31

How sad then these lines of Keifer really are, because he obviously is sincere, and clearly was trying to pursue some kind of belief in the Eucharist. He is typical of many unfortunate people in the Church. Having failed personally in the effort to experience a personal God "as friend, lover, companion, or parent," they resent others who have this blessing. If we say that this blessing is immature, "devotionalistic saccharine," then what do we do with Saint Augustine, Saint Francis, Saint Teresa of Ávila, Saint Thérèse of Lisieux, and most, if not all, of the canonized saints? What do we do with Saint Ignatius Loyola, Saint Alphonsus Liguori, and in our own time Blessed Edith Stein, all brilliant minds who experienced a deep personal devotion to Christ as friend and companion? What are we to do with Christ's admonition that we must receive the Kingdom of God as little children if we wish to enter it? At least the "brighter sort" of Catholics might be careful about depriving the little people of what brings them closer to Christ. And if these "brighter people" feel as alienated as Keifer seems to be, they might have something to learn from the "foolishness of God" that "is wiser than men"!

The Flap over Perpetual Adoration

A tradition of perpetual prayer in a given place can be traced back to Constantinople, where in the fifth century there was a place of worship called the Monastery of "those who do not sleep" ("*Akoimetoi*"). An endless recitation of psalms was maintained by relays of monks in this church. As we have seen (and will see in more detail in Chapter 8), perpetual prayer in the presence of the Eucharist may have appeared in Lugo, Spain, as early as the sixth century, and this practice is known to have arisen in at least two other locations by the middle of the thirteenth century. These latter cases are described in Chapter 12 by James Monti.

In more recent times, this extraordinary homage and intercession began to focus on the exposed Blessed Sacrament. A large number of communities of contemplative nuns chose this form of prayer as their principal work and charism. The Blessed Sacrament Fathers and Brothers founded by Saint Peter Julian Eymard did a great deal in the late nineteenth and early twentieth centuries to propagate the devotion to the exposed Blessed Sacrament. As a youngster I remember visiting the Church of St. Jean Baptiste in Manhattan, and being deeply impressed by the devotion of the hundreds of people who were often seen praying before the huge monstrance of that church.

We have already mentioned that perpetual adoration of the exposed Blessed Sacrament conducted by members of the laity has gone on in the Basilica of the Sacred Heart on Montmartre in Paris for well over a century. In the last forty years the establishment of perpetual adoration of the exposed Blessed Sacrament in parishes has steadily grown. Only rarely has the practice had to be discontinued because of a lack of support, sadly often occasioned by some of the clergy. Those who have taken the opportunity to responsibly form an association of the faithful for this work have had no trouble filling the hours of the day or month with volunteers. Usually a small chapel of reservation is set up apart from the church for liturgical as well as safety reasons. It is not unusual in the hours of the night to find several people praying very devoutly along with the volunteers assigned for that hour of the vigil. A sense of contemplative prayer usually pervades the chapel, and among the books in the benches one will often find works of great mystics, as well as devotional literature and meditations on charity and social responsibility. One pastor who initiated perpetual adoration several years ago, Father Richard Doheny of St. Mel's parish in Fair Oaks, California, found that it transformed the spiritual life of the parish and brought parishioners much closer together. This is a parish of people with a variety of ethnic backgrounds and economic situations, but they came together joyfully and without hesitation in making perpetual Eucharistic adoration an important part of their parish life.

Since priests investigating the possibility of initiating perpetual adoration in their parishes are often given the impression that there is some general disapproval of this practice, a review of the pertinent documents and some history may be helpful. Sometimes misunderstandings do arise, because only older documents are available and some of these are out of date.

For reasons that are obscure but perhaps related to the downplaying of Eucharistic devotion in general, the June-July 1986 *Newsletter* of the Bishops' Committee on the Liturgy (Volume 22) issued norms on perpetual adoration of the Blessed Sacrament that had, at best, a rather restrictive tone.[37] The Congregation for Divine Worship is quoted as saying, "If the sacrament were exposed continuously, there would be a lessening in the value of these occasions [exposition and adoration] as reminders of their proper place in the spiritual life and of their character as high points for reflection on the eucharist."[38]

The *Newsletter* went on to cite a 1973 document of the Congregation entitled *On Holy Communion and the Worship of the Eucharistic Mystery Outside of Mass.* According to the official English translation of this document published in 1976 (by ICEL), Paragraph 90 states: "According to the constitutions and regulations of their institute, some religious communities and other groups have the practice of perpetual eucharistic adoration or adoration over extended periods of time. It is strongly recommended that they pattern this holy practice in harmony with the spirit of the liturgy. . . ."[39]

The phrase "and other groups" in the above passage certainly indicates that perpetual adoration is not restricted to "religious communities" alone. Yet in citing the same paragraph, the Bishops' Committee on the Liturgy *Newsletter* interpreted it as follows: "With regard to perpetual exposition, this form is permitted only in the case of those religious communities of men or women who 'according to the constitutions and regulations of their institute have the general practice of perpetual eucharistic adoration or adoration over extended periods of time' (no. 90). In other instances perpetual exposition is not permitted."[40]

The *Newsletter* proceeds to use this interpretation of Paragraph 90 to conclude that "perpetual adoration of the blessed sacrament in parish churches and other oratories, except where permitted by law, is not permitted."[41] Fortunately, this defective definition of the current status of perpetual adoration was not allowed to stand unclarified for long. The Prefect of the Congregation for Divine Worship, Cardinal Paul Mayer, OSB, wrote back in regard to the *Newsletter* that there had been an omission of a phrase that "cannot be considered as an omission of no consequence" (Letter, November 12, 1986). It appeared that the statement was "over-restrictive." The correction pertains to this omission. "When all conditions are observed a bishop can grant permission for a pious association to have perpetual exposition."

In January of 1987 the *Newsletter* of the Bishops' Committee on the Liturgy published a correction (Volume 23).[42] It admitted that there had been an omission of pious associations from the list of those who could have perpetual adoration. The *Newsletter* deemed this an "inadvertent non-substantive omission." If some of the faithful had gained much spiritual strength from being a member of a parish where perpetual adoration was held, I suppose the omission would have seemed to them to be quite substantive. But was there now a further impasse insofar as a parish wishing to have perpetual adoration needed to have a pious association? The Prefect of the Pontifical Council for the Laity essentially removed this impasse in a decree dated June 2, 1991 (Feast of Corpus Christi), signed by Cardinal Eduardo Pironio and Bishop Paul Cordes, establishing a pontifical pious association for perpetual Eucharistic adoration. This document can be seen in Appendix 1.

The obvious conclusion is that a pastor wishing to begin perpetual adoration should obtain from the diocesan bishop permission to establish such an Association of Perpetual Eucharistic Adoration in the parish. Thus, not only should there be a request made to have perpetual adoration, but along with it should be a petition to establish an association of the faithful with responsible officers to oversee all the requirements of this devotion, such as a suitable place, the care of the oratory, and a sufficient number of members or volunteers to see to it that the exposed Blessed Sacrament is never left without worshipers.

With certain questions remaining as to precisely when, where, and how perpetual adoration could be carried out, the Bishops' Committee on the Liturgy issued a comprehensive document updating the whole matter in the June 1995 issue of its *Newsletter* (Volume 31).[43] Acknowledging that perpetual exposition can "for some good reason" take place in parish churches, the document states that there is to be an appropriate association in the parish for such adoration to be permitted, and that its activities "should be seen as separate from that of the parish, although all members of the parish are free to participate in it." If the Eucharist is exposed in a monstrance or ciborium, the permission of the bishop is required (this regulation is nothing new — it existed long before Vatican II). Perpetual exposition is of course not permitted during the Easter Triduum, or during the celebration of Mass in the chapel of exposition. The document wisely suggests that two worshipers be assigned at all times, and that the exposed Eucharist should never be left unattended. The entire document can be found in Appendix 2.

In response to the question "Must the local bishop permit perpetual exposition?" the following answer is given in the June 1995 *Newsletter*. While the tone of the response may still seem restrictive, it must be borne in mind that the bishop is responsible for his diocese. He might decline or withdraw permission if a neighbor-hood is unsafe at night, or place other restrictions — for example, adoration only during the day: "The bishop is responsible for all matters pertaining to the right ordering of the celebration of the Eucharist and adoration and devotion to the Eucharist outside Mass. It is his duty to promote and guide the liturgical life of the diocese. Consequently, he alone determines the pastoral appropri-ateness of perpetual exposition in his diocese and accordingly may permit it or not and may limit the number of places where it takes place."[44]

The Encouragement of the Holy Father for Perpetual Adoration

On the other hand, a very strong encouragement for perpetual adoration was given to the whole Church by Pope John Paul II at the Eucharistic Congress in Seville during June of 1993. In his homily at Seville's cathedral on June 12, the Holy Father stated: ". . . the continual adoration — which took place in many churches throughout the city, and in some even at night — was an enriching feature that distinguished this Congress. If only this form of adora-tion, which ends tonight in a solemn Eucharistic vigil, would con-tinue in the future too, so that in all the parishes and Christian communities the custom of some form of adoration of the Eucha-rist might take root."[45]

Further excerpts from this landmark homily on Eucharistic devotion appear in Chapter 12.

It would seem that a blanket denial of permission for perpetual Eucharistic adoration would be consistent neither with the spirit of the law nor with the wishes of the Holy Father. Perpetual adora-tion of the exposed Eucharist has come into its own. We are in-formed by Father Martin Lucia, Director of the Apostolate for Per-petual Adoration, that more than a thousand parishes in one hun-dred fourteen dioceses throughout the United States have estab-lished perpetual Eucharistic adoration.[46] Another thousand have Eucharistic adoration for a substantial part of the day, even though not "perpetual." I would be remiss if I did not mention those devout clergy and laity who have struggled to maintain and expand per-petual adoration at a time when there has been a certain diffidence about it among diocesan officials. These ambiguities seem to have arisen from the same trends in the Liturgical Movement that we have documented earlier in this chapter. Obviously there has been a turn in the tide. We ought to commend the efforts of Father Martin Lucia and his associates, as well as all others who have worked for the spread of this devotion.

A number of publications and associations throughout the country have dedicated considerable time and effort to spreading this practice in many parishes. As a result, large numbers of people who may not have made quiet interior prayer an important part of their spiritual lives are now being drawn by the presence of Christ Himself to spend an occasional hour in quiet contemplative prayer and self-examination. It is my impression that these people have also grown in their love and appreciation of their neighbor whom they also see drawn, knowingly or unknowingly, by the loving mercy of Jesus Christ.

The Future of Eucharistic Devotion

A number of the current citations given in this book suggest that Eucharistic devotions are emerging from the dark period that threatened to drag this important part of Catholic life into the dustbin of liturgical history. In several European countries and Asia, and certainly in North and South America, there is an increasing enthusiasm and desire for this kind of devotion. This is all the more impressive when one recalls that many of the clergy of every rank are diffident toward, if not opposed to, this devotion for various reasons. You can still get called nasty names for suggesting something as apparently harmless as Benediction. Certainly a new wave of Eucharistic devotion can and should be well received by all interested in the pastoral care of parishes. Consistent and effective efforts will be needed to link the devotion to the Eucharistic liturgy. Eccentricities, which are always a danger in devotions as well as liturgical practices, need to be avoided and curtailed. One need only think of some of the more bizarre spectacles observed at the liturgy during the past two decades to be convinced of this. Clergy, religious, and lay leaders should be aware of the history and significance of Eucharistic devotion, much of which is reviewed in this book.

Eucharistic devotions of all kinds are coming back. A legitimate question is why. One may give many reasons, from the inspiration of the Holy Spirit (if you are pleased by this comeback) to the decline of society (if you are not pleased). There is, I think, a historical reason that needs to be considered — especially by those interested in the pastoral life of the Church. We live in very lonely times. Modern people have more solitude in their lives than people did in the past. With the virtual end of the extended family, with the modern preference for privacy, with the solitude in the midst of a crowd that one sees as an obvious necessity in the multitudes of large cities — people spend much less time interacting in a personal way with one another. The impersonal one-way communication of the media now substitutes for the shared recreation and cultural activities of the past. One might compare the lively paintings of farm life in Pieter Bruegel or the friendly taverns of the Dutch masters to the lonely but commonplace urban scenes of Edward Hopper to get some sense of the loneliness of our times. There are still great public events where people experience each other with shared feelings, and they range from papal visits to rock concerts — but all in all we live in lonely times, and it appears that the coming age of virtual reality is even more likely to be an age of the solitary.

It should be no surprise then that the mysterious and personal presence of Christ should have a profound human appeal. Nor need there be any fear that this devotion could lead to any kind of spiritual isolation, so long as we carefully keep the Eucharistic Presence linked with the Paschal Mystery, which encompasses all men and women, and with Holy Communion, which draws together all the faithful disciples of Christ.

ENDNOTES

1. *The Persecution of the Catholic Church in the Third Reich: Facts and Documents Translated from the German*, 1940, pp. 212-218, 442.
2. Fr. L. Bouyer, *Liturgical Piety* (Liturgical Studies, Vol. 1), 1955, pp. 2-9, 248-251; Fr. H.A. Reinhold, *The American Parish and the Roman Liturgy*, 1958, pp. 10-13, 66-67.
3. Karl Rahner, *Everyday Faith*, 1967, pp. 90, 93-94.
4. In *Understanding the Eucharist*, ed. Patrick McGoldrick, 1969, p. 109.
5. Rahner, *Mission and Grace: Essays in Pastoral Theology*, Vol. I, 1963, pp. 312-313.
6. Ibid., pp. 301-302.

7. Rahner, "Eucharistic Worship" (originally published as an article in 1981), in *Theological Investigations: Volume XXIII: Final Writings*, 1992, p. 115.

8. Hans Urs von Balthasar, *"You Crown the Year with Your Goodness": Radio Sermons*, trans. Graham Harrison, 1989, p. 153.

9. Ibid., pp. 153-155.

10. *Encyclical Letter of His Holiness Pope Paul VI: Mystery of Faith: Mysterium Fidei*, n.d., p. 23.

11. Pope John Paul II, *Dominicae Cenae*, No. 3, in *Vatican Council II: More Postconciliar Documents* (Vatican Collection, Vol. II), ed. Austin Flannery, OP, 1982, p. 67.

12. Ralph A. Keifer, *Blessed and Broken: An Exploration of the Contemporary Experience of God in Eucharistic Celebration* (*Message of the Sacraments* series, Vol. 3), 1982, pp. 132-133.

13. "Eucharistic Exposition: An Obsolete Relic?" *America*, Feb. 25, 1989, Vol. 160, p. 168.

14. Ibid., p. 169.

15. "Preconciliar Agenda Seems to Surface," *Catholic Northwest Progress*, Oct. 19, 1995, p. 8.

16. Joseph Martos, *Doors to the Sacred: A Historical Introduction to Sacraments in the Catholic Church*, 1981, pp. 292-293.

17. "Eucharistic Devotions Today," *The Furrow*, Sept. 1994, Vol. 45, p. 505.

18. P.J. Fitzpatrick, *In Breaking of Bread: The Eucharist and Ritual*, 1993, p. 337.

19. "Eucharistic Presence: Introduction" (editorial), *Commonweal*, Jan. 27, 1995, p. 10.

20. Council of Trent, Session XIII, Oct. 1551, Canon II, in Msgr. James T. O'Connor, *The Hidden Manna: A Theology of the Eucharist*, 1988, p. 218. For Msgr. O'Connor's entire discussion of the subject and new theories, see ibid., pp. 219-222, and pp. 157-162.

21. P.J. Fitzpatrick and Paul Baumann, "Signs & Disguises: Sorting Out Transubstantiation," *Commonweal*, Jan. 27, 1995, p. 19.

22. Fitzpatrick, *In Breaking of Bread*, p. 219.

23. Nathan Mitchell, *Cult and Controversy: The Worship of the Eucharist Outside Mass* (*Studies in the Reformed Rites of the Catholic Church*, Vol. IV), 1982, p. 413.

24. Ibid., p. 388.

25. Erik H. Erikson, *Childhood and Society*, 1964.

26. Mitchell, p. 388. Citations of Rahner are from "Considerations on the Active Role of the Person in the Sacramental Event" in *Theological Investigations: Volume XIV: Ecclesiology, Questions in the Church, The Church in the World*, 1976, p. 169.

27. Mitchell, p. 389.

28. *Commonweal*, Jan. 27, 1995, pp. 10-15.

29. Ibid., p. 15.

30. This is said with apologies to T.S. Eliot, who uses some of these images in his poem cycle "Four Quartets," where the context gives them some sense; see Eliot, *Collected Poems: 1909-1962*, 1963, pp. 176ff.

31. Mitchell, "Who Is at the Table? Reclaiming Real Presence," p. 12.

32. Ibid.

33. Ven. John Henry Newman, *The Idea of a University, Defined and Illustrated*, 1901, Discourse IX, No. 2, pp. 217-218.

34. Dag Hammarskjöld, *Markings*, 1970.

35. See pp. 147-149 of this volume.

36. Keifer, pp. 134, 135.

37. "Perpetual Exposition of the Blessed Sacrament," in National Conference of Catholic Bishops, *Committee on the Liturgy: Newsletter*, June-July 1986, Vol. 22, pp. 24-25.

38. Ibid., p. 25, quoted from *Notitiae*, 1971, Vol. 7, pp. 414-415.

39. *On Holy Communion and the Worship of the Eucharistic Mystery Outside of Mass*, June 21, 1973, in *The Rites of the Catholic Church as Revised by the Second Vatican Ecumenical Council* (Vol. I), trans. International Commission on English in the Liturgy, 1976 and 1983, p. 508.

40. "Perpetual Exposition of the Blessed Sacrament," p. 25.

41. Ibid.

42. "Perpetual Adoration of the Blessed Sacrament: Clarification," National Conference of Catholic Bishops, *Committee on the Liturgy: Newsletter*, Jan. 1987, Vol. 23, p. 50.

43. "Perpetual Exposition of the Blessed Sacrament," National Conference of Catholic Bishops, *Committee on the Liturgy: Newsletter*, June 1995, Vol. 31, pp. 21-22.

44. Ibid., p. 22.

45. *L'Osservatore Romano*, June 23, 1993, p. 4.

46. For helpful information on this devotion write to: Apostolate for Perpetual Adoration, P.O. Box 46520, Mt. Clemens, MI 48046-6502.

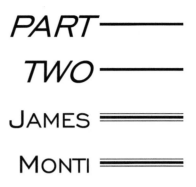

PART TWO

JAMES

MONTI

Chapter 7

The Eucharistic Presence of Christ in the Early Church

". . . the bread which I shall give for the life of the world is my flesh" (Jn 6:51)

From the beginning, the Church has taken Christ her Divine Spouse at His word when in the course of the Last Supper He took first bread, then wine, into His sacred hands and said, ". . . this is my body . . . this is my blood . . ." (Mt 26:26, 28); thus the Church has *always* spoken of and treated the Eucharist as the real Body and Blood of Christ. Of course the outward manifestations of this belief in the Real Presence have not remained static but rather have developed over the centuries in keeping with an ever deepening understanding of this mystery forged in the hearts of generation upon generation of believers and brought to fruition in the teachings of the Church's pastors and the lives of her saints.

In view of the overwhelming depth and breadth of the mystery that Holy Communion is nothing less than a communion with the risen Christ Himself, a communion in which the recipient partakes of his Divine Master's very Body and Blood, it should not come as a surprise that the practice of adoring this sacrament outside the immediate context of the Eucharistic liturgy would take time to appear; the riches of God's gift of the Eucharist are too vast to be fully plumbed in the span of one generation. Yet the doctrines and observances from which extraliturgical adoration is derived have been part of the deposit of faith since the apostolic era. The Church has always believed that the Eucharistic Presence of the Redeemer begins not at the moment of Communion but rather earlier, at the altar, brought about by the words and actions of Christ repeated by His ordained ministers. Coupled to this has been the belief that those unable to be present during the Mass itself were not to be deprived of receiving this sacrament but rather that Christ remained present in the consecrated Eucharistic Species even after the conclusion of the liturgy, making it possible to bring the sacrament to those who were ill or in prison. The testimony from the early centuries of the Church in regard to both these points is incontestable. Hence the recognition of the Eucharistic Presence of Christ on the altar during the liturgy and the directing of adoration toward that Presence is strikingly attested in the writings of Saint John Chrysostom (347-407):

> This body even when lying in the manger the Magi reverenced. Heathen and foreign men left their country and their home, and went [on] a long journey, and came and worshipped Him with fear and much trembling. Let us then, the citizens of heaven, imitate these foreigners. For they approached with great awe when they saw Him in the manger and in the cell, and saw Him in no way such as thou dost see Him now. For thou dost see Him not in a manger but on an altar, not with a woman holding Him but with a priest standing before Him, and the Spirit descending upon the offerings with great bounty. . . . For as in the palaces of kings what is most splendid of all is not the walls, or the golden roof, but the body of the king sitting on the throne, so also in heaven there is the body of the King; but this thou mayest now behold on earth. For I show to thee not angels, nor archangels, nor the heaven, nor the heaven of heavens, but Him who is the Lord of these Himself.[1]

Likewise, in another homily he states: "Not in vain do we at the holy mysteries make mention of the departed, and draw near on their behalf, beseeching the Lamb who is lying on the altar, who took away the sin of the world."[2]

Christ's Eucharistic Presence on the altar is also mentioned by

Saint Optatus of Mileve (died 400) in the course of rebuking the Donatist heretics for their vandalism of Catholic churches: "What has Jesus Christ done to you that you should destroy the altars on which he rests at certain times? Why do you break the sacred tables where Jesus Christ makes his abode?"[3]

In an often quoted passage from his commentary on Psalm 98 Saint Augustine (354-430) is most emphatic that we are to adore the Eucharist *prior* to receiving It: "No one eats this flesh unless he has first adored . . . not only do we not sin by adoring, but we would sin by not adoring."[4]

The significance of this citation is heightened by the subsequent words in the same passage, which speak of the adoration taking the form of an outward gesture of bowing or prostrating oneself before the Eucharist; thus Saint Augustine provides us with one of our two earliest extant testimonies of an outward act of reverence to the sacrament: "Therefore when you bow and prostrate yourself even down to the earth in whatever way you please, it is not as if you are venerating the earth, but the former Holy [One] whose footstool [i.e., flesh] you adore."[5]

Belief in the Real Presence necessarily engendered a deep reverence toward the Eucharist in the early Church, a reverence that recognized the abiding presence of Christ in even the smallest particles of the Eucharistic Species, as can be seen in a comment of Origen (184-254): "You who are wont to be present at the divine mysteries, understand here, when you receive the body of the Lord, you are to preserve it with all care and veneration, lest the smallest particle of it should fall."[6]

A similar vigilance regarding the smallest fragments of the Eucharist is enjoined in the instructions of Saint Cyril of Jerusalem (315-386) for the newly baptized: ". . . partake of it [the Eucharist], giving heed lest thou lose any part of it; for whatever thou shouldest lose would be evidently a loss to thee as from one of thine own members. For tell me, if any one gave thee grains of gold, wouldest thou not hold them with all care, taking heed lest thou shouldest lose any of them and suffer loss? Wilt thou not much more carefully be on thy guard lest a crumb fall from thee of what is more precious than gold and precious stones?"[7]

As one further illustration of the early Church's profound veneration of every portion of the Eucharistic Species we offer the instructions in this regard of the fifth-century Syrian Orthodox Bishop Rabulas: "Let any crumb of the holy Body which falls to the ground be carefully searched for, and if it be found, let the place, supposing it to be earth, be scraped and the dust therefrom be mixed with water and given to the faithful as a draught of blessing. If it should not be found, let the place still be scraped as before. Similarly if anything of the Blood be spilt, supposing the spot to be of stone, let (hot) coals be laid upon it."[8]

But what of the practice of bringing the Eucharist to those unable to come to Mass? Such reception of Holy Communion outside the Eucharistic liturgy was already an established practice by the second century, as can be seen in the *First Apology* of Saint Justin Martyr (100-165), wherein he speaks of the deacons at the bishop's Mass taking some of the Eucharist in order to bring the sacrament to those who are absent from the assembly.[9] This documentary evidence is augmented by archaeological findings; from the Vatican catacombs there are surviving examples of the *arca*, a small box used by the early Church for carrying the reserved Blessed Sacrament, made of gold and thought to date from the second or third century.[10]

With the administration of Holy Communion outside of Mass necessitating the reservation of the Eucharist from an early date, it may seem difficult, in view of the early Church's firm belief in the Real Presence, to understand why the concept of prayer to the reserved Sacrament did not emerge in short order. But for such a devotion to develop it would first be necessary for the reserved Eucharist to be moved to a location in places of worship where It could become the focus of public and private prayer. Yet in the first centuries of Church history, the concept of placing the reserved Eucharist in a prominent and conspicuous place in the church would not have had the opportunity to arise for several reasons.

To begin with, the periodic persecutions under the pagan Roman emperors prevented the universal establishment of permanent places of worship until the fourth century; such persecutions would have also increased the danger of sacrileges against the reserved Blessed Sacrament. Moreover, in view of the early Church's practice of dismissing the catechumens from the Eucharistic liturgy before the Offertory began, thereby reserving the sight of the consecration and Holy Communion exclusively for the eyes of the baptized, it would not have seemed appropriate to leave the Eucharist exposed to the eyes of the unbaptized by reserving it permanently in a readily visible location in the place of worship. This custom of dismissing the catechumens as well as other manifestations of the "secrecy" with which the early Church surrounded the Eucharistic liturgy amply demonstrates that the lack of any special devotions to the reserved Eucharist was not due to a more casual, less reverential view of the sacrament, but rather can be explained at least in part by an atmosphere of profound awe that would have reserved the sight of the Eucharistic Species to baptized believers.

"... where I am, there shall my servant be ..." (Jn 12:26)

The eventual development of prayer before the reserved Blessed Sacrament owed its origins not only to the Church's faith regarding the nature of the Eucharist itself but also to a concept of prayer rooted in the Old Testament that came to flourish in Christian spirituality by the fourth century — "*compositio loci,*" that is, composition of place — the "placing" of oneself in the presence of God. Of course the soul is always and everywhere in the presence of God; yet by meditation, especially upon the mysteries of our Lord's life, the soul can direct and focus its attention upon this Divine Presence, and this is what is meant by *compositio loci.*

In the Old Testament God chose to manifest His presence in particular places such as on Mount Sinai and in the Sanctuary of the Ark of the Covenant. The people of Israel responded to the latter manifestation of God's presence by converging yearly upon the Temple in Jerusalem for the Feast of Passover, seeing the Temple as the house where God dwelt among men. But under the New Covenant God came to dwell among His people in a far more extraordinary way — "And the Word became flesh and dwelt among us ..." (Jn 1:14). The Incarnate Son of God came to live, die, and rise from the dead in a particular time and place — early first-century Palestine. Subsequent generations of Christians were not to have the consolation of seeing with their bodily eyes the face of their Redeemer, yet they knew and believed Christ's promise that

He would not leave them orphans (Jn 14:18), that He would come to them (*ibid.*), and remain with His Church always, even to the end of the world (Mt 28:20). How, then, were the Christians of later ages to come to a deep recognition of this abiding presence? In their desire to draw near their Savior they set out from their homes and journeyed in growing numbers to the land that He had trodden — to "walk in the footsteps of the Master," as Origen explained.[11]

Origen's testimony certainly suggests that *compositio loci* existed in the hearts of the faithful long before 300, but it was in the fourth century that the concept truly came to the fore. Our earliest glimpse of the itinerary of those who came to the Holy Land for this purpose is afforded by an individual known to history as the "Burgundian pilgrim," who visited Jerusalem in 333. The desire to see every landmark associated with the particulars of our Lord's passion is manifest in the sights he lists: a palm tree from which the children took branches to greet Christ on Palm Sunday; the spot in the Garden of Gethsemane where Judas betrayed his Master; the house of Caiaphas where Christ was tried by the Sanhedrin; the Praetorium of Pilate; the pillar where the Romans scourged our Lord; the Mount of Golgotha; and the Holy Sepulchre.[12] Later in the same century, Saint Paulinus of Nola (353-431) was to articulate the motivations of those who came to the Holy City:

> No other sentiment draws men to Jerusalem than the desire to see and touch the places where Christ was physically present, and to be able to say from our very own experience "we have gone into his tabernacle and adored in the very places where his feet have stood" (Ps. CXXXII. 7). . . . Theirs is a truly spiritual desire to see the places where Christ suffered, rose from the dead, and ascended into heaven. . . . The manger of His birth, the river of His baptism, the garden of His betrayal, the palace of His condemnation, the column of His scourging, the thorns of His crowning, the wood of His crucifixion, the stone of His burial: all these things recall God's former presence on earth and demonstrate the ancient basis of our modern beliefs.[13]

Implicit in the above observation is the desire to pray, to adore, in places that readily bring to mind the presence of God. And it is this exercise of prayer in the particular places where the events of Christ's life could be most readily and vividly recalled that characterizes page after page of the remarkable fourth-century diary of the pilgrim Egeria, a woman of Spain who came to Jerusalem around the year 380. She tells of the Christians of this city celebrating Holy Week as a journey in the footsteps of Christ, with the times and places of their liturgical services from Palm Sunday to Easter closely following the Passion narratives of the Four Gospels. Thus on the first day of Holy Week, following a reading of one of the Gospel accounts of Christ's triumphant entry into Jerusalem, the clergy and people of the city participated in what is our earliest known example of the "procession of palms": "At this the bishop and all the people rise from their places, and start off on foot down from the summit of the Mount of Olives. All the people go before him with psalms and antiphons, all the time repeating, 'Blessed is he that cometh in the name of the Lord.' The babies and the ones too young to walk are carried on their parents' shoulders. Everyone is carrying branches, either palm or olive, and they accompany the bishop in the very way the people did when once they went down with the Lord. They go on foot all down the Mount to the city, and all through the city to the Anastasis, but they have to go pretty gently on account of the older women and men among them who might get tired."[14]

Jerusalem was indeed an ideal setting for those who came to the city to enter more deeply into the presence of their Redeemer. Yet many others were unable to make such an arduous journey to the Holy Land, and those who did could do so only once or a few times in the course of their lives. Hence the longing to place oneself in the presence of the Lord would need to be satisfied in more accessible ways. The churches of the faithful were the *loci* of public liturgical prayer; yet it was not long before they became preferred places for private prayer as well, where Christians could withdraw for a time from the distracting activities of their daily lives and mentally prostrate themselves at the feet of their God.

The identification of the altar as a symbol of Christ and, more importantly, the awareness that it was upon the altar that Christ became truly present during the Eucharistic liturgy, would have made the altar the focus of attention for those who came for silent prayer, especially in the quiet of the night. An early example of this is provided by Saint Gregory Nazianzus (329-390), who relates how on one occasion, when gravely ill, his sister Gorgonia during the night "betook herself to the Physician of all," and "fell before the altar with faith . . . calling on Him who is honoured thereon with a great cry and with every kind of entreaty, and pleading with Him. . . . Placing her head on the altar with another great cry and with a wealth of tears, like one who of old bedewed the feet of Christ, and declaring that she would not let go until she was made well, she then applied to her whole body this medicine which she had, even such a portion of the antitypes of the honourable body and blood as she treasured in her hand, and mingled with this act her tears."[15]

The significance of this passage is enhanced by the somewhat cryptic reference to Gorgonia, in her desperate plea for healing, touching to herself the Eucharistic Species, as one might touch a relic; it does appear to imply, albeit vaguely, an effort to invoke the intervention of Christ in the reserved Sacrament. The meaning of the text is not sufficiently clear for us to identify it as our earliest extant testimony of prayer to the reserved Eucharist. Nonetheless, with Gorgonia going into the church at night as if she could especially place herself at the feet of Christ there, we certainly find in this episode at the very least the concept of *compositio loci* in the form of private prayer before the altar that in the centuries to come was to fuse with the Church's belief in the Real Presence, and lead to the birth and development of extraliturgical Eucharistic adoration.

ENDNOTES

1. *In I Corinthians*, Homily 24, No. 5, quoted in Darwell Stone, *A History of the Doctrine of the Holy Eucharist*, 1909, Vol. I, p. 107.
2. *In I Corinthians*, Homily 41, No. 4, quoted in ibid.
3. St. Optatus of Mileve, *Contra Parmenianum Donatistam*, Bk. VI, Ch. 1, quoted in Most Rev. W. Walsh, *Eucharistica; or a Series of Pieces, Original and Translated, of the Most Holy and Adorable Sacrament of the Eucharist*, 1854, p. 53. Original Latin text in *Corpus Scriptorum Ecclesiasticorum Latinorum, Vol. XXVI: S. Optati Milevitani Libri VII*, ed. Carolus Ziwsa, 1893, p. 143.
4. *Enarratio in Ps. 98*, Ch. 9, as quoted in Fr. Everett Diederich, SJ, "Eucharistic Worship Outside Mass," in *The New Dictionary of Sacramental Worship*, ed. Rev. Peter Fink, SJ, 1990, p. 459. For Latin text see citation in following note.

5. Translated into English from the Latin text in *Patrologia Latina*, Vol. 37, col. 1264. Strangely, this verse is simply omitted from the English translation of this work of Augustine made for the series, *A Select Library of the Nicene and Post-Nicene Fathers of the Christian Church (Volume VIII: Saint Augustin: Expositions on the Book of Psalms*, ed. A. Cleveland Coxe, rpt. 1974, p. 485). In a passage quoted earlier by Fr. Groeschel (pp. 41-42), St. Cyril of Jerusalem mentions bowing before the Precious Blood (the Eucharist under the species of wine) prior to receiving it, a reference that predates that of St. Augustine by a few years.

6. Origen, *Hom. 13 in Exodus*, No. 3, in Walsh, p. 45. Original text in *Patrologia Graeca*, Vol. 12, col. 391.

7. *Catechetical Lectures*, XXIII, Nos. 21-22, quoted in Stone, Vol. I, p. 106.

8. Quoted in Fr. Herbert Thurston, SJ, "Reservation in its Historical Aspects," *Month*, Sept. 1917, Vol. 130, p. 241.

9. *Apologies I*, No. 65, in Lucien Deiss, C.S.Sp., *Early Sources of the Liturgy*, 1975, p. 24.

10. Archdale King, *Eucharistic reservation in the Western Church*, 1965, p. 37.

11. *In Joannem*, VI, No. 24, quoted in Jonathan Sumption, *Pilgrimage: An Image of Medieval Religion*, 1976, p. 89. Original text in *Patrologia Graeca*, Vol. 14, col. 269.

12. *Itinerarium Burdigalense*, in *Corpus Christianorum, Series Latina: CLXXV: Itineraria et Alia Geographia*, 1965, pp. 16-17.

13. St. Paulinus of Nola (end of fourth century), Epistle 44, No. 14, in Sumption, pp. 89-90.

14. John Wilkinson, ed., *Egeria's Travels*, 1971, Ch. 31, p. 133.

15. St. Gregory Nazianzus, *Orations*, VIII, No. 18, in Stone, Vol. I, pp. 106-107.

Chapter 8

Eucharistic Presence Discovered Anew: Sixth-Twelfth Centuries

"How lovely is thy dwelling place, O Lord of hosts!" (Ps 84:1)

As we shift from the age of the early Church to the era of medieval Christianity, we gradually begin to see the Eucharistic teachings of the Church Fathers and the pilgrim longings of the Christian people converge and interact. These are the centuries that gave the world the Western monasticism of Saints Benedict and Scholastica, as well as the great missionary endeavors of Saint Columban, Saint Augustine of Canterbury, Saint Boniface, and Saints Cyril and Methodius; this was the era of the first noble Christian monarchs — France's Saint Clotilde, Bohemia's Saint Wenceslaus, Germany's Saint Henry, Hungary's Saint Stephen, and England's Saint Edward the Confessor. It was men and women such as these who transformed a largely pagan Europe into a Christian society — and as they did so, the Church's understanding of, and love for, Christ's inestimable gift of Himself in the Eucharist deepened and grew.

The practice of visiting churches for private prayer, which we have already noted was in evidence by the end of the early Christian era, continued through the early Middle Ages, becoming a favorite spiritual exercise of the devout. Thus the sixth-century French Bishop Saint Arey of Gap (circa 535-604) was wont to spend long hours prostrate in prayer on the floor of the church, according to Probus, a contemporary of his.[1] The seventh-century rule (*"Regula monachorum"*) of Fructuosus of Braga stipulated a visit to the chapel following meals so as to offer "thanksgiving to Christ before the altar."[2] In the late ninth century, King Alfred of England (871-901) and one Abbot John are recorded making nocturnal visits to churches,[3] as did another Englishman two centuries later, Saint Wulstan (circa 1008-1095), who went in the night to pray before the altar.[4] A most striking example of this practice is attested by Bishop Gumpold (episcopate 967-985) in his life of the famous Bohemian king Saint Wenceslaus (circa 907-935): ". . . during the nighttime . . . so soon as deep silence settled down upon all, he [Wenceslaus] scorned the comfort of his luxurious chamber, rose from his bed by stealth, silently awakened his page, snatched up his dog-eared prayer book, quitted the palace unknown to the guards, and then with only his page for companion traversed the steep mountain heights or the perilous descents of the valleys, hastening barefoot from hamlet to hamlet along roads and by-paths rough with stones or frozen with ice, busied the while with the continuous recitation of psalms and other prayers, in order to seek out one by one the various churches."[5]

Of course there was always a Eucharistic element implicit in such prayer, for the church, and the altar in particular, was revered as the setting for the offering of the sacrifice of the Mass. But for the reserved Eucharist to become the focus of this prayer, it was first necessary that the church, and especially the altar, become the normal place of the sacrament's reservation. Our earliest testimony regarding the location of the reserved Eucharist is that found in the fourth-century *Apostolic Constitutions*, which directed that when "all the men and women have communicated, the deacons are to take what is left over and carry it to the sacristy."[6] Over a span of several centuries the sacristy remained the single most common repository for the Blessed Sacrament — a location that did not lend itself to private prayer.

Yet sacristy reservation should not be misunderstood to connote a casual attitude to the Eucharistic Species; there was never any backing off from the Church's constant teaching that the presence of Christ in the reserved Eucharist was no less real than that of Christ on the altar during the Eucharistic liturgy itself. Indeed, it was during the fifth to seventh centuries that there appeared in the East a liturgy for the weekdays of Lent wherein the reserved Sacrament consecrated at an earlier Mass was administered to the faithful gathered in church for a Communion service — the "Mass of the Presanctified." This service is a familiar part of our present-day Good Friday liturgy, having first appeared in the Holy Week rites of Rome by the seventh century (in the *Gelasian Sacramentary*).[7] Such a service could not have been introduced if there was not a firm belief that the presence of Christ in the Eucharistic Species remained beyond the end of the liturgy at which the sacrament was originally consecrated.

In the seventh-century Eastern document entitled the *Chronicles of Alexandria* we find this belief clearly expressed in an antiphon that was chanted by the people as the reserved Blessed Sacrament was carried from the sacristy to the altar during the Lenten "Mass of the Presanctified": "In this moment, the Virtuous of the heavens invisibly adore God with us. Behold that the King of Glory makes His entrance, behold that the mystic sacrifice is presented: approach with faith and with fear, in order to become participants of the life eternal. Alleluia."[8]

The sacristy was not to remain the only place of Eucharistic reservation. There is a passage in the writings of Saint Peter Chrysologus (400-450) that, in addition to confirming that the early Church made no distinction between Christ's Real Presence in the Eucharist during the Mass and His presence in the reserved Sacrament afterward, suggests that already in the first half of the fifth century the Blessed Sacrament was being kept within the church edifice proper: "He [Christ] is the bread which was sown in the Virgin, fermented in the flesh, made on the cross, baked in the furnace of the tomb, *which is preserved in the churches*, brought to the altars, and daily administered as heavenly food to the faithful."[9]

Of course it must be admitted that in this case Peter Chrysologus may have considered the sacristy a part of the church itself, and hence could have meant sacristy reservation in speaking of the Eucharist as "preserved in the churches." Yet there is unambiguous archaeological evidence dating from the next century — the sixth — that reservation not only within churches but even at altars had been introduced in at least some places before the seventh century. There is the hollow stone stem from an altar erected probably between the years 525 and 550 by Bishop Eufrasius for the Baptistry of Parenzo Cathedral (Istria) that has toward its base what is obviously an aumbry, an aperture for reserving the Eucharist. The aperture is beautifully sculpted in the form of a portal with a cross over the lintel, flanked by two doves; over a triangular arch above the cross and doves are two fish. These are unmistakably Eucharistic symbols, and their location makes it clear that they were intended specifically for the aumbry, rather than being merely decorations for the overall altar. The monument dates from a period when the Eucharist was often received immediately after the sacrament of Baptism — from this it becomes evident why the Blessed Sacrament would have been reserved at a baptistry altar as it was in this case.[10]

As to further literary evidence in this regard, the earliest fairly explicit reference to the reservation of the Eucharist within the church (instead of the sacristy) is to be found in the life of Saint Guthlac (died 714) — a reference that also implies reservation at the altar. His biographer states that on the final night of the saint's life, in the English Abbey of Croyland, Guthlac "sat throughout the night in his oratory. . . . He stretched out his hand to the altar, and strengthened himself with the communion of the body and blood of Christ and, raising his eyes to heaven and stretching out his arms, he breathed forth his soul into the joys of everlasting beatitude."[11] A biographical account of Saint Basil (329-379), written about the eighth century by an individual known only as Pseudo-Amphilochus, speaks of the Eucharist being reserved in a dove-shaped gold vessel hanging over the altar.[12] Such dove-shaped Eucharistic vessels were to become quite common in the centuries to come, especially in France, and may have been in use as early as the fourth century — the donations of silver, gold, or gilded "doves" as church furnishings are mentioned in the ancient biographies of several fourth- and fifth-century Popes, although their probable Eucharistic function is not explicitly stated in these cases.[13]

It should also be borne in mind that if Pseudo-Amphilochus's reference to the keeping of the Eucharist in a gold dove over the altar is not merely his own eighth-century gloss upon his earlier sources but is actually traceable to the time of Saint Basil, it would mean that reservation at the altar — albeit above it — already existed in the fourth century, and could therefore be as old a practice as sacristy reservation. The significance of the Pseudo-Amphilochus text is heightened by the fact that it is of Eastern provenance,[14] thus indicating that Eucharistic reservation in close proximity to the altar existed in the East, as well as the West, by the eighth century.

Toward the end of the ninth century, directives stipulating reservation at the altar began to appear, emerging for the first time in an anonymous document known as the *Admonitio Synodalis*: "The altar should be covered with clean linen; nothing should be placed on the altar except reliquaries and relics and the four gospel-books, and a pyx with the body of the Lord for the viaticum of the sick; other things should be kept in some seemly place."[15]

An identically worded injunction is found in the synodal constitutions given by Bishop Ratherius of Liège (died 974) in the year 966 to the clergy of his Diocese of Verona, Italy.[16] Some years earlier, Regino, Abbot of Prumm (died 915), had stipulated in his *De ecclesiasticis disciplinis*: "Let inquiry be made whether the pyx is always *super altare* [on or over the altar] with the sacred oblation for the *viaticum* of the sick."[17]

Elsewhere Regino provides a canon from what two later medieval authors (Burchard of Worms, died 1025, and Ivo of Chartres, died 1116) tell us was a council of the French Diocese of Tours, which specified that "the pyx or other vessel should always be kept locked *super altare*, on account of mice or impious men."[18]

The transferal of the reserved Eucharist from the sacristy to a position on or above the altar in at least some places during the ninth and tenth centuries raises an interesting question. Such a move would seem to run counter to the Middle Ages' growing concern for the safeguarding of the reserved Sacrament, as it shifted the Eucharist from the security of a closed room — the sacristy — to what was a more vulnerable location in an open church. It certainly suggests that the decision to implement altar reservation was dictated by some overriding consideration that took precedence even over the need to protect the Blessed Sacrament from sacrilege. What was this overriding consideration? We cannot rule out the possibility of a devotional motive behind the move. It was certainly the presence of the reserved Eucharist on or near the altar that two to three centuries later contributed to the transformation of private prayer before the altar into the practice we now know as "visiting the Blessed Sacrament."

During the early medieval period there were other more certain indications of a growing outward manifestation in words and actions of the Church's unchanging belief in the Real Presence of Christ in the Eucharist. Thus in the *Regula coenobialis* of Saint Columban (died 615), those coming forward to receive Holy Communion were directed to make three prostrations before receiving, obviously as an act of adoration directed toward the sacrament itself.[19] An eighth-century document of the Roman liturgy — *Roman Ordo I* — speaks of the Pope "saluting" with a bow of his head the reserved Blessed Sacrament carried at the beginning of Mass in a Eucharistic vessel identified as a *capsa*.[20] About the end of the seventh century, Pope Sergius I (687-701) introduced into the Roman Liturgy a prayer to be said during the "fraction" of the Eucharist shortly before Communion — the *Agnus Dei*,[21] or as it is translated in the present liturgy, "Lamb of God, you take away the sins of the world: have mercy on us."[22] The eminent twentieth-century liturgist Father Josef Jungmann, SJ, described this addition by Pope Sergius as "the first indication of a more personal intercourse with Christ present in the Eucharist."[23]

In the ninth century, private prayers were introduced for the celebrant of Mass to say immediately before Holy Communion[24]; at least some of these prayers were addressed directly to Christ (rather than to the Father), and thus implicitly constituted a form of prayer to the Eucharist. This aspect of the private Communion prayers was to be made particularly explicit hundreds of years later in one such text found in a fifteenth-century English Missal of the Sarum Rite (at least one liturgist believes the prayer is far older than the Missal it is found in[25]); the accompanying rubrics (emphasized below) leave no doubt as to the focus of the prayer:

> *Here the priest bows and speaks to the host:*
> I adore you; I glorify you;

with all the intensity of my heart I praise you.

And I pray that you will not leave your servants,

but that you will forgive our sins. . . .

Before he receives, let him humbly say to the body:

Hail forever, most holy flesh of Christ, before all else and above all else the highest sweetness! . . .

Then, with great devotion, let him say to the blood:

Hail forever, heavenly drink, before all else and above all else the highest sweetness![26]

The Mystery of Lugo, Spain

In view of all these intimations of a deepening Eucharistic devotion, is there any evidence whatsoever that in at least one or two isolated places extraliturgical prayer before the reserved Sacrament *may* have begun to develop before the tenth century? For the answer to this question we must enter a world shrouded in the mists of history and legend — the world of medieval northern Spain. It was into the mountainous terrain of northeastern Spain that the chalice believed to be that of the Last Supper was in the eighth century carried for safety from Muslim invaders and where, over the centuries to follow, it was to become the inspiration for many a legend of the "Holy Grail."[27]

Further to the west, it was in the northwestern Spanish city of Santiago de Compostela that the tomb of the Apostle James the Greater was discovered in the first years of the ninth century,[28] transforming the city into the atrium of the heavenly Jerusalem for countless medieval pilgrims. A short distance to the north and east of Santiago de Compostela stands an ancient walled city — Lugo, where in a twelfth-century cathedral there has been for untold hundreds of years unceasing prayer offered, day and night, hour after hour, before the Blessed Sacrament. It is the possibility that Lugo's perpetual Eucharistic adoration can be traced back over fourteen centuries that here commands our attention. In 1910 the writer E. Boyle O'Reilly described what he observed upon visiting for himself this extraordinary Eucharistic shrine:

No matter what hour you enter the Cathedral, there are worshipers; two priests always kneel before the tabernacle, and they never kneel alone. The scenes of humble piety drew me back to the church again and again with compelling attraction. To me a Spaniard praying unconsciously before the altar is unequaled by any act of worship I have witnessed; not even the touching Russian pilgrims in Jerusalem kissing the pavement in the Church of the Holy Sepulchre, nor the Arab at sunset kneeling alone in the desert, can impress more powerfully. It seemed as if this tranquil shrine of Lugo spread an influence of uplifting thought through the whole contented little town; in the quiet afternoon a withered grandmother knelt with her hands on the head of a little tot of six who repeated the prayers that fell from the old lips, or three young women of the upper class sought a retired corner of the church to repeat together their daily chaplet; now in a side chapel, a peasant thinking herself unobserved, in a glow of devotion, encircled the altar on her knees.[29]

In 1615 Lugo's Bishop Lopez Gallo made a search of his diocesan archives in an effort to discover the origins of this ongoing observance of perpetual Eucharistic adoration, which was universally believed by the inhabitants of the ancient city to date from time immemorial. His investigation yielded records indicating a papal privilege being granted for this custom in the sixth century — during the reign of the Suevian King Theodomiro, who converted to Catholicism in the year 550.[30] At first glance such a finding by Bishop Gallo would seem impossible in view of the lack of any other firm evidence of such extraliturgical prayer before the reserved Eucharist earlier than the twelfth and thirteenth centuries. Moreover, Bishop Gallo lived in a period when the standards for evaluating the dates and authenticity of historical documents were not as highly developed as they are in our own century.

But there are several factors that lend a certain plausibility to Bishop Gallo's claim — a claim that cannot be simply summarily dismissed, as the bishop may well have had access to documents that over the past three and a half centuries have been lost. It is known that two Church councils were convened in Lugo during the reign of King Theodomiro,[31] and the suggestion has been made that the institution of Lugo's Eucharistic adoration stemmed from the decisions of these councils, which were called in an effort to reaffirm Catholic doctrines at a time when this region of Spain was ridding itself of a heresy known as Priscillianism.[32] Thus we have reason to explore the possibility that there existed in Lugo in the early medieval period Eucharistic adoration of a far more ancient form than that found centuries later elsewhere. We must begin by considering Lugo's relationship with the Portuguese city of Braga.

A diocese dating back to the fifth century and perhaps far earlier, Lugo became for a time a suffragan see of the Diocese of Braga, until in 561 — during the reign of King Theodomiro — the city's earlier status as an independent see was restored. Nevertheless, Lugo's bond with Braga resumed in 666 when it was yet again made a *suffragan* diocese under the overriding jurisdiction of Braga.[33] Hence it is highly significant that in 675 — only nine years after the "reunion" with Lugo — the Fourth Council of Braga provided what is our earliest surviving record of the reserved Eucharist being carried in an outdoor procession. Likening this practice to the carrying of the "Ark of God" in the Old Testament, the sixth canon of the council specified that when in festal processions the reserved Eucharist, the "relics of holy God," was to be borne by the bishop instead of the priests, he was to carry the sacrament on foot.[34]

Such a practice was unparalleled for its era. Elsewhere, when the reserved Blessed Sacrament needed to be carried to or from the altar, deacons performed the task; but in this case from Braga it was the higher-ranking clergy — the priests, and on special occasions the bishop — who carried the sacrament. The importance of this detail is heightened by the fact that centuries later the carrying of the reserved Sacrament by the Pope himself rather than a lesser cleric in the papal Holy Thursday liturgy was to be one of the manifestations of deepening Eucharistic devotion toward the close of the Middle Ages.[35] Moreover, there is no other comparable reference to the Eucharist being carried in processions prior to the tenth century — hence it is not implausible that there existed at Braga a more developed cultus of the reserved Sacrament than elsewhere, a cultus it may have derived from or shared with its suffragan Diocese of Lugo.

As for the subsequent history of what practices of this nature, if any, existed in Lugo or Braga during the eighth to tenth centuries, our sources are very limited, for it was during this period that Islamic forces overran Spain, conquering Lugo in 714. Although Lugo along with other cities of northern Spain was liberated from the Muslim invaders by the end of the same century, much of the country remained under Islamic rule. Even in the northern regions a dearth of literary activity continued for some time to come, leaving the scholars of future generations with little material for investigating the history of such cities as Lugo during this period.[36]

But there is one piece of evidence from eighth-century Lugo — a document testifying that during the episcopate of Odoarius (circa 740-786), there were in the city's cathedral church altars dedicated to "the Savior and holy Mary."[37] Paired with Lugo's devotion to the Eucharist has always been a special devotion to the Blessed Virgin, with the principal church of the city being referred to as "Santa Maria de Lugo" as early as the tenth century[38]; hence the eighth-century reference may imply that the old cathedral church was the home of two special devotions — one centering upon Christ, the other upon the Blessed Mother. Four centuries later, we find the same pairing expressed more explicitly in a donation from the Spanish Queen Urraca dating from 1107, which speaks of "the most glorious Mother of Our Lord Jesus Christ, the glory of whose relics honor with admiration the city of Lugo, with a great celebration of the Divinity, inspired by God in the same place."[39]

What is this cultus to the "Divinity" of which Queen Urraca's donation document speaks? In the same century, an English cleric named Honorius referred to the reserved Eucharist on the altar (in churches where it was kept in this location) as the "Divinity of Christ."[40] In virtue of Lugo's subsequent history of Eucharistic adoration, and in the absence of any known twelfth-century cultus focusing in a particular manner upon the divinity of Christ, it does not appear possible to explain Lugo's "celebration of the Divinity" as anything else but a devotion to the Eucharist, which as we have seen in the case of Honorius, is known to have been referred to in at least one other case as simply the "Divinity." The use of this term may also cast some light on the antiquity of Lugo's Eucharistic adoration; notice that in contrast to the term "*Corpus Christi*" (Body of Christ) that prevailed during the Middle Ages, the seventh-century Council of Braga, of which we spoke earlier, refers to the Eucharist carried in procession with a term likewise focused upon the Divinity — "the relics of Holy God."

Two other pieces of evidence lend a certain degree of additional support to the existence of perpetual Eucharistic adoration in Lugo by the twelfth century. In 1130, only four years after construction of the present cathedral church began, a donation was given to the monastery attached to the cathedral, stating, "They celebrate the divine ministries [in] the times of the night and the day."[41] The passage may constitute a reference to perpetual Eucharistic prayer, although it must be admitted that this text could simply be referring to the recital of the different hours of the Divine Office. Over the portal of the north transept of the present cathedral there is a sculpted depiction of the Last Supper that, like the cathedral itself, dates from the twelfth century[42]; the inclusion of such a Eucharistic theme in the design of the medieval edifice would be consonant with the existence of a special Eucharistic devotion in the cathedral.

There are two further sources, albeit of uncertain reliability, that may give additional weight to Bishop Gallo's extraordinary claim of sixth-century beginnings for Lugo's Eucharistic adoration. Appended to a chronicle mistakenly or fraudulently attributed to the tenth-century Bishop Liutprand of Cremona is a text that among other things contains the following remarkable statement: "Before the devastation of Spain by the Moors, the Eucharist was always exposed ['*patens*'] in the cathedral churches. To what extent the ancient Churches may have preserved the custom as for example Toledo, Braga, Lugo, and others, which were not captured by the Moors, but either deserted or let loose [*lacuna* in text at this point]. . . . In other Churches, where the Saracens most frequently passed [through], and the Churches were crippled, it sometimes was done, but rarely."[43]

The above passage certainly appears to contain untenable exaggerations of whatever truth it may be based upon — for example, the assertion that *all* of Spain's cathedral churches had adoration at an early date; there is no extant evidence for such a wholesale claim. Moreover, it is highly unlikely that the Eucharist would have been "exposed" in the modern sense of the term, with the Host directly visible to adorers as it is in a monstrance. Nonetheless, if

there is at least a kernel of truth in these words, it could add significant support to Bishop Gallo's findings, for the above passage
does speak of Eucharistic adoration existing in Spain before the
Moorish invasion — that is, before 711 — and it does specifically
name Lugo as one of the cities that would have had such adoration. Only two other cities are mentioned, and significantly, one of
these is Lugo's sister diocese, Braga. Again, we must stress that
the text this passage is excerpted from is of uncertain historical
reliability, especially as it is known to contain interpolations of
questionable validity made by the sixteenth-century Spanish Jesuit Geronimo Roman de la Higuera (1538-1611).[44] However, even
if Father Higuera did add or modify this passage, the question would
still remain as to where he obtained his information (we could not
be sure it was merely a fabrication).

It has also been claimed that Saint Antonine, Archbishop of
Florence (died 1459), respected for his scholarship as well as his
holiness, testified to the early existence of Eucharistic adoration in
Lugo.[45] Without a verifiable source for this assertion, it is unfortunately not possible for us to assess its value, but it certainly is
significant when seen in the light of the other intimations that Lugo
has been devoted to the Eucharistic Presence of its God and Savior
for well over a thousand years.

The Tenth and Eleventh Centuries

Whatever may or may not have transpired in Lugo during the
early medieval period, we do know for certain that an identifiable
devotion to the reserved Sacrament did begin to appear elsewhere
in Europe, especially northern Europe, during the tenth and eleventh centuries, although in the rites we are about to consider there
is still no explicit mention of extraliturgical prayer to the reserved
Eucharist. These developments took place within the context of
Holy Week, the summit of the Church's liturgical calendar. In the
course of a tenth-century biography of Saint Ulrich (893-973), the
German Bishop of Augsburg, we are told for the first time of a ceremony that reenacted the burial of Christ by symbolically "bury-
ing" the reserved Eucharist on Good Friday in a location that, like
the Holy Sepulchre itself, was closed with a stone until Easter Sunday: "On Good Friday ... early in the morning, he [Saint Ulrich]

hastened to complete the Psalm service; and, when the holy mystery of God was completed, the people fed with the holy Corpus Christi, and the remainder buried in the customary manner, he finished the Psalm service while walking from church to church. . . . When the most delectable day of Easter arrived, he entered the church of St. Ambrose after prime, where he had placed the Corpus Christi on Good Friday, covering it with a stone. And there with a few clerks he celebrated the Mass of the Holy Trinity. When the Mass was completed, he took the Corpus Christi and the Gospels [Gospel book] with him, along with candles and incense. And . . . he proceeded to the church of St. John the Baptist."[46]

This "deposition" of the Blessed Sacrament in a symbolic tomb on Good Friday and its subsequent "elevation" on Easter Sunday, mentioned again briefly in an eleventh-century breviary of St. Gall, Switzerland,[47] was eventually to become a commonplace Holy Week observance across much of medieval Europe. By making the reserved Sacrament the focus of attention in a way that was distinct from, although not divorced from, Mass and Holy Communion, these "deposition" ceremonies inaugurated a new era in the history of Eucharistic adoration. Of additional importance in the tenth-century text from the life of Saint Ulrich is the mention of accompanying the reserved Sacrament with "candles and incense."

The veneration of the Eucharist with incense, the same fragrant offering that the Magi had brought with gold and myrrh to the Christ Child nine hundred years earlier, likewise appears in the tenth-century *Regularis Concordia*, a document for regulating England's monastic communities; in this case incense helped to transform the bringing of Holy Communion to the sick into a solemn procession, yet another practice that was to become in the future a catalyst for expressions of Eucharistic devotion: "Thenceforth daily after the Morrow Mass the celebrant, having taken off his chasuble, and the other ministers of that Mass, bearing with them the Eucharist, preceded by acolytes and thurifer, with the whole community shall go to visit the sick brother . . . the sick brother shall then receive Communion."[48]

While we cannot determine precisely when candles were first introduced as a mark of honor to the reserved Blessed Sacrament, it is known that in 904 a synod of the Nestorian Church in Baghdad specified that a lamp be kept burning before the reserved Eucharist.[49] Although Nestorian theology differs widely from that of the Catholic Church, the existence of such a practice among the Nestorians in this era may point to its existence in at least some of the other Eastern churches during or even before this time. In the present Byzantine liturgy there is a tradition of keeping a light known as the "sleepless light" burning before the *Artophorion*, the Byzantine equivalent of our tabernacles (the *Artophorion* is usually located on the altar).[50] The mention of candles in the case of Saint Ulrich indicates such a usage may not have been unknown in the tenth-century West.

During the eleventh century the maintenance of burning candles or lamps before the reserved Eucharist is repeatedly mentioned in the context of Holy Week. In the ordinances of Bernhardus (1068), Abbot of the famous reformed French Monastery of Cluny, we find the earliest explicit stipulation that a lamp be kept burning before the reserved Sacrament from the Mass of the Lord's Supper on Holy Thursday until the Mass of the Presanctified on Good Friday.[51] It was also by the eleventh century that the carrying of the Blessed Sacrament to the repository on Holy Thursday had become a solemn Eucharistic procession, with incense and candles, as can be seen in the following rubrics from Cluny's *Constitutions* of Sigibert: "After mass let the deacon and the secretary and the lay brethren come with candles and thurible, and take the chalice and the paten which has the Lord's body, putting another paten upon it, and wrap it in most clean linen, and put it away upon some altar, or in a most clean coffer, and let there be a light before it all day and all night until matins."[52]

Another text of eleventh-century Holy Thursday rubrics, Ulrich's *Constitutions*, also from Cluny, is noteworthy for the care and attention given to enclosing the reserved Eucharist with a paten and plates of precious metal: "Meanwhile the Lord's body is put away by the priest behind the altar on a golden paten, and the paten between golden plates, and the plates again between silver tablets which were made for the text of the gospel. And thus it is carried from the altar with candles and very much incense."[53]

We come now to an eleventh-century text (circa 1070-1089)

that marks one of the defining moments in the history of Eucharistic adoration — a Eucharistic procession for the celebration of Palm Sunday — introduced by the Archbishop of Canterbury, Lanfranc (circa 1010-1089), who had led the Church's battle to defend the doctrine of the Real Presence against the heterodox opinions of the theologian Berengarius of Tours (circa 1010-1088). In the Palm Sunday processions of tenth-century Europe the Gospel Book or a statue of Christ riding a donkey had been carried to represent our Lord entering Jerusalem. But in what must have been to the people of the time a powerful new affirmation of the doctrine of the Real Presence, Lanfranc replaced such symbols in the procession with the living presence of the risen Christ in the Eucharist:

> When they reach the starting-point of the procession all the community halts in position; when the cantor begins the antiphon *Occurrunt turbae* two priests shall come forward, vested in albs, to carry the shrine, which shall have been brought thither by these same priests a little before daybreak; in it the Body of Christ shall have been laid. Those who carry the banners and cross and the rest as above shall go straight to this shrine, and when those who carry it halt they too shall halt on the left and right of it in the same order as they have been walking. . . .
>
> When this is done, the abbot or cantor shall intone the antiphon *Ave, rex noster*, and those who bear the shrine shall pass down between the ranks of the *statio*, preceded by those who carry the banners and by the other servers before mentioned, all keeping the same order in returning that they had in going. As they pass, all shall genuflect, not all together but in turn on the right and left as the shrine passes them. When this antiphon is finished, they shall sing another, if the time taken demands this. When they come to the gates of the city they shall halt, forming two ranks with such space between as the place may provide; the shrine shall be set upon a table covered with a cloth before the gates in such manner that the bearers standing on either side shall face the shrine in their midst. There shall be fair hangings and curtains prepared above the gateway . . . as the procession enters the city the two great bells shall ring and continue till the

others begin when the procession enters the choir and the bells ring for Mass. . . . Here again the shrine shall be set down upon a table covered with a rich cloth.[54]

In the above ceremony from Lanfranc's *Constitutions* the reserved Sacrament is clearly made the focus of devotion, and provides us with perhaps our earliest explicit example of the reserved Eucharist being venerated outside the context of Mass with the act of genuflection. Notice that the brothers are instructed not to genuflect all at once but rather individually at the moment the Blessed Sacrament passes each of them. In view of Lanfranc's pivotal role as an outspoken defender of the Real Presence, there can be little doubt that his placement of the Eucharist in Canterbury's Palm Sunday processions was indeed a precursor to the Eucharistic devotion of subsequent ages. Moreover, the inclusion of a solemn Holy Thursday Eucharistic procession in Lanfranc's *Constitutions*[55] comparable to the two examples from Cluny that we have already cited refutes any argument that the carrying of the Eucharist on Palm Sunday was nothing more than a variant of the older practice of carrying relics in these processions.

The Twelfth Century: The Advent of Prayer Before the Reserved Eucharist

Lanfranc's Holy Thursday rubrics are of added interest in that they and another eleventh-century document of Rouen, France,[56] provide us with our earliest indications of special adornments for the repository where the Blessed Sacrament was kept until the liturgy of Good Friday. The construction and decoration of elaborate Holy Thursday repositories was to become one of the hallmarks of burgeoning Eucharistic devotion in the centuries to come, and perhaps the earliest catalyst for prayer before the reserved Sacrament. Something of this nature is implied in the twelfth-century *Ordo of Beroldus*, a liturgical book for Milan's Ambrosian Rite (a Western rite similar to, but distinct from, the Roman Rite), which instructs that after Mass on Holy Thursday the bishop is to "go into the sacristy, where he bids the subdeacons diligently guard the sacrament of the body and blood of the Lord."[57]

It is evident that the subdeacons were expected to mount a

watch before the sacrament in the sacristy until Communion on Good Friday; such a watch must have included prayer. Around the year 1177 the Croatian city of Zara was granted by papal privilege the right to conduct forty hours of what was evidently Eucharistic adoration during Holy Week each year.[58] A later record of Zara's Forty Hours Prayer from 1380 indicates that the prayer was maintained with relays of watchers, beginning around eight on the evening of Holy Thursday and concluding at midday on Holy Saturday.[59] Although the documentation from Zara does not explicitly mention the Eucharist, the timing and circumstances of this devotion strongly suggest that the Forty Hours Prayer did indeed constitute Eucharistic adoration — a conclusion endorsed by the eminent twentieth-century liturgist Father Josef Jungmann, S.J.[60]

Two other pieces of evidence lend support to the assertion that prayer before the reserved Sacrament existed by the close of the twelfth century. An anecdote from the life of the English Cistercian Saint Walthen of Melrose (died 1159) speaks of this monk on one occasion praying before the altar where the Blessed Sacrament was reserved; assaulted by a temptation, he put the devil to flight by making the sign of the cross with the pyx containing the Eucharist. The whole incident implies that Saint Walthen was praying to Christ in the Eucharist, thus providing one of the earliest probable examples of this practice.[61] More compelling is a comment made by the illustrious English martyr Saint Thomas Becket in a letter dating from 1166 to the man that would ultimately bring about his death, King Henry II: "If you do not hearken to me, who have been wont to pray for you in an abundance of tears and with groanings not a few before the majesty of the Body of Christ, most surely I shall lodge my appeal there also against you, and shall say, 'Arise, O God, and judge Thy cause.' "[62]

It is believed that Thomas Becket is here probably speaking not of prayers offered to the Eucharist during the Mass but rather prayers said before the reserved Eucharist; nonetheless, as the text is not sufficiently explicit to rule out the first possibility (prayer offered during Mass), we must admit that this and indeed all the evidence for prayer before the reserved Sacrament in regard to the twelfth century should be considered probable, but none of it is absolutely conclusive. The Rule of the Carthusian Order, believed to have been formulated before 1200, contains a provision for spending a quarter of an hour in adoration before the altar prior to the conventual Mass[63]; it seems plausible that this adoration was directed to the reserved Eucharist, for a text of the Carthusian Rule as it existed around 1130 specifically states that the usual place for the reserved Eucharist in Carthusian churches was at the high altar.[64] There was also (evidently) a pre-thirteenth-century Carthusian custom of bowing deeply when passing before the Eucharist.[65]

Yet another sign of the increasing attention that the reserved Eucharist was receiving in the twelfth century is provided by a comment to which we briefly referred earlier — that of Honorius, who had served as praelector of Canterbury's Christ Church but subsequently took up the life of a hermit in Ratisbon, Germany. In his work *Gemma animae*, he applies to the reserved Blessed Sacrament situated on the altar an Old Testament "type" — the Mercy-Seat, the cover for the Ark of the Covenant — the "*propitiatorium*": "*Propitiatorium*, which is located on the altar, is the divinity of Christ, who is the mediator for the human race."[66]

This word seems to have become a standard term in at least some quarters for the place of Eucharistic reservation on the altar, as we find it again used in this way during the next century by one of the greatest liturgists of the Middle Ages, the French Bishop Durandus of Metz (died 1296). In his classic work, the *Rationale Divinorum Officiorum*, he observes that the *propitiatorium*, as found in some churches (altar reservation was not as yet a universal practice), was reminiscent of the Temple of Solomon.[67] Such a comparison is pregnant with meaning, for it readily brings to mind the Letter to the Hebrews' commentary on Christ's fulfillment of Old Testament types, and in particular the following allusion to the Mercy-Seat: "Let us then with confidence draw near to the throne of grace, that we may receive mercy and find grace to help in time of need" (Heb 4:16).

It was also during the twelfth century that the Cistercian theologian Baldwin of Ford (died 1190) was to speak of the continual Eucharistic Presence of Christ as a fulfillment of our Lord's promise to be with us always, even to the end of the world (Mt 28:20), an observation that we will encounter time and again in subsequent discussions of Eucharistic adoration down through the centuries.[68]

ENDNOTES

1. Msgr. Paul Guerin, *Les Petits Bollandistes: Vies des Saints: Tome Neuvieme: Du 24 Juilet au 17 Aout*, 1872-1874, pp. 603-604.
2. Robert Cabie, *The Church at Prayer: An Introduction to the Liturgy: Volume II: The Eucharist* (Series ed., Msgr. A.G. Martimort), 1986, p. 247.
3. According to "Asser," in Fr. Herbert Thurston, SJ, "The Early Cultus of the Blessed Sacrament," *Month*, April 1907, Vol. 109, p. 386.
4. Fr. T.E. Bridgett, CSSR, *History of the Holy Eucharist in Great Britain*, 1908, p. 169; Fr. Alban Butler, *The Lives of the Fathers, Martyrs and Other Principal Saints*, ed. Fr. Bernard Kelly, 1961, Vol. I, pp. 67-68.
5. Thurston, p. 385.
6. *Apostolic Constitutions*, VIII, 13, quoted in Lucien Deiss, C.S.Sp., ed., *Early Sources of the Liturgy*, 1975, p. 180.
7. See James Monti, *The Week of Salvation: History and Traditions of Holy Week*, 1993, p. 237.
8. *Chron. Alexandr.*, Olymp. CCCCXLVIII, anno X, quoted in Abbé Jules Corblet, *Histoire Dogmatique, Liturgique et Archeologique du Sacrement de l'Eucharistie*, 1885, Vol. 2, p. 346 (James Monti's trans.).
9. St. Peter Chrysologus, Sermon 67, quoted in Most Rev. W. Walsh, *Eucharistica; or a Series of Pieces, Original and Translated, of the Most Holy and Adorable Sacrament of the Eucharist*, 1854, p. 52 (emphasis added).
10. S.J.P. Van Dijk and J. Hazelden Walker, *The Myth of the Aumbry: Notes on Medieval Reservation Practice and Eucharistic Devotion*, 1957, pp. 26, 46, plus Plate 8.
11. *Acta Sanctorum*, 1866 ed., April, Tome II, p. 47 (April 11), quoted in Archdale King, *Eucharistic reservation in the Western Church*, 1965, p. 32.
12. King, p. 43.
13. Ibid., p. 40.
14. The original text of this biography of St. Basil is in Greek (W.H. Freestone, *The Sacrament Reserved* [Alcuin Club Collections, No. 21], 1917, p. 195, n. 1).
15. *Admonitio Synodalis*, No. 6, quoted in ibid., p. 32.
16. *Patrologia Latina*, Vol. 136, col. 559, cited in Van Dijk and Walker, pp. 33, 47.
17. *De ecclesiasticis disciplinis*, No. 9, quoted in Freestone, p. 193.
18. King, p. 33.
19. Felim O'Briain, OFM, "The Blessed Eucharist in Irish Liturgy and History," in *Studia Eucharistica: DCC Anni a Condito Festo Sanctissimi Corporis Christi, 1246-1946*, 1946, p. 236.

20. *Patrologia Latina*, Vol. 78, col. 941b.
21. Fr. Josef Jungmann, SJ, *The Place of Christ in Liturgical Prayer*, 1965, p. 259.
22. *The Roman Missal: The Sacramentary*, Catholic Book Publishing Co., 1974, p. 563.
23. Jungmann, p. 259.
24. Nathan Mitchell, *Cult and Controversy: The Worship of the Eucharist Outside Mass*, 1982, pp. 104-105; Fr. Josef Jungmann, SJ, *The Mass of the Roman Rite: Its Origins and Development*, Vol. II, 1955, pp. 344-346.
25. Mitchell, pp. 105-106, who implies the text dates from the ninth to tenth centuries. Msgr. A.G. Martimort identifies the Missal as dating from the fifteenth century (*La Documentation liturgique de Dom Edmund Martene* [Studi e Testi, No. 279], 1967, pp. 199-200).
26. Ibid., p. 106, translated from the original Latin text in Dom Edmund Martene, *De Antiquis Ecclesiae Ritibus*, 1763 ed., Tome I, Bk. I, Ch. 4, Art. 12 (Ordo 35), p. 241. The parentheses placed by Mitchell around the rubrics in his translation have been removed here for greater clarity.
27. Joan Carroll Cruz, *Relics*, 1984, p. 30; Juan Angel Onate Ojeda, *El Santo Grial: Su historia, su culto y sus destinos*, 1952, pp. 34-37.
28. Joseph O'Callaghan, *A History of Medieval Spain*, 1975, p. 185.
29. E. Boyle O'Reilly, *Heroic Spain*, 1910, pp. 123-124.
30. Secretary General, Diocese of Lugo, "Santuario Eucarístico y Mariano," manuscript submitted for publication in forthcoming book, 1995, p. 3. As for Theodomiro's conversion, see Ramon Otero Pedrayo, *Galicia: Una Cultura de Occidente*, 1985, pp. 94, 96.
31. J.D. Mansi, ed., *Sacrorum Conciliorum Nova et Amplissima Collectio*, Tome 9, 1766 and 1901, cols. 815-817, 845-846.
32. Secretary General of Lugo, p. 3.
33. A.A. MacErlean, "Lugo," *Catholic Encyclopedia*, 1907 ed., Vol. 9, p. 417.
34. Mansi, Tome 11, cols. 157-158.
35. Monti, p. 126.
36. O'Callaghan, pp. 93, 188-189, 190; "Lugo," *Encyclopedia Universal Ilustrada*, 1958 ed., Vol. 31, p. 577.
37. Amador Lopez Valcarcel, "Lucus Augusti, Locus Sacramenti: El Culto Eucarístico en Lugo. Notas para su historia," *El Progresso*, June 8, 1969, reprinted in *Historias Luguesas*, ed. Excma. Disputación Provincial de Lugo, 1975, p. 42.
38. Fr. Enrique Llamas Martinez, OCD, "El Culto Mariano en España, a través de las Iglesias y Santuarios dedicados a la Virgen María, antes del Siglo XII," in *Du Cultu Mariano Saeculis VI-XI: Acta Congressus Mariologici-Mariani Int. in Croatia Anno 1971 Celebrati, Vol. V: De Culto Mariano saeculis VI-XI apud Varias Nationes et Secundum Fontes Islamicos*, 1972, p. 190.

39. Valcarcel, p. 44.
40. *Gemma animae*, quoted in King, p. 75.
41. Valcarcel, p. 44.
42. Pedrayo, pp. 100-101; Amador Lopez Valcarcel, *La Cathedral de Lugo*, n.d. (pages unnumbered).
43. "Pseudo-Liutprandi Adversaria," No. 29, in *Patrologia Latina*, Vol. 136, col. 1137.
44. Secretary General of Lugo, p. 4; "Higuera (Geronimo Roman)," *Biografia Eclesiástica*, Vol. 9 (1855), pp. 1021-1023; "Liutprando," *Biografia Eclesiástica*, Vol. 12 (1862), p. 459.
45. Ibid., pp. 3, 4. For this reference to St. Antonine of Florence the Secretary General cites an author he simply identifies as "Pallares."
46. O.B. Hardison, Jr., *Christian Rite and Christian Drama in the Middle Ages*, 1965, p. 136; Latin text in *Patrologia Latina*, Vol. 135, cols. 1020b, d-1021a.
47. Karl Young, *The Drama of the Medieval Church*, 1933, Vol. I, pp. 130-131.
48. *Regularis Concordia: The Monastic Agreement of the Monks and Nuns of the English Nation (Medieval Classics)*, trans. Dom Thomas Symons, 1953, Ch. 12, p. 64.
49. Mario Righetti, *Manuale di Storia Liturgica*, Vol. III, 1949, pp. 492-493 (note).
50. W.H. Freestone, *The Sacrament Reserved* (Alcuin Club Collections, No. 21), 1917, pp. 194, 249.
51. Righetti, Vol. III, p. 493.
52. W. Lockton, *The Treatment of the Remains at the Eucharist after Holy Communion and the Time of the Ablutions*, 1920, pp. 76-77.
53. Ibid., p. 77.
54. *The Monastic Constitutions of Lanfranc*, trans./ed. David Knowles, 1951, pp. 23-25.
55. Ibid., p. 31.
56. John of Avranches, *Liber de Officiis Ecclesiasticis*, in *Patrologia Latina*, Vol. 147, col. 50b.
57. Lockton, p. 96.
58. Giuseppe Barbiero, "L'Origine delle Confraternite del SS.mo Sacramento in Italia," in *Studia Eucharistica: DCC Anni a Condito Festo Sanctissimi Corporis Christi, 1246-1946*, 1946, p. 190; Fr. Herbert Thurston, SJ, "Easter Sepulchre, or Altar of Repose?" *Month*, April 1903, Vol. 101, p. 404.
59. Thurston, "Easter Sepulchre. . . ," p. 405.
60. Jungmann, *Pastoral Liturgy*, 1962, pp. 235-236, 237.
61. Righetti, Vol. III, p. 491.
62. Thurston, "The Early Cultus of the Blessed Sacrament," pp. 387-388.
63. Barbiero, p. 188.
64. Lockton, p. 77, who quotes the relevant passage of Carthusian legisla-

tion from Martene, Tome IV (containing Martene's *De Antiquis Monachorum Ritibus*), Bk. III, Ch. 13, No. 47, p. 129. Martene in turn quotes the text from the *Ordinarium Cartusiense* (Ch. 49, No. 6), published in 1582.

65. Barbiero, p. 188.

66. *Gemma animae*, Bk. I, Ch. 136, quoted in King, p. 75. Original Latin text in *Patrologia Latina*, Vol. 172, col. 587.

67. *Rationale Divinorum Officiorum*, Bk. 1, Ch. 2, No. 16; Bk. 4, Ch. 1, No. 15, as cited in King, p. 75.

68. G. Vassalli, "Santissimo Sacramento," in *Dizionario degli Istituti di Perfezione*, Vol. 8, 1988, col. 825; Fr. M. Camille Hontoir, OCR, "Le Devotion au Sacrement chez les Premiers Cisterciens (XII-XIII siecles)," in *Studia Eucharistica: DCC Anni a Condito Festo Sanctissimi Corporis Christi 1246-1946*, 1946, pp. 137-138.

Chapter 9

The Thirteenth Century:
A Eucharistic Renaissance

"The glory of the Lord settled on Mount Sinai . . ." (Ex 24:16)

> *The Holy Grail entered through the great door, and at once the*
> *palace was filled with fragrance as though all the spices of the*
> *earth had been spilled abroad.*
> — Helinand of Froidmont, Abbot, *Estoire del Graal*, 1215[1]

It was in the waning years of the twelfth century that the
poets of France and Germany began to compose haunting legends about a mysterious sacred object — the Holy Grail — that
gradually emerged as the chalice of the Last Supper. In these
accounts the Grail is depicted as a relic that was far more than
a relic — enveloped in a mystical aura of brilliant light and flickering candles,[2] and guarded by an elite corps of dedicated
knights. It was as if the soul of medieval man in majestic alle-
gory had found a voice for its highest aspirations — a quest to
kneel before the face of God. The New Testament's Joseph of
Arimathea, who assisted in the burial of Christ, figures promi-
nently in the Grail legends, and so it is that in the *Grand St.
Graal* (circa 1210) Joseph is instructed to venerate the Grail in
the ark where it is kept: "And each day thou shalt make thy

genuflections on both knees before this ark and thou shalt say thy prayers in order to have the love of God thy Lord."[3]

The more we seek to penetrate the mystery of the Holy Grail, the more we come to recognize amidst the blaze of candlelight and clouds of incense the figure of something far holier than any relic — that the quest to see and venerate this vessel of the Last Supper was but a parable of a grand new quest to gaze upon and adore the Priceless Divine Gift of that Supper — a quest to adore the Eucharist. Fittingly enough, it is in the text of a Grail legend composed in the first years of the thirteenth century — the *Grand St. Graal* (the same cited above) that we find what is one of the earliest explicit descriptions of prayer before the reserved Eucharist, wherein a mother on her deathbed, living in a pagan land, exhorts her daughter to pray regularly before the Blessed Sacrament to be entrusted to her by a hermit priest and reserved for Viaticum in a white case within their home:

> And whanne ye haven It [the Eucharist]
> in your keeping,
> Looketh that every day over all thing
> That to this holy boist [box] ye go,
> And your devocions doth therto,
> With weping and with sore sighing
> With bonching [beating] on breast and repenting
> Of all the sinnes that ye haven ido,
> With high contricion, daughter, evermo,
> And he wolde send you such grace and powere
> Never other God to worshipen here.[4]

Although the Grail legends were an eclectic mixture of fact and fiction, they eloquently mirrored the greater realities that were unfolding in the life of the Church during this period. For it was in the last years of the twelfth century that two key figures in what would prove to be a Renaissance in the worship of the Eucharist were to enter the world — Saint Francis of Assisi, the great apostle of poverty for the sake of Christ, in 1182; and the Belgian Augustinian mystic Blessed Juliana of Cornillon, in 1192. As the role of Blessed Juliana belongs more properly to a later section of this chapter, we will begin with Saint Francis.

Saint Francis and the Eucharist

It is a largely unappreciated fact that bound up with Saint Francis' legacy of service to the poor was his passionate love for the Holy Eucharist, a love that did not cease with the concluding *"Ite, missa est"* of the Mass, but rather lingered in the presence of the reserved Sacrament. It is believed that Francis' earliest formulation of his devotion to the reserved Eucharist is the ejaculatory prayer he first taught his brothers in the years before the death of Pope Innocent III in 1216[5] — a prayer of which he speaks in his 1226 deathbed *Testament*: "And God inspired me with such faith in his churches that I used to pray with all simplicity, saying, 'We adore you, Lord Jesus Christ, here and in all your churches in the whole world, and we bless you, because by your holy cross you have redeemed the world.' "[6]

The above is a clear expression of the prayer of composition of place, for it addresses God in a particular place — "here," the church where the worshiper is praying. As to the presence of God that Francis speaks of as being found in every church, the wording does not explicitly indicate that this presence is the Real Presence of the reserved Eucharist. Yet in the context of the saint's known zeal for the reverential reservation of the Blessed Sacrament, of which there is ample proof in his recorded words and actions, as well as the incontestable manifestations of extraliturgical Eucharistic worship in the lives and writings of other early Franciscans, there can be little doubt that Francis intended his brothers to direct this prayer to the reserved Eucharist. With the words of this pious ejaculation echoing in the hearts of Francis' thousands of followers whenever they approached a church, the means were in place for such Eucharistic adoration to radiate outward from the Umbrian region of Italy during the first quarter of the thirteenth century.[7]

Francis' devotion to the Eucharist did not develop in isolation but rather in conjunction with a steady stream of new measures introduced from Paris to Rome regarding the worship of this sacrament, not the least of which was the advent of the "major elevation," the raising of the Host above the head of the celebrating priest immediately following the words of consecration during the Mass. First appearing in Paris during or shortly after the episcopate of Eudes de Sully (1196-1208),[8] this practice proved a major impetus to Eucharistic devotion by giving the laity a totally unobstructed view of the newly consecrated Host, serving as an invitation to adore the unseen God in the sacrament. But there were also developments with a direct bearing upon the worship and reverential care of the reserved Blessed Sacrament outside of Mass. Thus the carrying of the Eucharist to the sick, which as we saw earlier had already begun to take on solemn processional characteristics in the Benedictine monasteries of England during the tenth century, became by the early years of the thirteenth century a focal point of Eucharistic devotion.

In the same *Constitutions* attributed to the Parisian Bishop Eudes de Sully that mandated the major elevation at Mass, there is likewise an instruction that the people are to kneel when a priest carrying the Blessed Sacrament to the sick passes them.[9] The practice of keeping a light burning before the reserved Sacrament, first found in the West during the eleventh century in association with the Eucharistic reservation of Holy Thursday, was at this time becoming the norm for reservation throughout the year, as can be seen in the case of Eustace, Abbot of Flai, who in his preaching during the year 1200 "laid it down that in London and in many other places, there should be in every church where it was practicable, a burning lamp or some other perpetual light before the Lord's Body."[10]

Coupled to the growing concern for the veneration of the reserved Sacrament was a concern for its security and protection from sacrilege. Thus it was that at the Fourth Lateran Council under Pope Innocent III in 1215 the safe reservation of the Eucharist was mandated for the Universal Church: "We decree that in all churches the chrism and the Eucharist be kept under faithful guard and be locked up, so that no presumptuous hand can be laid on them for any horrible or wicked purpose."[11]

Significantly, Saint Francis is thought to have been present at this council. There is also a tradition that a year or so earlier he had journeyed to the great Spanish pilgrimage shrine of Santiago de Compostela,[12] and that as he journeyed home along the older northern branch of the great pilgrimage route to and from Santiago de Compostela known as the Camino Real, he stopped in one of the cities along the way — Lugo — founding the thirteenth-century

Franciscan church that can be seen there to the present day.[13] If indeed Francis did visit Lugo, it would have afforded him an opportunity to observe the city's Eucharistic adoration, undoubtedly bolstering his own devotion to the sacrament, a devotion that became all the more pronounced in the later years of his life.

Whatever may be said for the possible influences of the Fourth Lateran Council and Lugo upon Francis, there can be no doubt as to the zeal of the saint for the honorable reservation of the Eucharist. This concern is most definitively expressed in his "Letter to All Clerics," addressed to all the clerical members of his young order: ". . . many clerics reserve the Blessed Sacrament in unsuitable places, or carry It about irreverently. . . . If the Body of our Lord Jesus Christ has been left abandoned somewhere contrary to all the laws, It should be removed and put in a place that is prepared properly for It, where It can be kept safe."[14]

In another letter, addressed to a chapter of his order and dating from his final years, Francis makes an emphatic personal appeal to his brethren, striving to impress upon them the importance of this matter to him: "Kissing your feet with all the love I am capable of, I beg you to show the greatest possible reverence and honour for the most holy Body and Blood of our Lord Jesus Christ through whom *all things, whether on the earth or in the heavens*, have been brought to peace and reconciled with Almighty God (cf. Col. 1:20)."[15]

In yet another letter, directed to the superiors of his friaries, Francis enjoins the same act of worship that Bishop Eudes of Paris had prescribed only a few years earlier for those in the presence of a priest carrying the Eucharist to the sick: "When the priest is offering sacrifice at the altar *or the Blessed Sacrament is being carried about*, everyone should kneel down and give praise, glory, and honour to our Lord and God, living and true."[16]

But for Francis it was not enough that his brethren exercise such reverence on their own; he also wanted them to be apostles of Eucharistic worship, ready to admonish others respectfully in the veneration of the sacrament: "With everything I am capable of and more, I beg you to ask the clergy with all humility, when it is called for and you think it is a good idea, to have the greatest possible reverence for the Body and Blood of our Lord Jesus Christ. . . ."[17]

In his work entitled *Speculum Perfectionis*, Brother Leo, one of

Francis' early followers, likewise testifies to the depth of his master's commitment in this regard: "For Blessed Francis had the highest reverence and devotion for the body of Christ, and wished to have it inserted in the rule, that the Friars in every province where they dwelt, should show great care and solicitude in this matter, exhorting all clerics and priests that they should reserve the body of Christ in good and decent places, and if they neglected this, the Friars were to do so for them."[18]

Francis' admiration of those who shared his solicitude for the Eucharist is manifest in his professed esteem for the nation of France, a country he described as the "Friend of the Eucharist":[19] "In the name of Our Lord Jesus Christ and of the glorious Virgin Mary, His Mother, I choose the province of France, where there is a Catholic people who more than other Catholics greatly reverence the body of Christ, which is to me a great joy, and therefore do I desire to converse with them."[20]

In his deathbed *Testament* Francis urged his followers one final time to make their own his devotion to the reserved Eucharist: "Above everything else, I want this most holy Sacrament to be honoured and venerated and reserved in places which are richly ornamented."[21]

A decision reached three years earlier by the saint would have ensured the practical means for Franciscan churches to become models of honorable Eucharistic reservation; in the rule for his order, which he composed in 1223, Francis stipulated that the liturgical practices of the papal court as observed in the Roman Church of St. John Lateran were to be followed by his congregation.[22] With reservation on the altar evidently the standard practice at the Lateran, Francis' rule implicitly made altar reservation the norm for his order as well.[23]

The Franciscans of the thirteenth century were not slow to prove their fidelity to their founder's legacy of love for the reserved Sacrament. In 1230, at the order's chapter in Assisi, their minister general John Parenti issued a statute that "the Most Holy Sacrament be preserved in all places in ivory or silver ciboria and that these be placed in well-locked tabernacles, because neither in heaven nor on earth can anything be found which deserves similar veneration."[24] Friar Mansuetus of Castiglion Fiorentino — who served in an official capacity three consecutive Popes: Alexander IV (1254-1261), Urban IV (1261-1264), and Clement IV (1265-1268) — told of being taught as a ten-year-old boy by the first Franciscans to revere the Holy Eucharist with particular veneration.[25] With the order spreading across Europe, and with the eventual elevation of some members to high ecclesiastical offices, conditions were ripe for the propagation of Francis' Eucharistic devotion throughout medieval Christendom.

Perhaps the single most compelling example of such Franciscan influence can be seen in the case of Eudes Rigaud, a Franciscan of exceptional piety who, after studying under the renowned scholar Alexander of Hales in Paris, became Archbishop of the key northern French Archdiocese of Rouen in 1248. According to one quasi-legendary account of Rigaud's election to this office, the chapter of Rouen, unable to reach a consensus as to who to nominate for their diocese, came to the decision that they would select the first cleric they saw entering the cathedral to pray. In the course of going to preach, Rigaud entered to visit the Blessed Sacrament; it was thus that he was chosen.[26] What is of particular interest in this account, regardless of whether or not Rigaud was actually selected in this manner, is the mention of the practice of visiting the Blessed Sacrament, and the attribution of such a practice to Rigaud.

Throughout the course of his episcopacy (1248-1275) as the Ordinary of Rouen, Archbishop Rigaud proved himself to be a most zealous guardian of the reserved Eucharist. Thus in a visitation to the Monastery of St.-Ouen-de-Rouen in December of 1249, the archbishop expressed his concern that the sacrament was not being reserved with sufficient reverence:

> As part of the duty imposed upon us by our office, we made a visitation of your monastery, and we found certain things which we neither can nor should overlook by way of dissimulation, and which must be corrected. Since we found that the sacrosanct and venerable Blessed Sacrament which should be kept with all care and diligence and treated with reverence and honor according to the canons was being improperly cared for, we will and decree that every effort be made to assure its proper care.
>
> Item, we will and decree that you remove the unsuitable and

shameful altar ornaments, especially the corporals, in which the real Body of Christ is wrapped, and that each altar be furnished with clean and decent cloths.[27]

It is in another of Rigaud's visitations in July of 1250 that we find our first explicit testimony linking the location of the reserved Sacrament on or near the altar to the exercise of devotion toward the Eucharist. Commenting upon what he found in the Church of St.-Gervais, the cathedral of Rouen's suffragan Diocese of Seez, the archbishop said: "Coming to the church at Seez for the purpose of making a visitation, a duty which our office demands of us, we found certain matters requiring correction, at which we neither could nor should connive. . . . We found that the sacrosanct and venerable Blessed Sacrament is so placed on the high altar that those passing through the choir, or praying there, do not have It before their eyes as is meet, so that their devotion may be increased."[28]

It is clear from the above text that Rigaud was dissatisfied, not with the placing of the Eucharist on the high altar, but rather that the reserved Sacrament was not located in a sufficiently prominent position upon the altar to stimulate the devotion of those in the choir of the church. Rigaud obviously wished the eyes of those at prayer to rest upon the reserved Eucharist; implicit in this desire is the concept of directing, addressing one's prayer to the reserved Sacrament — a fusion of the prayer of composition of place with the worship of the Eucharist outside of Mass. This same concern to relate prayer in church to the continual Eucharistic Presence surfaces in the archbishop's complaint regarding the Priory of Sacey, which he visited in May of 1256: "Item, since we found that in the church the Blessed Sacrament was placed in a window in such a way that they [the monks] must turn their backs upon it whenever they say their Hours, we ordered them to place it honorably upon the altar, in some tabernacle or pyx."[29]

In the above passage we see Rigaud desirous that monks saying the official prayer of the Church — the Divine Office — should not turn away from the Blessed Sacrament while doing so, with the implication that just as those in the presence of a king are not permitted by court protocol to turn their backs upon him, so too monks in prayer to their Divine King should not turn their backs upon Him either. It should also be noted that here again the situating of the reserved Eucharist on the altar is explicitly linked to the honor of the sacrament.

From Rigaud's visitation records there emerges a consistent campaign to make the Franciscan practice of altar reservation the norm for the Archdiocese of Rouen — a clear demonstration of Franciscan Eucharistic devotion shaping the overall direction of medieval spirituality. Thus in a visitation of the chapter at Gournay in September of 1258, Archbishop Rigaud noted: "We ordered them to hang something, or to have something constructed, beside the High Altar to receive the pyx wherein the Body of the Lord rests."[30]

Rigaud's professed amazement upon failing to find the Blessed Sacrament reserved on or near the altar in a priory at Bohon during September of 1266 serves to confirm that he considered altar reservation a norm to be universally observed, at least within the confines of his own archdiocese. The archbishop's comments on this occasion also illustrate yet again that he — and undoubtedly the Franciscans in general — specifically wanted the reserved Sacrament on or near the altar so that it could become a visual focal point there: "We requested the prior to arrange and see to it that the Blessed Sacrament was placed in a vase, pyx, or other such vessel and *set in a noticeable and prominent place* above the altar or vicinity. This had never as yet been done, which amazed us" (emphasis added).[31]

Eudes Rigaud was not the only thirteenth-century Franciscan to disseminate his order's Eucharistic devotion upon being raised to a high ecclesiastical station in life. The English Franciscan John Pecham (circa 1240-1292) did not fail to exert his authority in this regard during his episcopate as Archbishop of Canterbury (1279-1292); thus at a council he convened at Lambeth in 1281, Pecham issued the following mandate:[32] "We decree . . . that in every parish church there be a tabernacle with a lock, fair and comely according to the greatness of the cure and the value of the church, in which the body of the Lord itself is to be placed in a beautiful pyx and with linen coverings. . . ."[33]

Archbishop Pecham also directed at this same council that bells were to be rung at the consecration; in his *Statutes* of the preceding year (1280) he ordered a more reverently conducted procession for carrying the Eucharist to those who are ill, prescribing that the people were to "prostrate themselves, or at least pray humbly, wherever it might happen that the King of glory was carried under the covering of bread."[34] Even before his accession to the See of Canterbury, Pecham while in Rome about the year 1276 composed two poems saluting the Eucharist elevated at the consecration, *Ave vivens hostia* and *Hostia viva, vale, fidei*, both of which became widely disseminated in medieval Europe.[35] The earliest text of the famous *Ave verum corpus*, likewise serving as a salutation to the elevated Eucharist, is believed to date from the late thirteenth century, and, significantly, is preserved in a Franciscan manuscript.[36]

We have seen how early Franciscan Eucharistic devotion expressed itself in outward actions, of which we will be considering still more examples shortly. But in addition to the visual testimony of such practices there would have been a need to instruct the clergy and people as to the rationale underlying the worship of the reserved Sacrament. As to this aspect of thirteenth-century Eucharistic adoration we are most fortunate to find a cogent, scripturally underpinned presentation in what is in certain respects a most unlikely source. In the course of his *Chronicle*, the Franciscan Salimbene de Adam (1221-circa 1288), who was somewhat of a gossipy eccentric in his writings, digresses from his account of recent history to address the subject of the Eucharist; it is this digression that provides us with perhaps the clearest exposition of the thirteenth century's growing devotion to the reserved Blessed Sacrament. Salimbene begins by citing the following text from the Book of Exodus regarding the manna that God had given to His people in the desert (here and in the passage to follow, the Douay-Rheims Bible translation is used, to reflect Salimbene's use of the Latin Vulgate):

> And Moses said: This is the word, which the Lord hath commanded: Fill a gomor of it [the manna], and let it be kept unto generations to come here-after, that they may know the bread, wherewith I fed you in the wilderness, when you were brought forth out of the land of Egypt.
> And Moses said to Aaron: Take a vessel, and put manna into

it, as much as a gomor can hold [about a tenth of a bushel]: and lay it up before the Lord to keep unto your generations,

As the Lord commanded Moses. And Aaron put it in the tabernacle to be kept.

— Exodus 16:32-34

Salimbene now proceeds to compare this reservation of the manna in the Old Testament with what he sees as its New Covenant counterpart, the reservation of the Eucharist in churches, giving three reasons for this practice and interlacing his explanation with further scriptural citations (emphasized below). Of particular importance to the history of Eucharistic adoration are the second and third reasons he offers in this regard:

In a similar way ecclesiastical men reserve the Body of the Lord in their churches and oratories on account of three [reasons]. First, in order that for the infirm It can be retained for the purpose of communicating them, whenever it may have been necessary. Secondly, that we may exhibit to It due and devout reverence to which any Christian is held all the time [of] his life. Which also he is able to say to the angel with Tobias 9: *"If I should give myself to be thy servant I should not make a worthy return for thy care."* [Tob 9:2]. Here Isaiah 63 says: *"I will remember the tender mercies of the Lord, the praise of the Lord for all the things that the Lord hath bestowed upon us, and for the multitude of his good things to the house of Israel, which he hath given them according to his kindness, and according to the multitude of his mercies. And he said: Surely they are my people, children that will not deny: so he became their saviour. In all their affliction he was not troubled, and the angel of his presence saved them: in his love, and in his mercy he redeemed them, and he carried them and lifted them up all the days of old."* [Is 63:7-9]. . . . Thirdly, because the Lord promised to dwell with us, as He does in the Sacrament of the Altar. Whence says Jeremiah 7: *"Make your ways and your doings good: and I will dwell with you in this place."* [Jer 7:3]. Likewise the end of Matthew: *". . . behold I am with you all days, even to the consummation of the world."* [Mt 28:20]. Here Solomon says [in] 2 Chronicles 6: *"Is it credible then that God should dwell with men on the earth?"* [2 Chron 6:18]. Unquestionably it is credible, because *"the Word was made flesh, and dwelt among us,"* John 1 [verse 14].[37]

Here for the first time we find it explicitly stated that one of the reasons for reserving the sacrament (the second) is to facilitate the worship of the Eucharist. The third reason offered by Salimbene fleshes this out further by specifically seeing the reserved Eucharist as Christ's fulfillment of His promise to remain with us always, a concept first broached by the Cistercian Baldwin of Ford nearly a century earlier. Three of the Scripture texts cited by Salimbene to illustrate his third reason also bring to the fore the understanding of the reserved Sacrament as nothing less than God *dwelling* among us.

Throughout the thirteenth century, Franciscan liturgical legislation served to perpetuate and propagate Saint Francis' reverence for the Eucharist both within and outside the context of Mass. Thus the Franciscans' fourth minister general, Haymo of Faversham, produced an ordo of Mass rubrics for his order in 1243 (a document known as the *Indutus plancta*) that included the major elevation of the Host immediately following the consecration; the presence of this practice in Haymo's text as well as in a thirteenth-century ceremonial of the Augustinian Order indicates that it existed previously in the liturgy that both orders emulated — that of the papal court.[38] A few years later (between 1245 and 1254) another rubrical book for the Friars Minor appeared — the Franciscan Ceremonial — stipulating that at the major elevation the friars were to bare their heads and kneel in adoration before the Eucharist[39]; the ringing of bells was also specified for this occasion.[40] Moreover, the friars were directed to receive Holy Communion "on bended knee."[41] In 1266 the Franciscan chapter at Paris stipulated the raising aloft of candles at the elevation[42]; it was during the later 1200s that a sizable candelabra was donated to the Franciscans of Reggio (Italy) for this very purpose.[43] As to the honor of the sacrament outside of Mass, the Franciscan Ceremonial of 1245-1254 mandated that in carrying the Eucharist two vested acolytes were to accompany it with lighted candles.[44]

In the lives of the first Franciscan saints we find several episodes that evince the worship of the reserved Blessed Sacrament. There is a Franciscan Psalter, a book of psalms for the recitation of the Divine Office dating from about the years 1250-1275 and produced in northern France, that includes an image of what is thought to be an early monstrance, a vessel for exhibiting the reserved Eucharist to the devotion of the people. Such vessels we will be discussing at length in the next chapter; for the present our attention is drawn to the figure depicted holding the monstrance in this thirteenth-century illumination — Saint Clare (1193-1253).[45] The portrayal of this foundress of the Franciscans' family of consecrated women with a monstrance in her hands stems directly from one remarkable episode. When in 1240 Frederick II's Saracen soldiers attacked Assisi's Convent of San Damiano, Clare took "the silver casket (pyx) enclosed in ivory, in which the body of the Holy of Holies was most devoutly kept," and brought it to the door to protect the convent.[46] Implicit in this action of the saint is the invocation of Christ in the reserved Sacrament for protection from harm. The event is likewise depicted in a thirteenth-century painted panel from Siena showing Clare holding the pyx as the attackers fall in terror from the roof of the convent.[47]

Another early Franciscan who has been portrayed with a monstrance in his hand is Saint Anthony of Padua (1195-1231), a native of Portugal who in joining the Friars Minor brought to the order his scholarship and talents as a preacher. As in the case of Saint Clare, such a depiction appears to have been inspired by one incident in particular, recorded by the Franciscan John Rigaldus in his life of the saint, which was written no later than the early 1300s.[48] In a dramatic confrontation with a man who refused to believe the doctrine of the Real Presence, Anthony took the bold step of carrying the Eucharist into a public square, where the man's horse, having been deprived of any nourishment for over two days, was tested to see whether he would turn his attention to an inviting pile of fresh hay on one side or rather to the sacrament in Anthony's hands; ignoring the hay, the horse went down on its knees before the Eucharist.[49] Later writers identify the city where the episode transpired as Bourges, France; and in Bourges there is a Church of St. Peter, consecrated in 1231, that is said to have been built by the man whom Anthony had converted in this remarkable manner. The discovery in 1850 of a marble slab embedded in the façade of this church depicting an adoring mule lends credence to the city's claims in this regard.[50]

The above incident readily brings to mind the practice of kneeling before the Eucharist as it was carried to the sick that served as one of the major manifestations of deepening devotion to the reserved Sacrament during the thirteenth century. Little wonder is it that on his deathbed the renowned Franciscan theologian Saint Bonaventure (1215-1274), unable to receive Viaticum, requested that the Blessed Sacrament, enclosed within a pyx, be placed upon his heart.[51] The carrying of the Viaticum evoked from the Franciscan penitent Saint Margaret of Cortona (1247-1297) the beautiful comment that "the streets through which the body of Jesus passed should be paved with the purest gold, that that sacred Body might thus be honored by us and welcomed. . . . This honor and reverence towards him was, she said, precisely one of the principal aims of the institution of that great Sacrament."[52] In a similar vein the Franciscan preacher Berthold of Regensburg (died 1272) stated in one of his sermons: "Grant now that our dear Lady saint Mary, mother of God, stood here on this fair meadow, while all the saints and all the angels found room around her, and that I were found worthy to see this sight . . . I would rather turn and bow the knee before a priest bearing the Lord's Body to the sick, than before our Lady saint Mary and all the saints of the whole host of heaven."[53]

As one final testament of early Franciscan Eucharistic devotion, there is the example of the knight Blessed Benvenute of Gubbio who, after hearing Francis preach (in 1222), presented himself a few days later to the saint, attired in his full armor, requesting admission into his order. During the remaining ten years of his life this Franciscan was known to pass whole nights prostrate before the altar in prayer to Christ in the Blessed Sacrament.[54]

The Development of Devotion to the Reserved Eucharist in Other Segments of Thirteenth-Century Society

While Saint Francis and his first brethren were bringing extraliturgical Eucharistic devotion to fruition in southern Europe, a parallel development was taking place to the north under the influence of a religious movement born in the twelfth-century Netherlands

— the Beguines. Beguines were women who chose to live a state of life similar in many ways to formal religious orders while remaining in the world. Like religious they lived in community following the evangelical counsels of chastity and obedience, although usually without taking permanent vows. Their apostolate often took the form of caring for the sick and disabled. Although their unusual state of life aroused suspicion and criticism in certain quarters, and abuses did arise among some of their number, in the majority of cases the Beguines were considered by the Church to be faithful daughters living in a praiseworthy manner, whose spirituality could best be described as Cistercian, a reformed version of the Benedictine life.[55]

In view of the increasing acts of reverence toward the reserved Eucharist that appeared in Benedictine communities during the tenth and eleventh centuries, it is not surprising that the Beguines, imbued with the Benedictine heritage, would have taken Eucharistic devotion a step further with the practice of prayer specifically directed to the reserved Sacrament. There is an implicit reference to this new observance in the life of the single most important figure in the Beguine movement, the Belgian Blessed Mary of Oignies (circa 1175-1213) who, according to her major biographer and friend Cardinal James de Vitry, was wont before feast days to spend day and night "in the presence of Christ in the church."[56] Another biographer of Mary who was evidently also a contemporary of hers, Nicholas of Cantimpre, serves to confirm the implicit Eucharistic meaning of Cardinal Vitry's comment by providing a fairly obvious instance of prayer to the reserved Blessed Sacrament in connection with Mary of Oignies: he tells of a man who, having been instructed by Mary to go to a nearby church, entered, and "falling on his knees before the holy altar, directed his mental gaze intently upon the pyx, with the Body of Christ, which hung above it."[57]

Eucharistic adoration is incontestably manifest in the life of Venerable Ida of Louvain (died 1300), another Belgian Beguine who eventually became a Cistercian nun of the Convent of Mechelen. Such prayer is explicitly mentioned three times in her biography, as on one occasion when kneeling on the floor of the chapel, "venerating the Price of our Redemption, namely the honorable Sacrament of the Body of the Lord, reserved respectfully in a vessel on the top of the altar," she saluted the Eucharist in these words: "Hail, benign, merciful and kind Jesus: you who longed for our Redemption, and redeemed us from the bonds of perpetual death with your precious Blood."[58] In another episode from her life she is described as praying "before the ciborium, in which the very Body of the Lord was kept."[59]

Similar in certain respects to the Beguines were the medieval hermits known as anchoresses, women who led a life of prayer and penance in relative solitude, although they were gathered into communities where they each lived in their own cells. It was for just such communities in England that a guidebook was composed during the first years of the thirteenth century — before 1220 — a work known as the *Ancrene Riwle*, which, aside from the evidence regarding Blessed Mary of Oignies and the example in one of the Grail legends we noted earlier, can be considered the earliest *absolutely explicit* description of prayer clearly addressed to the reserved Sacrament: "When ye are quite dressed, sprinkle yourselves with holy water, which ye should have always with you, and think upon God's flesh and on His blood, which is over the high altar, and fall on your knees towards It with this salutation, 'Hail Thou author of our creation, Hail Thou price of our redemption! Hail Thou who art our support (*viaticum*) during our pilgrimage! Hail O reward of our expectation!' "[60]

Elsewhere in the text the anchoresses are reminded of the uninterrupted continuity of Christ's presence in the reserved Eucharist: "Ye have with you night and day, the same Blood and the same blessed Body that came of the maiden and died on the cross, there is only a wall intervening. . . . And He showeth Himself to you thus [in the Mass], as if He said: 'Behold! I am here. What would ye? Tell Me what you greatly desire; of what you are in want. Complain to Me of your distress.' "[61]

Devotion to the reserved Eucharist came to permeate thirteenth-century Catholic piety with remarkable swiftness. The practice of perpetual prayer before the reserved Eucharist — perpetual adoration — that as we have already seen appears to have developed first in Lugo, Spain, was introduced in Avignon, France, in September of 1226 by King Louis VIII.[62] Four years later perpetual adoration was established at the Cistercian Monastery of Santa Maria d'Alcobaça in Portugal.[63] In 1238 Robert Grossetete, Bishop of Lincoln, ordering that the Eucharist "should always be kept with honour in a place set apart . . . and there be devoutly and faithfully reserved," sought to stimulate devotion to the Blessed Sacrament outside Mass by further instructing that a priest bearing the Eucharist to the sick was to "carry it openly and with honour before his breast with reverence and dread," preceded by a light, for that which he bears "is 'the brightness of the everlasting light [cf. Wis. 7:26],' by which means faith and devotion may be increased among all." Moreover, a bell was to be carried along with the light and rung "that by the sound thereof the devotion of the faithful may be kindled to render the adoration due to so great a sacrament."[64]

Similarly, in 1279 a Church council in Reading, England, stipulated that the Eucharist was to be reserved in "a beautiful pyx lined with the fairest linen, in which we charge that the Lord's body be laid and be covered with a veil of silk or fine cloth or most pure linen"; moreover, the people were to "prostrate themselves, or at least humbly pray, wherever it may happen that the King of Glory is carried under the covering of bread" to the sick.[65]

Corpus Christi, Blessed Juliana of Cornillon, and Saint Thomas Aquinas

In 1208, four years after the young Francis of Assisi renounced everything to give himself to his distinctive calling in the Church, a sixteen-year-old Belgian girl first learned of hers. An orphan from the age of five, Juliana was taken in as a pupil by the Augustinian nuns of Cornillon, a convent bordering upon Liège, the city of her birth. Developing a pronounced devotion to the Eucharist as a child, she became an Augustinian novice in 1206, and shared in the sisters' life of prayer and the service of lepers.[66] Two years later Juliana experienced a mysterious vision, the meaning of which eluded her — while at prayer she saw the full moon, the disk of which was darkened in one area.[67] Two more years would pass before she received an interior message explaining the vision — "The moon, which is appearing to you, is a figure of My Church. The dark line passing over it, and veiling some of its brightness, is to signify that a great feast in honour of the Blessed Sacrament is wanting to complete its glory."[68] Although there was already a feast day on the Church's calendar that constituted in a certain sense the feast of the Eucharist *par excellence* — Holy Thursday — the celebration of the latter rightly takes place within the context of the mystery of the Passion — hence the need for a separate feast that, in the words of Pope John Paul II, can express "all that the Eucharist is for the Church" not only as a *"mysterium passionis"* but also as a *"mysterium gloriae."*[69]

Although Juliana did confide her original, inexplicable vision to her superior, it would be another eighteen years before the young nun could bring herself to reveal the subsequent explanation she had received. Among those to whom she finally divulged the message was the archdeacon of Liège, Jacques Pantaléon. At the time neither she nor he could have imagined that he would eventually become a Successor of Saint Peter, and that as Pope Urban IV he would in 1264 make the feast first spoken of within the recesses of Juliana's heart a feast of the universal Church — Corpus Christi.[70]

Juliana, however, did not live to see this vindication of her mission. Her last years were fraught with the scorn and persecution of others who did not believe her; finally driven from her own convent, she became an outcast. But He for whom she had suffered all these things did not leave her to die alone; she passed to His Kingdom while kneeling in adoration upon her straw bed as a priest held the Blessed Sacrament before her. The date was April 3, 1258.[71]

The establishment of a new feast on the Church's calendar necessitated the composition of a new office for it — a selection of psalms, readings, antiphons, prayers, and hymns with which to mark the occasion in the Mass and in the recitation of the Divine Office. Some years earlier a young monk had composed an office for the first local celebration (in 1247) of the feast in Juliana's own Diocese of Liège,[72] but for the universal Church a more impressive effort was requisite. To meet this need, Pope Urban IV enlisted the services of the brilliant Dominican scholar Saint Thomas Aquinas (circa 1225-1274). And Thomas did not disappoint his Pontiff — the office he produced has been hailed as a masterpiece of literary art.[73] His achievement is exemplified by the hymn he composed for the first Vespers of Corpus Christi, perhaps the most widely known Eucharistic canticle ever written, the *Pange Lingua*:

> Sing, my tongue, the Savior's glory,
> Of his Flesh the mystery sing;

Of the Blood, all price exceeding,
Shed by our immortal King,
Destined, for the world's redemption,
From a noble womb to spring. . . .[74]

Saint Thomas's office antiphon *O sacrum convivium* encompasses in one stanza the breadth and depth of the Eucharistic mystery:

O sacred banquet, wherein Christ is received;
the memorial of his passion is celebrated;
the mind is filled with grace; and a pledge
of future glory is given to us, alleluia.[75]

Another of Thomas Aquinas's Corpus Christi antiphons and one of his prayers for the office have become a permanent part of the rite of Eucharistic Benediction. In the current Mass of Corpus Christi the entrance antiphon, opening prayer, prayer over the gifts, and prayer after Communion are all from Saint Thomas's pen, as is the special hymn preceding the Gospel, the "sequence" *Lauda Sion*:

Laud, O Zion, your salvation,
Laud with hymns of exultation,
   Christ, your king and shepherd true. . . .[76]

The implementation of Pope Urban's decree establishing the Feast of Corpus Christi was slow in coming; it was eventually necessary for a later Pontiff, Clement V, to promulgate a new decree in 1314 mandating its universal observance.[77] In 1319 the Franciscans became the first religious order to stipulate observance of the Feast of Corpus Christi in its legislation.[78]

While Corpus Christi is indeed a celebration of the Eucharist in all its aspects, it is especially a celebration of the Real Presence. And it is this dimension of the feast that eventually expressed itself in a new Eucharistic devotion — the Corpus Christi procession — a phenomenon that was to reach its zenith in the centuries to come, as we shall see hereafter.

ENDNOTES

1. Noel Currer-Briggs, *The Shroud and the Grail: A Modern Quest for the True Grail*, 1987, p. 13.
2. Fr. Herbert Thurston, SJ, "The Blessed Sacrament and the Holy Grail," *Month*, Dec. 1907, Vol. 110, pp. 627-628.
3. Ibid., p. 627.
4. Ibid., p. 629.
5. S.J.P. Van Dijk and J. Hazelden Walker, *The Myth of the Aumbry: Notes on Medieval Reservation Practice and Eucharistic Devotion*, 1957, p. 69.
6. *St. Francis of Assisi: Writings and Early Biographies: English Omnibus of the Sources for the Life of St. Francis*, ed. Marion A. Habig, OFM, 1973, p. 67.
7. Van Dijk and Walker, p. 69.
8. Thurston, p. 618; V.L. Kennedy, CSB, "The Date of the Parisian Decree on the Elevation of the Host," *Medieval Studies*, 1948, Vol. 8, pp. 87-96.
9. *Synodicae Constitutiones*, Ch. 5, No. 6, in J.D. Mansi, ed., *Sacrorum Conciliorum Nova et Amplissima Collectio*, Tome 22, 1766 and 1901, col. 678.
10. Walter of Coventry, *Memoriale*, II, quoted in Fr. Herbert Thurston, SJ, "The Early Cultus of the Blessed Sacrament," *Month*, April 1907, Vol. 109, pp. 383-384.
11. Ch. 20, in Darwell Stone, *The Reserved Sacrament*, 1917, pp. 131-132.
12. *Annales Franciscorum*, III, p. 9, cited in Johannes Jorgensen, *Saint Francis of Assisi: A Biography*, Image Books, 1955, p. 314.
13. "Lugo," *Enciclopedia Universal Ilustrada*, 1958 ed., Vol. 31, p. 576.
14. *St. Francis of Assisi: Writings and Early Biographies*, p. 101.
15. "Letter to a General Chapter," in ibid., p. 104.
16. "Letter to All Superiors of the Friars Minor," in ibid., p. 113 (emphasis added).
17. Ibid.
18. Ch. 65, quoted in Fr. Hilarin Felder, OFM Cap., *The Ideals of St. Francis of Assisi*, 1925, p. 53.
19. Thomas of Celano, Bk. II, No. 201, quoted in ibid., p. 39.
20. St. Francis, in Brother Leo, *Speculum Perfectionis*, Ch. 65, quoted in ibid.
21. *St. Francis of Assisi: Writings and Early Biographies*, p. 67.
22. Van Dijk and Walker, p. 49.
23. Ibid., pp. 49-51; S.J.P. Van Dijk, OFM, and J. Hazelden Walker, *The Origins of the Modern Roman Liturgy: The Liturgy of the Papal Court and the Franciscan Order in the Thirteenth Century*, 1960, p. 369.
24. Felder, p. 55; slightly different and shorter translation in Van Dijk and Walker, *Origins of the Modern Roman Liturgy*, p. 368.
25. Van Dijk and Walker, *The Myth of the Aumbry*, p. 70.

26. Introduction, Sydney M. Brown, trans., *The Register of Eudes of Rouen*, 1964, p. xviii; Introduction, T. Bonnin, ed., *Regestrum Visitationum Archiepiscopi Rothomagensis: Journal des Visites Pastorales d'Eude Rigaud*, 1852, p. iii.

27. Visitation of Dec. 22, 1249, in Brown, p. 62 (English trans.); Latin text in Bonnin, pp. 56-57.

28. July 16, 1250, in Brown, p. 92; Bonnin, p. 81.

29. May 8, 1256, Brown, p. 274; Bonnin, p. 246.

30. Sept. 17, 1258, Brown, p. 364; Bonnin, p. 319.

31. Sept. 16, 1266, Brown, p. 637; Bonnin, p. 556.

32. Van Dijk and Walker, *The Myth of the Aumbry*, pp. 19-20.

33. Council of Lambeth, Ch. 1, in Stone, p. 133.

34. Darwell Stone, *A History of the Doctrine of the Holy Eucharist*, 1909, Vol. I, p. 354 (quotation); Van Dijk and Walker, *The Myth of the Aumbry*, p. 67.

35. Van Dijk and Walker, *The Myth of the Aumbry*, pp. 67, 90.

36. Ibid., pp. 90-91.

37. *Chronica Fratris Salimbene de Adam, Ordinis Minorum*, ed. Oswald Holder-Egger (*Monumenta Germaniae Historica, Scriptorum*, Vol. 32), 1905-1913, p. 338. (Salimbene's words trans. by James Monti.)

38. Van Dijk and Walker, *The Myth of the Aumbry*, pp. 49, 88-89; for dating and relevant passage of Haymo's *Indutus plancta* see S.J.P. Van Dijk and J. Hazelden Walker, *Sources of the Modern Roman Liturgy: The Ordinals of Haymo of Faversham and Related Documents (1243-1307)*, 1963, Vol. I, pp. 60-63, Vol. II, p. 11.

39. Van Dijk and Walker, *Origins of the Modern Roman Liturgy*, pp. 318-319, 362.

40. Ibid., p. 362.

41. Van Dijk and Walker, *Origins of the Modern Roman Liturgy*, p. 365.

42. Van Dijk and Walker, *The Myth of the Aumbry*, p. 89 (footnote).

43. *Chronica Fratris Salimbene de Adam*, p. 589; Van Dijk and Walker, *The Myth of the Aumbry*, pp. 89-90.

44. Van Dijk and Walker, *Sources of the Modern Roman Liturgy*, Vol. II, p. 351.

45. Archdale King, *Eucharistic Reservation in the Western Church*, 1965, p. 136; Van Dijk and Walker, *The Myth of the Aumbry*, plate facing title page.

46. King, pp. 96-97; Arnaldo Fortini, *Francis of Assisi*, 1992, pp. 361-362, especially note on p. 362.

47. Van Dijk and Walker, *The Myth of the Aumbry*, Plate 1 (facing p. 16).

48. Ernest Gilliat-Smith, *Saint Anthony of Padua, According to His Contemporaries*, 1926, pp. 62-63.

49. John Rigaldus's version of the incident, as given in Olive M. Scanlan, *St. Anthony of Padua*, 1958, p. 33.

50. Charles W. Stoddard, *The Wonder-Worker of Padua*, 1896, pp. 113-114.

51. Van Dijk and Walker, *The Myth of the Aumbry*, p. 76.
52. Canon Anthony Francis Giovagnoli, *The Life of Saint Margaret of Cortona*, n.d. (1800s), p. 138.
53. Van Dijk and Walker, *The Myth of the Aumbry*, p. 83.
54. Fr. Candido Mariotti, *L'Eucaristia ed i Francescani*, 1908, p. 44; Marion Habig, OFM, *The Franciscan Book of Saints*, 1959, pp. 459-460.
55. Ernest W. McDonnell, "Beguines and Beghards," in *New Catholic Encyclopedia*, 1967 ed., Vol. 2, p. 225; E.W. McDonnell, *The Beguines and Beghards in Medieval Culture, With Special Emphasis on the Belgian Scene*, 1954, p. 312.
56. Fr. Herbert Thurston, SJ, "The Transition Period of Catholic Mysticism," *Month*, June 1922, Vol. 139, p. 530.
57. Ibid., pp. 530-531.
58. *Vita* of Ven. Ida of Louvain, Bk. II, Ch. 4, No. 6, in *Acta Sanctorum*, April, Tome II, 1738 (2nd ed.), p. 172.
59. *Vita*, Bk. III, Ch. 4, No. 22, in ibid., p. 188.
60. Thurston, "The Early Cultus of the Blessed Sacrament," p. 388; Fr. Michael Gaudoin-Parker, *The Real Presence Through the Ages*, 1993, pp. 93-94.
61. Ibid.
62. Abbé Jules Corblet, *Histoire Dogmatique, Liturgique et Archeologique du Sacrement de l'Eucharistie*, 1885, Vol. II, pp. 415, 420.
63. Fr. Paul H. O'Sullivan, OP, "Portugal and the Eucharist," in *Thirty-First International Eucharistic Congress, Dublin: Sectional Meetings, Papers and Addresses* (Vol. II of the Book of the Congress), ed. Very Rev. Patrick Canon Boylan, PP, 1934, p. 307.
64. Freestone, p. 263.
65. Ch. 7 of this Council's decrees, in Stone, *The Reserved Sacrament*, pp. 132-133.
66. M.H. Allies, "Blessed Juliana of Cornillon and Corpus Christi," *Irish Ecclesiastical Review*, Vol. 14, 3rd series, Nov. 1893, pp. 1011-1013.
67. Ibid., p. 1013; Miri Rubin, *Corpus Christi: The Eucharist in Late Medieval Culture*, 1991, p. 170.
68. Allies, p. 1013.
69. Homily, Solemnity of Corpus Christi, June 15, 1995, No. 2, in *L'Osservatore Romano*, June 21, 1995, p. 2.
70. Allies, p. 1013; Francis Mershman, "Corpus Christi (Body of Christ)," *Catholic Encyclopedia*, 1907 ed., Vol. 4, p. 391.
71. Allies, pp. 1014-1015; William Preston, *The Blessed Sacrament and the Church of St. Martin at Liège*, 1890, p. 61.
72. Mershman, p. 391.
73. Yrjo Hirn, *The Sacred Shrine*, 1912, pp. 143-144; Mershman, p. 391.
74. *Roman Breviary in English: Summer*, ed. Rt. Rev. Msgr. Joseph A. Nelson, 1951, p. 260.
75. Ibid., p. 261.

76. *The Roman Missal: Lectionary for Mass*, Catholic Book Publishing Co., 1970, p. 265.
77. Fr. Francis X. Weiser, SJ, *Handbook of Christian Feasts and Customs: The Year of the Lord in Liturgy and Folklore*, 1958, pp. 260, 266 (footnote).
78. Van Dijk and Walker, *The Myth of the Aumbry*, p. 79.

Chapter 10

"All nations shall serve him":
Fourteenth-Fifteenth Centuries

> *"Arise, O Lord, and go to thy resting place, thou and the ark of thy might."*
> — Psalm 132:8

Over the course of the fourteenth and fifteenth centuries, medieval Christendom's "discovery" of the continual Eucharistic Presence of its God and King in its very midst — in churches and cathedrals from the bustling streets of London to the tranquillity of Swiss mountain hamlets — inexorably matured into an integral component of Western spirituality. In the lives of the saints and blessed from this period, references to Eucharistic adoration grow increasingly commonplace, while at the same time manifesting an ever deepening consciousness of the ramifications of the unceasing Real Presence. It can be seen, for instance, in the life of the Dominican Blessed Henry Suso (circa 1300-1365), whom we find habitually visiting the Blessed Sacrament: "It was the Servitor's [Henry's] practice when he left his cell, or returned to it, to pass through the choir before the Sacrament; for he thought within himself that he who has a very dear friend anywhere upon his road, is very glad to make his journey a little longer in order to hold some loving converse with him."[1]

The comparison of Eucharistic adoration with the visiting of a beloved friend in the above passage is highly significant, for it is an early indication of that sense of consoling intimacy in the living presence of their Lord and Redeemer that the faithful were to experience in visiting the reserved Sacrament over the centuries to come. In this practice the sons and daughters of the Church had found a most compelling way to share in the peace that Mary of Bethany had found as she "sat at the Lord's feet and listened to his teaching" (Lk 10:39). Moreover, as medieval Christians came to seek union with Christ in abiding before the reserved Blessed Sacrament, they likewise began to discover in the presence of their God a deeper union with their family and friends, as did Saint Elzéar of Sabran, a Third Order Franciscan (1286-1323), who, in a letter to his wife, Saint Delphina, wrote: "You desire to hear often of me. Go often to visit our amiable Lord Jesus Christ in the holy sacrament. Enter in spirit his sacred heart. You know that to be my constant dwelling. You will always find me there."[2]

As Christ in the reserved Eucharist increasingly drew human hearts to His own, the devout soon found that a brief visit to the church was often not enough to satisfy their love — hence there arose the longing to spend as much time as possible with the Master. Such was the custom of the young Portuguese prince Saint Ferdinand (1402-1443), who kept a continuous watch day and night before the Blessed Sacrament from Holy Thursday to Easter.[3] So reluctant was the Third Order Franciscan Blessed Mary de Malliaco (1332-1414) to leave her Lord's presence that sleep would finally overtake her, "but on solemn feasts she watched in the church before the Body of Christ, assiduously . . . devoted to prayer; and after the withdrawal of the Brothers, her diminutive body fatigued, on the stone step of the high altar she slept a little while."[4]

But if the peoples of medieval Europe recognized in the reserved Sacrament a focal point for silent worship, they likewise saw in this newly appreciated mystery a cause for celebration. For just as the victories of earthly kings had been commemorated with parades and pageantry, even more so should the victory of the King of the Universe over sin and death be celebrated with fitting glory, majesty, and splendor, not only within the confines of the church edifice, but outside as well, under the brilliant canopy of skies He had created, where the Eucharistic Christ could be borne like a triumphant Victor through the streets and byways, visiting and sanctifying the places where His people lived and worked in His service.

As we have already seen, the carrying of the Eucharist in procession had existed for centuries, especially within the framework of Holy Week, yet until the end of the thirteenth century the practice had always been situated within the wider context of a liturgical feast or action of which the worship of the reserved Blessed Sacrament was not the specific purpose. But with the establishment of the Feast of Corpus Christi in the mid-thirteenth century, there appeared for the first time on the Church's calendar a commemoration that focused the attention of the faithful in a most particular manner upon the mystery of the Real Presence. When in the first quarter of the fourteenth century the universal observance of this feast became at last firmly established, a host of medieval cities in rapid succession harnessed the growing popular devotion surrounding the Holy Week and Viaticum Eucharistic processions by instituting just such a procession for the day of Corpus Christi as well. One case of this practice — the earliest known — appeared at the Church of St. Gereon in the German city of Cologne, sometime during the years 1264-1279[5]; instructions for the Benedictines of Hildesheim, Germany, dating from 1301, contain another very early Corpus Christi procession that includes the first extant reference to Benediction of the Blessed Sacrament — the blessing of the participants with the reserved Eucharist.[6] Elsewhere Aachen, Germany, had a Corpus Christi procession by 1319,[7] and by 1320 Gerona, Spain; it was also in 1320 that a council of the French Diocese of Sens stipulated the conducting of a Eucharistic procession on the Feast of Corpus Christi,[8] a decision likewise made by a diocesan synod of Paris three years later.[9]

It was in the second half of the thirteenth century that there began to appear a new form of Eucharistic vessel that was to become a defining feature of Corpus Christi processions for centuries to come, a vessel that would allow the faithful to gaze upon the Blessed Sacrament outside of Mass — the "monstrance." Not surprisingly, the earliest testimony to the existence of these vessels is to be found in a Franciscan manuscript — a French thirteenth-century psalter (circa 1250-1275) that contains a depiction of a monstrance in the hands of Saint Clare.[10] The earliest surviving monstrance, in the shape of a hexagonal tower, surmounted by a small crucifix with flanking statuettes of the Blessed Virgin Mary and Saint John, bears the date 1286, having originally belonged to the Abbey of Herckenrode but now kept in Limbourg, Belgium.[11] Generally the first monstrances were modeled after medieval reliquaries (vessels for displaying relics), with the Host often mounted in a crescent-shaped holder within a tube of glass that rested atop an ornate base; in many instances these were really reliquaries that had been modified to fit their new purpose, or which served simultaneously as reliquaries and monstrances, with the Host enshrined above and the relics below.[12] In the case of one such vessel from Bayeux, France (circa 1400), the cross-shaped reliquary was designed to be removable from its molded pedestal of six small lions, which on the Feast of Corpus Christi served as the base for a monstrance.[13]

In 1429 Pope Martin V granted an indulgence to those who participated in the Corpus Christi procession,[14] further enhancing the status of an observance that by the fifteenth century had grown to splendid proportions across medieval Europe. The use of flowers and plants in the adornment of the church and the procession route for this feast was common; thus in 1490 or 1491 the Church of St. Mary at Hill in London was festooned with rose garlands and woodruff.[15] In the southern Spanish city of Jaen, branches and French cloth adorned the procession route, according to an account from 1463.[16] Often church bells were rung continuously during the procession, as was the case in the English towns of Walden (1443) and Yeovil (circa 1457).[17] Religious banners and flags were carried, as in Walden, which in 1449 possessed seven Corpus Christi flags.[18] In southern Germany there existed as early as 1479 (in the vicinity of Bamberg) a format for the annual Corpus Christi procession that was to endure in this region for centuries to come: along the procession route were four "stations," stopping places where the procession would pause, with the Blessed Sacrament placed upon a temporary altar as a Gospel passage was read.[19] What were these readings? A liturgical book of the Bavarian Diocese of Regensburg, published centuries later (in 1876, to be exact) but undoubtedly reflecting an unbroken tradition, assigns the beginnings of each of the Four Gospels to the four stations of the Corpus Christi procession: Matthew 1:1-16, Mark 1:1-8, Luke 1:1-17, and John 1:1-14. It also specifies the giving of Benediction at each of the four stational altars.[20]

The monstrances for carrying and exposing the Eucharist in Europe's Corpus Christi processions continued to develop in splendor during the fifteenth century, exemplified by Barcelona's *custodia* from this period, studded with two thousand pearls and over twelve hundred diamonds. Use of this magnificent monstrance has continued into the twentieth century: during the Corpus Christi procession the Eucharist, enshrined in this vessel, is borne on a silver-gilt, Gothic-style throne chair, carried by eight priests; the chair had once served as the earthly throne of King Martin of Aragon (1393-1412).[21]

Throughout fifteenth-century Europe the sacrament was borne beneath a lavish canopy of rich cloth, adorned with fringes and mounted on poles, conveying so pronounced an aura of majesty that the earthly rulers of medieval Europe subsequently incorporated canopies into the assertion of their own royal prerogatives.[22] The beauty of such Corpus Christi canopies is well illustrated by that of Bassingbourn, England, as described in 1498: "Item a cloth of velvet of purple color for the canopy to be borne over the blessed Sacrament with the image of the crucifix embroidered in the midst of the said cloth and the names of the givers in the four corners."[23]

The development of medieval Europe's festive outdoor Corpus Christi processions mirrored developments taking place within the walls of the churches, where the reserved Eucharist was becoming the primary focus of worship outside of Mass. During the first half of the fourteenth century, an altar tabernacle was erected in Cologne's *Franciscan* Church of St. Clara, Germany's earliest "tabernacle" in the modern sense of the word; it was subsequently moved to the city's magnificent cathedral.[24] It was likewise in Germany toward the end of the 1300s that there appeared an extraordinary new manner of reservation that facilitated Eucharistic worship as never before — the sacrament-house. Usually erected in or near the sanctuary but set apart from the altar, these structures often took the form of ornate towerlike monuments, carved from stone or fashioned from other materials, including marble, metal, wood, brass, and even bronze. The Eucharist was placed within the structure in a ciborium or monstrance that could be seen at all times through the latticework grille of a metal door; the floor immediately surrounding the sacrament-house was elevated in the same manner as around an altar, with a railing encircling it to form what has been termed an "enclosed garden." Flickering candles lined the railing, and a light was sometimes placed in an upper tier of the structure, presumably to serve as the perpetual lamp that had become customary wherever the Eucharist was kept.[25] It was probably within a sacrament-house that the Eucharist was reserved in a small chapel near what is now Gdánsk, Poland, where Blessed Dorothy of Montau (1347-1394), a widow after twenty-five years of marriage and nine children, went "in order that there she might gaze on the Body of Christ which used to be kept there open to view in a monstrance. . . ."[26]

During the fifteenth and sixteenth centuries, sacrament-houses became common not only in Germany but also in Belgium, the Netherlands, and Luxembourg, appearing in Sweden, France, Austria, and Italy as well.[27] Some of these structures have survived into the twentieth century, as has that of the Church of St. Leonard in Leau, Belgium, a magnificent Gothic-style tower fifty-eight feet high, dating from 1552. At present it is used quite appropriately as the repository for the Blessed Sacrament from Holy Thursday to Good Friday.[28]

In Chapter 8 we outlined how many of the earliest manifestations of devotion to the reserved Sacrament first developed during the tenth to twelfth centuries within the context of the Holy Week liturgy. Throughout the later Middle Ages the celebrations of Palm Sunday and in particular the Easter Triduum (Holy Thursday to Easter Sunday) remained among the most likely occasions for the faithful to exhibit their devotion in this regard. Thus a diary of life in the court of the Italian prince Ercole I d'Este (1471-1505), dating from 1497, describes the splendor of a Holy Thursday repository in the city of Ferrara; for this occasion the Eucharist was reserved in a vessel of gold and silver, resting within a larger structure of figured wood and porphyry, atop a rocky "mountain" covered with mosses. Above was a canopy of gold brocade, with curtains of Spanish linen and a beautiful carpet further enhancing the majesty of the scene.[29]

So numerous and varied are such Holy Week manifestations of Eucharistic piety that a thorough review of them would be beyond the scope of the present discussion (we have treated them at length elsewhere).[30] A few brief comments will suffice. While many readers are undoubtedly familiar with the popular practice of visiting the repositories on Holy Thursday, a custom whose origins can be traced to the eleventh and twelfth centuries, few would be aware that during the fifteenth and sixteenth centuries (at least until the Protestant Reformation) a comparable tradition for Good Friday and Easter Saturday existed and thrived in many of the parishes of England, Germany, and France — the "Easter Sepulchre."

As we have already seen, this practice had been introduced by the tenth century in Germany; by the fifteenth century, prayer before the Blessed Sacrament reserved within the Easter Sepulchre, in memory of Christ's burial, had become a commonplace and extraordinarily popular devotion. Late medieval records abound in references to the faithful donating to the adornment of Easter Sepulchres, with bequests often specifying the burning of candles at these special Eucharistic shrines. To the present day the custom of the Easter Sepulchre lingers on in certain parts of Germany and Austria, where the Blessed Sacrament is now brought and enthroned atop the "Sepulchre" in a monstrance shrouded with a translucent veil.

In Christendom's capital the Successors of Saint Peter incorporated the Middle Ages' burgeoning devotion to the reserved Eucharist into the austere framework of the Roman liturgy, a process of assimilation that had begun in the thirteenth century and continued onward through the fourteenth and fifteenth centuries. By the end of the 1400s the papal liturgies for Holy Thursday and the Feast of Corpus Christi had fully come to reflect the Church's ever deepening love for the reserved Sacrament. From the detailed diary of the papal master of ceremonies Johann Burchard we learn how these rites were celebrated by Pope Innocent VIII in the spring of 1486. At the end of Mass on Holy Thursday the Pontiff carried the Eucharist — a single consecrated Host — in a chalice from the high altar in St. Peter's Basilica to St. Peter's "small chapel." Sixteen torches were borne before the Eucharist, while eight bishops and archbishops served as pole-bearers for the canopy carried over the sacrament along the route. Upon reaching the "small chapel" the Blessed Sacrament was taken from the hands of the Pontiff by a cardinal vice-chancellor assisting him, and placed into a *capsa* (the special tabernacle for this occasion) on the altar, where it was censed by the Pope on his knees before the door of the *capsa* was closed and locked.[31]

On the Feast of Corpus Christi the procession began at about ten o'clock in the morning. After kneeling in St. Peter's "small chapel" for a short prayer before the Blessed Sacrament enshrined in a vessel that was evidently a monstrance (called here a *tabernaculum*), the Pontiff rose and censed the Eucharist three times. Taking the vessel from the altar into his hands, he was then seated upon the portable papal throne for the procession, which traveled from St. Peter's Basilica along the street known as the "*via Nova*" to the Castel Sant' Angelo and then returned to the basilica along another street, the "*Sancta.*" Throughout the procession a canopy was borne over the Eucharist in the hands of the Pope, as he himself was carried on his papal throne. Upon arriving at St. Peter's, he placed the Blessed Sacrament upon the altar and, genuflecting, censed it again. The celebration of Mass followed.[32]

ENDNOTES

1. *The Life of Blessed Henry Suso*, trans. Fr. Thomas F. Knox, 1865, Ch. 38, p. 184.
2. Fr. Alban Butler, *The Lives of the Fathers, Martyrs and Other Principal Saints*, ed. Fr. Bernard Kelly, 1961, Vol. III, p. 1149.
3. Solange Corbin, *La Déposition Liturgique du Christ au Vendredi Saint: Sa Place dans l'histoire des rites et du théâtre religieux*, 1960, pp. 135, 259.
4. *Acta Sanctorum*, March, Tome 3, 1668 (1st ed.), p. 742; Msgr. Paul Guerin, *Les Petits Bollandistes: Vies des Saints: Tome Quatrieme: Du 26 Mars au 23 Avril*, c. 1880, pp. 28-40.
5. Archdale King, *Eucharistic reservation in the Western Church*, 1965, p. 158.
6. Mario Righetti, *Manuale di Storia Liturgica*, 1949, Vol. III, pp. 506-507.
7. Miri Rubin, *Corpus Christi: The Eucharist in Late Medieval Culture*, 1991, p. 258.
8. Rubin, p. 243; "Custodia," *Enciclopedia Universal Ilustrada*, 1958 ed., Vol. 16, p. 1295.
9. Rubin, p. 243.
10. S.J.P. Van Dijk, OFM, and J. Hazelden Walker, *The Myth of the Aumbry:*

Notes on Medieval Reservation Practice and Eucharistic Devotion, 1957, title page; King, p. 136.

11. Michel Andrieu, "Aux Origines du Culte du Saint-Sacrement: Reliquaires et Monstrances Eucharistiques," *Analecta Bollandiana*, 1950, Vol. 68, p. 403; Fr. Herbert Thurston, SJ, "Our Popular Devotions: IV. Benediction of the Blessed Sacrament: II. Exposition," *Month*, July 1901, Vol. 98, p. 65; King, p. 136. The discussion of monstrances that here follows is based largely upon James Monti's article "Sacred Vessels" that appeared in the May-June 1995 issue of *Catholic Heritage* magazine (p. 14).

12. See Andrieu, pp. 397-418; C.W. Howell, "Monstrance," *New Catholic Encyclopedia*, 1967 ed., Vol. 9, pp. 1070-1071.

13. Andrieu, pp. 402-403 (footnote).

14. Papal Bull of May 26, 1429, in *Magnum Bullarium Romanum, A.B. Leone Magno usque ad S.D.N. Clementem X*, ed. Laertius Cherubini, 1673, Tome I, pp. 327-328.

15. Rubin, p. 249.

16. Ibid.

17. Ibid., p. 248.

18. Ibid., p. 249.

19. Dr. Theol. Xavier Haimerl, *Das Prozessionswesen des Bistums Bamberg im Mittelalter* (*Munchener Studien zur Historischen Theologie*, Vol. 14), 1937, pp. 54-55.

20. *Euchologium Ratisbonense sive Ordo Sacri Ministerii Servandus in Processionibus cum S.S. Eucharistiae Sacramento et in Sacris Officiis Publicisque coram eodem Exposito Praecendis*, 1876, 3-17.

21. "Custodia," p. 1295 plus Plate I; Abbé Jules Corblet, *Histoire Dogmatique Liturgique et Archeologique du Sacrement de l'Eucharistie*, 1885, Vol. 2, p. 323.

22. Rubin, pp. 252-253, 259.

23. Ibid., p. 254 (spelling modernized by James Monti).

24. King, p. 78.

25. Ibid., pp. 104-110.

26. Fr. Herbert Thurston, SJ, "Our Popular Devotions: IV. Benediction of the Blessed Sacrament: II. Exposition," *Month*, July 1901, Vol. 98, p. 59; *Butler's Lives of the Saints*, ed. Fr. H. Thurston, SJ, and Donald Attwater, 1956 ed., Vol. 4, p. 224.

27. King, pp. 105-110.

28. Ibid., pp. 108-109.

29. Giovanni Sabadino degli Arienti, *De triumphis religionis*, in Werner L. Gundersheimer, ed., *Art and Life at the Court of Ercole I d'Este: The 'De triumphis religionis' of Giovanni Sabadino degli Arienti* (Travaux d'Humanisme et Renaissance, No. 127), 1972, pp. 90-91. Also quoted in Claudio Bernardi, *La Drammaturgia della Settimana Santa in Italia*, 1991, p. 226.

30. James Monti, *The Week of Salvation: History and Traditions of Holy Week*, 1993, pp. 43-46, 124-137, 143-146, 270-275, 282, 309-314, 392-395, 402-403.
31. Johann Burchard, *Diarium sive Rerum Urbanarum Commentarii (1483-1506): Tome Premier (1483-1492)*, ed. L. Thuasne, 1883, p. 180.
32. Ibid., p. 203.

Chapter 11

"Before him all kings shall fall prostrate": Sixteenth-Seventeenth Centuries

"The Lord is in his holy temple . . ."
— Psalm 11:4

The sixteenth century proved to be a decisive epoch in the history of Christianity — a time of both brilliant light and impenetrable darkness — an age of saints and heretics, of great artists and brutal tyrants. As this new century dawned, there arose a new form of monstrance for the adoration of the Eucharist, the "sunburst," with the Host appearing in a sunlike setting of dazzling, outwardly radiating molded rays. Its introduction seemed to foreshadow the beginning of another great age of the Eucharist — and indeed it did, although just how this new Eucharistic Renaissance was to unfold could scarcely have been imagined by those living at its outset.

Perhaps no event defined the 1500s more than the phenomenon of the Reformation, a conflict that opened a breach in Christianity that even after four and a half centuries remains unhealed. In the Protestant reformers' war of words against the doctrines of the Catholic Church, the sacraments came under some of their heaviest attacks. While the reformers as a whole did acknowledge the Eucharist as a sacrament, they were almost universally convinced that in one way or another the Church had misunderstood what Christ had intended when at the Last Supper He took bread and said, ". . . this is my body . . . this is my blood . . ." (Mt 26:26-28). Their Eucharistic theories were wide-ranging: Martin Luther (1483-1546) denied the doctrine of transubstantiation, insisting that while the Body and Blood of Christ really did become present in the Eucharist, the bread and wine nonetheless continued to be present after consecration; far more radical in his Eucharistic theology was Ulrich Zwingli (1484-1531), who saw the Eucharist as little more than a symbol of Christ's spiritual presence. Whatever their differing definitions of the sacrament, however, the reformers were united in their opposition to the adoration of the reserved Eucharist. And this opposition sometimes inspired vicious acts of sacrilege against the Hosts in the tabernacles of Catholic churches, including the feeding of the Eucharist to animals as a blasphemous amusement. On the printed page, Protestant writers turned out ugly satires aimed at making Eucharistic adoration appear ridiculous and idolatrous.

Yet again, Christ's teaching in His Eucharistic discourse at Capernaum — that the Bread He would give was to be His very own Flesh (cf. Jn 6:51) — was proving to be a "hard saying" (Jn 6:60) that some would not endure. Those who refused to believe were once more "voting with their feet" and leaving the Church. And again could be heard Christ's haunting and poignant question to His remaining followers — "Will you also go away?" (Jn 6:67). The answer that He received from His faithful sons and daughters in strife-torn sixteenth-century Europe has endured to the present, and it is a testament of love — a hymn of praise in the form of communal and continuous prayer before the reserved Blessed Sacrament.

The Forty Hours Prayer

It was in 1527 — only ten years after Martin Luther had posted his ninety-five theses on the door of the German castle church of Wittenberg, inaugurating the Reformation — that there began at Milan's Church of the Holy Sepulchre the seminal form of what would eventually come to be known as the Forty Hours Prayer. Introduced by Antonio Bellotto, a priest from Ravenna, the devotion was held four times during the year in an oratory where the Blessed Sacrament was reserved but without the continuous exposition of the Eucharist that would afterward characterize this devotion.[1] While the observance of forty hours of prayer before the reserved Sacrament during Holy Week probably existed as early as the twelfth century in the Croatian city of Zara (see Chapter 8), Father Bellotto was the first known to have expanded such a concept beyond the confines of the Easter Triduum. Two years later (1529), in response to a crisis brought on by the invading troops of Emperor Charles V together with a fever epidemic, the Forty Hours Prayer was conducted during the final days of the Corpus Christi octave in all the churches of Milan, beginning with a penitential procession in which the Blessed Sacrament was carried; this city-wide observance of the "*Quarant' Ore*" ("Forty Hours") was repeated in September.[2]

Thanks to the decisive initiative of a zealous Capuchin preacher, Father Joseph Plantida of Fermo (died 1566), 1537 saw the establishment of this devotion on a continuous, year-round basis in Milan, with the observance successively carried from one parish to another; at the conclusion of the prayer in one parish the Blessed Sacrament was evidently borne in procession to the next parish where it was to be conducted. During the prayer in each parish the Eucharist was placed on the main altar, although not necessarily exposed in a monstrance.[3] We should add that along with Father Joseph of Fermo, two other figures from this period are credited with playing a major role in the development of the Forty Hours Prayer — Saint Anthony Mary Zaccaria (1502-1539), founder of the Barnabite Order and an ardent advocate of frequent Communion, and the hermit Bonus of Cremona (died 1547).[4]

What began as a local observance during the first half of the sixteenth century spread rapidly across Catholic Europe in the second half of the century. In 1550 Saint Philip Neri introduced the Forty Hours devotion to Rome[5]; three years later the newly founded Jesuit Order began to observe and promote the *Quarant' Ore* as well.[6] The "Forty Hours" first came to France in 1574, when it was introduced in Paris by the Jesuit Edmond Auger.[7] It was while a member of the Capuchin Order during the period 1577-1584 that Joseph de Rocaberti introduced the *Quarant' Ore* in Spain.[8]

By 1574 there had appeared in the Diocese of Milan another practice similar to, but distinct from, the Forty Hours devotion.

Known as the "prayer without interruption," this practice, to be carried out on those occasions when the city was threatened by an imminent danger, comprised a series of one-hour periods of exposition and adoration of the Eucharist, with each hour assigned to a different parish so that from sunrise to sunset there was at all times adoration being conducted in at least one of the city's churches. The format prescribed for each of the one-hour services is clearly the precursor of what we now know as the "holy hour": "The priest who presides at the service then rises alone, while the rest of the clergy and people remain upon their knees; he says *Dominus vobiscum*, intones the antiphon of the Psalm *Benedictus*, and recites the prayers following which are printed upon a card. . . . After an entire hour has been consumed in exercises of this description, the senior priest, as above explained, will give the Benediction to the people with the Blessed Sacrament and afterward replace It, while the people sing what is printed on the card."[9]

Although the earliest accounts of the Forty Hours Prayer are sketchy at best in revealing the visual details of this increasingly popular devotion, regulations issued in 1577 by the Archbishop of Milan, Saint Charles Borromeo, provide a considerably more complete picture in this regard. The Blessed Sacrament was to be placed on the *mensa* (tabletop) of the altar in a veiled vessel. The altar was to be appropriately adorned, to the exclusion of anything profane. Up to ten large candles or up to thirteen lamps were to be kept lit around the Eucharist; all other illumination of the place of reposition could be suppressed to foster recollection. At least two clerics were to maintain a continuous watch before the sacrament during the day, with at least one doing so throughout the night. A sign was to be posted with the texts of suitable prayers and intentions. The *Quarant' Ore* was to begin and end with a procession and the singing of the Litany of the Saints; it was to conclude with Benediction of the Blessed Sacrament. To ensure continuity, the Forty Hours devotion was to begin in one parish an hour before it ended in another. Brief devotional sermons of a quarter of an hour or less could be given by preachers authorized to do so by the bishop.[10]

In 1592, in his bull *Graves et diuturnae*, Pope Clement VIII made the continuous observance of the Forty Hours devotion obligatory for the Diocese of Rome. From the diary of the papal master of ceremonies for this same year (Giampaolo Mucanti) we learn that the directives accompanying this bull specified exposition of the Blessed Sacrament in a monstrance that was to be mounted on a silk-covered wooden throne resting on the *mensa* of the altar, with the monstrance itself veiled by a large cloth stretching from it in two wings to either side. Six candles and six lamps were to be kept lighted on the altar, with the surroundings darkened if possible, as in Milan, to foster recollection. A schedule was to be drawn up of those committing themselves to keep successive watches before the sacrament. Again as in Milan, the Roman instruction permitted short devotional sermons during the *Quarant' Ore*, and specified processions and the Litany of Saints to begin and end the devotion, as well as Benediction at the conclusion.[11] Mucanti's 1592 diary also mentions that the *Quarant' Ore* at the papal palace both began and ended with the celebration of Mass — a practice that appears to have become the norm by the third quarter of the seventeenth century.[12]

At the Jesuits' Church of the Jesu in Rome (in 1593), the altar of exposition for the Forty Hours devotion was decorated lavishly, ringed by a multitude of candles, lamps, and gold and silver vases, as well as statues, with a painted backdrop erected in the apse.[13] In March of 1597 Bologna's Confraternity of Santa Maria della Morte decorated the place of exposition for the *Quarant' Ore* with a perspective painting behind the altar, augmented with gold and veils, while above was a "blue heaven full of veils and roses of various colours." The altar was flanked on the right by a statue of the Blessed Virgin Mary, and on the left by the Angel Gabriel; the altar rail was adorned with further statues of angels, as well as candles and lamps, which cast their reflections in mirrors to their rear. When the monstrance was lifted up (evidently at the moment of Benediction), the Eucharist was saluted with a trumpet blast.[14]

In October of 1598 the Forty Hours devotion was celebrated in full grandeur in Thonon, France (near Lake Geneva), with the provost of Geneva, Saint Francis de Sales, the celebrant. The devotion began with Mass at Thonon's Church of St. Hippolytus, after which the provost (Francis de Sales) carried the Blessed Sacrament in procession from St. Hippolytus to the Church of St. Augustine along a street route adorned with abundant flowers and plants, hang-

ings, and pictures. The Eucharist was borne in a monstrance studded with pearls, diamonds, and other precious gems under a canopy
carried by four prominent laymen, including the Duke of Savoy
and his brother. Behind the canopy walked the visiting cardinal
legate from Rome together with other prelates and noblemen, who
in turn were followed by a great concourse of the laity who had
converged upon the city from the surrounding villages. Entering
the brilliantly lit destination church (St. Augustine's), the participants carried the Blessed Sacrament to a chapel where it was enthroned for adoration. Over the course of the next two days Saint
Francis de Sales preached during the *Quarant' Ore* no less than
ten times. On the final night of the devotion the Duke of Savoy
remained before the Blessed Sacrament until two o'clock in the
morning. Thonon's *Quarant' Ore* concluded with Francis carrying
the Eucharist from St. Augustine's back to the Church of St.
Hippolytus in a procession illuminated by torches, lanterns, and
candles.[15]

The Age of the Baroque

The image of Christ as a universal King is a biblical one — indeed, our Lord does not hesitate to speak of Himself as "the King"
in describing to His disciples the Last Judgment (cf. Mt 25:34).
Moreover, Saint John's Gospel account of the Passion is replete
with allusions to Christ's kingship, as modern biblical scholars are
wont to remind us. Hence, as Christological prayer — prayer directed to Christ — became from the Middle Ages onward increasingly focused upon our Lord's presence in the reserved Sacrament,
it came as a natural development that the outward artistic expressions of kingship were enlisted in manifesting the kingship of Christ
in the Eucharist. Already a dominant theme in the fourteenth and
fifteenth centuries, this motif was to come even more to the fore in
the seventeenth century, during which the various forms of Eucharistic devotion outside of Mass — the Corpus Christi procession, exposition of the Blessed Sacrament, the Forty Hours Prayer,
perpetual adoration, adoration before the repository on Holy Thursday, and personal visits to the tabernacle — had all fully matured
after centuries of gradual development.

Drawing upon the splendors of baroque art, architecture, and music, seventeenth-century Catholics lavished upon the reserved Eucharist an atmosphere of stately majesty and colorful pageantry. And why not? What they were doing was a perfectly natural application of the teachings from the Gospels. Christ had taught that He was the Son of God, and that He was truly present in the Eucharist; He had allowed the Magi to do Him homage with costly gifts of gold, frankincense, and myrrh (Mt 2:11), and welcomed Mary of Bethany's anointing of His feet with precious aromatic nard (Jn 12:3). Even in death Nicodemus saw fit to bestow upon the lifeless Body of our Lord taken down from the cross a hundred pounds of fragrant aloes and myrrh (Jn 19:39), an incredible amount such as would have only been lavished upon a dead king. Is it then any wonder that as the faithful progressed in the realization that in their churches dwelt their God incarnate under the appearances of bread, they would have brought the finest gifts of their culture to adorn the dwelling place of their Lord? Moreover, if baroque church furnishings were designed to inspire in the worshiper a sense of awe in the Eucharistic Presence of God, what was wrong with this? By no means foreign to the Roman liturgy, the sense of awe has been an integral element of the Eastern liturgies from the early centuries onward, epitomized in the iconostasis that screens the altar from the rest of an Eastern church.

For the Catholics of the seventeenth century, the Eucharist was likewise a cause for great rejoicing. This aspect of "baroque piety," as well as the others of which we have spoken, are well illustrated in the Corpus Christi celebrations of seventeenth-century Spain. Thus for the Corpus Christi procession of 1613 in Seville, pine trees were placed in the streets and plazas along the procession route, with rushes, green poplar twigs, and fresh reeds spread upon the street surface; houses were adorned all along the route, with "awnings" suspended above the route to shield the participants and spectators from the sun. Moreover, all horses and carriages were banned from the procession route.[16]

For the Corpus Christi procession of Madrid in 1623, the streets were decked with hangings and tapestries, and temporary altars were erected before the palatial homes of two dukes and a count, as well as before the palace of the king. The altar before the latter was adorned with jewels and a silk frontal interwoven with gold and silver thread.[17] Among the notable features of Madrid's 1679 procession were the awnings spread from one side of the street to the other, as well as the profuse carpeting of the street route with flowers, after the road surface had been sanded and sprinkled with water. From time to time the awnings were watered, so as to cool the air. Many of the women carried baskets of flowers and vessels of perfume to scatter upon the procession, as was undoubtedly done by some of those watching from the balconies along the route that were festooned with hangings.[18]

Across seventeenth-century Spain, on the evening before the Feast of Corpus Christi, the sound of continuously tolling bells accompanied the solemn chanting of Vespers in the principal churches. The firing of artillery and the lighting of great illuminations likewise heralded the coming of this feast. Thus a decree for the city of Granada dating from June of 1637 ordered the placement and lighting of lights in all the houses along the procession route as well as in the town hall on the eve of the feast, accompanied by the sounding of trumpets and hornpipes. A visitor to the city over a hundred years later (in 1751) described that when the afternoon sun had descended to the horizon on the eve of Corpus Christi there was heard the "harmonious clamor of the bells (innumerable in this town) with the violent din of the artillery, which crowns the walls of the Royal Fortress . . . of the Alhambra."[19]

The procession itself was usually, although not always, held or at least begun in the morning of the feast; thus that of Madrid in 1623 commenced at nine o'clock and continued until almost three in the afternoon.[20] In this 1623 procession those preceding the monstrance included the Spanish government's counselors for the Indies, Aragon, Portugal, Castile, the Exchequer, the Military Orders, the Inquisition, and Italy. They were followed by the chapter general for the clergy and twenty-four priests vested in copes and carrying censers. Behind them came the clerics of the Royal Chapel, then three chaplains of the Archbishop of Santiago, with the middle one carrying the crozier, and finally the archbishop himself. The king's pages, carrying lighted candles, immediately preceded the Eucharist, borne on a *carro triumphale* under a canopy carried by members of the city council. Immediately behind the monstrance walked the King of Spain, his son the prince at his side.[21] From another source we learn that, following the conclusion of Madrid's Corpus Christi processions, the Blessed Sacrament remained exposed on the high altar, while veiled women kept watch, holding lighted candles in their hands as they prayed.[22]

The splendors of baroque piety converged like golden rays upon the vessel that exposed to the eyes of the faithful the priceless Body of Christ — the monstrance. As beautiful as were the monstrances of the Middle Ages, baroque artisans strove to surpass the achievements of their forefathers by giving to the vessels of exposition even more magnificent forms. In this age of the French "Sun King," Louis XIV, brilliant sunburst monstrances came to prevail by the end of the seventeenth century.[23] The men who crafted these vessels manifested an ingenious propensity for incorporating scriptural themes into their works, as in the case of a silver sunburst monstrance from Augsburg, Germany (circa 1700), wherein the Host fills the actual place of Christ at table with His disciples in a depiction of the Last Supper across the front of the vessel.[24] In another sunburst monstrance from Bruges, Belgium (1685), the Host is positioned so as to be the focal point in a depiction of the Transfiguration.[25] In Spain, vessels of truly epic proportions were constructed for exposition — what the Spanish call the *custodia*. That of Seville, dating from 1587, nearly twelve feet high and weighing over half a ton, is in the form of a five-story circular Roman temple, into which is placed a gold sunburst monstrance containing the Eucharist.[26] The pyramid-shaped *custodia* of Toledo's cathedral (sixteenth century) is over fourteen feet high.[27]

The missionaries of sixteenth- and seventeenth-century Catholic Europe carried their love for the Blessed Sacrament with them to the shores of the New World, relying upon this devotion both to sustain themselves amid many hardships and to enrich the lives of the Native American peoples they had come to serve and even die for. Indeed, it was Eucharistic adoration that sustained the faith of the Jesuits' great North American martyr Saint Isaac Jogues (1607-1646), as one of his contemporaries relates: "He seemed, as it were, a soul glued to the Blessed Sacrament. Before this hidden God he made all his spiritual exercises — prayers, examens, Office — no matter how intense the rigor of the cold nor the importunity of the insects."[28]

In the *Jesuit Relations*, the Jesuits' official accounts of their missionary endeavors in seventeenth-century New France (what is now southeastern Canada), there is a colorful account of the Corpus Christi procession held in Quebec City on May 31, 1646, less than five months before Isaac Jogues's martyrdom. At the conclusion of Mass, which began at seven-thirty in the morning, the procession followed a course from the parish church onward past the fort, where a temporary altar was erected, the first of four "stations" along the route; here the Blessed Sacrament was saluted with pealing bells and three cannon shots. Bells tolled again, and guns and muskets were fired to salute the Eucharist at both the second station, which was erected at the hospital, and at the third, before the residence of a prominent citizen.

Greeted by bells once more at the fourth station (the Ursuline Convent), the sacrament was given a second salute of cannon fire as the procession passed a second time near the fort, before finally ending around eleven o'clock at the parish church where it had begun. Here the Blessed Sacrament remained exposed throughout the day to the end of Vespers; at the city's religious houses there was likewise day-long exposition on each of the succeeding days of the Corpus Christi octave. As for the order of the procession itself, the account states that a representative of the governor, two church wardens, and one native American carried the four poles of the canopy over the Eucharist, with the other participants described as follows:

> Two bell-ringers marched in front, then the banner: the one who carried it had a hat of flowers. The Cross followed, borne by a youth of 20 years, in alb and silk sash — on either side of him, two boys in surplices and sashes. The torches followed, 6 in number; for the 1st time we appointed the local crafts to bear them — to wit, carpenters, masons, sailors, toolmakers, brewers, and bakers; to whom this time we sent, on the day before, some torches made by our skill and of our wax. These they hung with festoons; and Jean Guion, a mason, put an escutcheon on his, on which were the arms of his trade, hammer, compasses, and rule. After the torches followed four lay choristers; then Monsieur de St. Sauveur and Monsieur Nicolet, in surplice and stole; then Father

Vimont and Father Dendemare; then 6 French angels, and two little savages in their costume: all carried candlesticks or tapers, except the last two, who bore corporal-cases. After these came two of our brethren in surplices, with smoking censers; then beneath the canopy, on either side of the Blessed Sacrament, Father Druilletes serving as deacon in dalmatic, and Monsieur the prior as subdeacon in alb and stole; our Brother Liegeois, in surplice, marched last, behind the Blessed Sacrament, and officiated as master of ceremonies.[29]

Eucharistic devotions thrived in seventeenth-century Latin America, where they nourished the spirituality of the Third Order Dominican Saint Rose of Lima (1586-1617). During Holy Week, Rose would spend an uninterrupted twenty-four hours before the Blessed Sacrament from the moment the Eucharist was placed in the repository (the *monumento*) at the conclusion of Mass on Holy Thursday until It was removed for the Mass of the Presanctified on Good Friday; throughout this period she remained kneeling, never stirring from her place or sitting. She also took delight in personally assisting with the work of preparing the silken and floral adornments for the repository. During the exposition of the Blessed Sacrament for the Forty Hours devotion, Rose remained immovable before the Eucharist from morning to nightfall, not even interrupting her adoration for any food or drink.[30] In July of 1615 Rose played a decisive role in rallying the people of Lima during a special city-wide exposition of the Blessed Sacrament that is believed to have averted a potentially catastrophic attack on the city by pirates.[31]

During the seventeenth and eighteenth centuries, devotional books promoting Eucharistic adoration abounded in France and Italy. The subject of Eucharistic devotion even emerged in the "recusant" literature produced for England's underground Catholic community, who were living under the threat of persecution and death for their faith. Thus in 1625 there appeared in print an English translation of the Spanish Carthusian Andrew Capella's *Manual of Spiritual Exercises* (originally published as three separate works during the years 1572-1580),[32] which exhorts the reader to visit the Blessed Sacrament whenever possible:

When we pass by a Church.

Verily our Lord is in this place; this place is no other than the house of God, and the gate of heaven [Gen. 28:16].

Is it therefore to be thought, that God doth truly dwell upon the earth [1 Kings 8:27]?

If the heavens, and the heavens of heavens cannot contain thee, how much less this house? [ibid.].

My house shall be called, the house of prayer [Mt 21:13].

An Instruction.

As often as we pass by a Church, unless we are in great haste, we should go into it, and there worship and adore almighty God, truly and really present in the most holy Sacrament of the Altar, and humbly commend our selves unto that Saint, unto whom the Church is dedicated: & whether we go into the Church or no, we may exercise ourselves in these points following.

The Consideration.

We will consider the goodness of God, who departing from us, leaveth himself present with us, in the most holy Sacrament of the Eucharist, and ordained Temples to be built, wherein the same Sacrament might be continually kept, which should be unto us as places of refuge, whereunto we might have recourse in all our necessities, and implore the assistance of God. . . .

The Confusion.

We will be ashamed, that we have been so slack, and negligent in visiting of Churches, and that we have carried our selves so unreverently, and undevoutly in them, when we were therein.[33]

In the first years of the seventeenth century the rubrics of the Corpus Christi procession were codified in the official liturgical books of the Roman Rite, beginning with the publication in 1600 of the first edition of the *Caeremoniale Episcoporum*, a manual that supplemented the *Roman Missal* by providing instructions for ceremonies in which the bishop was the celebrant or a participant. The 1600 *Caeremoniale*'s description of Benediction with the Blessed Sacrament at the conclusion of the Corpus Christi procession can scarcely be distinguished from the manner in which this ceremony is performed in our own day: ". . . he [the bishop celebrating] shall ascend to the altar, and taking the tabernacle [i.e., the monstrance] with the Most Holy Sacrament, holding it upraised with both hands and turning round to the people, he shall make with it the sign of the cross over the people, saying nothing meanwhile. After which, the Bishop shall set the Blessed Sacrament down again upon the altar and shall genuflect as above."[34]

In 1614 the first edition of another liturgical book, the *Roman Ritual*, was published, providing parish priests with rubrics for the Corpus Christi procession essentially the same as those formulated for bishops in the *Caeremoniale Episcoporum* (including instructions regarding exposition and Benediction of the Blessed Sacrament).[35] Throughout the seventeenth century the Vatican's Congregation of Sacred Rites issued a host of decrees further defining the proper celebration of these processions.

The codification of the Forty Hours Prayer was accomplished during the first half of the eighteenth century with the promulgation in 1705 of the *Clementine Instruction*, a detailed document governing the proper celebration of this devotion for the Diocese of Rome, issued by authority of Pope Clement XI (1700-1721); under a later Pontiff, Clement XII (1730-1740), the document was revised twice, first in 1730 and again in 1736, the latter becoming the definitive edition of the *Clementine Instruction*.[36] Although issued specifically for Rome, the instruction set the standard for the Forty Hours Prayer throughout the world. Concessions were eventually granted allowing the substitution of three days of daytime adoration in place of forty continuous hours of exposition in parishes where nocturnal adoration was not feasible. Among the more beautiful features of this devotion enjoined in the *Clementine Instruction* were the requirement of at least twenty lit candles on or around the altar, and the ringing of church bells the day before exposition began.[37]

Austria's Royal Family, the Hapsburgs, were in the eighteenth century great proponents and defenders of Eucharistic devotion, with the reigning monarch regularly participating in the annual Corpus Christi procession. Nor was this dedication to Eucharistic adoration divorced from or in competition with participation in the liturgical celebration of this sacrament; thus the famed Queen Maria Teresa (1717-1780) insisted that her children attend daily Mass, and it was essentially the norm for Austria's sovereigns to receive

Holy Communion daily. Among the general population it was largely through the efforts of the Jesuits, encouraging frequent reception of the sacrament during the seventeenth and eighteenth centuries, that the number of those approaching the altar for Holy Communion in Austria drastically rose over the period. Hence at the Jesuits' house in Graz the number of Communions increased from 45,000 in 1637 to 85,000 forty-six years later and to 120,000 by 1765. Similarly, at the Basilica of Maria Taferl near Melk, the number of communicants progressively increased from 36,000 in 1660 to 71,000 in 1702, 186,000 in 1751, and climbed to 250,000 by 1760. The Capuchins likewise contributed to this burgeoning Eucharistic renaissance among the peoples of Austria and Bohemia.[38]

In eighteenth-century Italy the members of the newly founded Passionist Order were key figures in the promotion of Eucharistic adoration outside the Mass, particularly evening adoration, which made it possible for those laboring in the fields during the day to participate.[39]

ENDNOTES

1. Fr. Joseph McKenna, "Quarant' Ore or the Forty Hours' Prayer," *Clergy Review*, Vol. 6, Sept. 1933, p. 186; Constanzo Cargnoni, "Quarante-Heures," *Dictionnaire de Spiritualité*, Vol. 12, Tome II, 1985-1986, col. 2703; Fr. Herbert Thurston, SJ, *Lent and Holy Week: Chapters on Catholic Observance and Ritual*, 1904, pp. 126-127.
2. McKenna, p. 187.
3. Ibid., p. 187; Fr. Fabian Fehring, OFM Cap., "Capuchin Origin and Propagation of the Quarant' Ore," *Round Table of Franciscan Research*, Vol. 17, Jan. 1952, pp. 15-16; Thurston, pp. 126-128.
4. Nathan Mitchell, *Cult and Controversy: The Worship of the Eucharist Outside Mass*, 1982, p. 312; McKenna, p. 187; Cargnoni, cols. 2703-2706.
5. Mitchell, p. 312.
6. Cargnoni, cols. 2707-2708.
7. Ibid., col. 2709.
8. Ibid., col. 2710.
9. Fr. Herbert Thurston, SJ, "Our Popular Devotions: IV.-Benediction of the Blessed Sacrament: III.-The Benediction," *Month*, Aug. 1901, Vol. 98, pp. 187-188 (quotation on p. 188).
10. McKenna, pp. 188-189.
11. Ibid., pp. 189-190.
12. Ibid., p. 191.

13. Ibid.
14. Christopher Black, *Italian Confraternities in the Sixteenth Century*, 1989, pp. 99-100.
15. Fr. Harold Burton, *The Life of St. Francis de Sales*, Vol. I, 1925, pp. 248-253.
16. Francis G. Very, *The Spanish Corpus Christi Procession: A Literary and Folkloric Study*, 1962, pp. 15-16, 19-20.
17. Ibid., pp. 12, 13.
18. Ibid.
19. Ibid., p. 21.
20. Ibid., p. 24.
21. Ibid., pp. 35-36.
22. Ibid., p. 43.
23. Archdale King, *Eucharistic reservation in the Western Church*, 1965, p. 215. The discussion of monstrances that here follows is based largely upon James Monti's article "Sacred Vessels" that appeared in the May-June 1995 issue of *Catholic Heritage* magazine (p. 14).
24. King, Plate 20 (facing p. 211).
25. Abbé Jules Corblet, *Histoire Dogmatique, Liturgique et Archeologique du Sacrement de l'Eucharistie*, 1885, Vol. 2, pp. 324-325.
26. Ibid., Vol. II, pp. 330-331.
27. Ibid., Vol. II, p. 332.
28. Fr. Buteux, quoted in François Roustang, SJ, *An Autobiography of Martyrdom: Spiritual Writings of the Jesuits in New France*, 1964, p. 28.
29. *The Jesuit Relations and Allied Documents: Travels and Explorations of the Jesuit Missionaries in New France 1610-1791: Vol. XXVIII: Hurons, Iroquois, Lower Canada, 1645-1646*, ed. Reuben Gold Thwaites, 1898, pp. 193-197 (quote on pp. 193-195; punctuation and capitalization modernized by James Monti).
30. *Acta Sanctorum*, August, Tome 5, 1863 ed., p. 959.
31. Sr. Mary Alphonsus, OSSR, *St. Rose of Lima: Patroness of the Americas*, 1968, pp. 274-278.
32. Joseph de Guibert, SJ, "Capilla (André)," *Dictionnaire de Spiritualité*, Tome 2, Pt. 1, 1937, col. 118.
33. Fr. Andrew Capella, *A Manual of Spiritual Exercises* (1625; rpt. 1971, Scholar Press [English Recusant Literature, 1558-1640, Vol. 59]), pp. 117-119.
34. Thurston, p. 187.
35. Mitchell, pp. 204, 341.
36. McKenna, p. 192.
37. *Clementine Instruction*, Nos. 6, 10, and 11, in Congregation of Sacred Rites, *Decreta Authentica Congregationis Sacrorum Rituum, Vol. IV: Commentaria ad Instructionem Clementis XI pro Expositione SS. Sacramenti in Forma XL Horarum et Suffragia atque Adnotationes*, 1900, pp. 22, 37.

38. Jean Berenger, "The Austrian Church," in *Church and Society in Catholic Europe of the Eighteenth Century*, ed. William Callahan and David Higgs, 1979, pp. 101-103.

39. Mario Rosa, "The Italian Churches," in *Church and Society in Catholic Europe of the Eighteenth Century*, p. 73.

Chapter 12

Eucharistic Adoration from the Eighteenth Century to the Present

> *One thing have I asked of the Lord,*
> *that will I seek after;*
> *that I may dwell in the house of the Lord*
> *all the days of my life,*
> *to behold the beauty of the Lord,*
> *and to inquire in his temple.*
>
> — Psalm 27:4

As we have already seen, the "rediscovery" of the living presence of our Lord in the reserved Eucharist prompted a massive response that evoked with sweeping grandeur the glory both of Christ's victory over sin and death in the Resurrection and of His long-awaited Second Coming when His triumph will be complete. But there was another dimension to the mystery of the abiding Eucharistic Presence, a dimension that revealed itself to those willing to venture into the restful quiet of a darkened church, where under the flicker of the sanctuary lamp the only voice to be heard was that which spoke within the deep recesses of the human heart. The realization steadily deepened that prayer before the Blessed Sacrament was nothing less than an intimate conversation with a living Person — the risen Christ — about as close as we can come in this life to talking with God face to face.

As this realization permeated the collective consciousness of the Church, it served to foster a spirituality that in a certain sense re-created so many of the beautiful scenes from the Gospels of troubled souls in need going to Christ to beg the healing of soul or body. Among the first to give voice to this new awareness was Saint Alphonsus Liguori (1696-1787), who discovered his calling to the priesthood on his knees before the monstrance, as had the first Apostles summoned by their Master along the Sea of Galilee. Thus in his classic *Visits to the Most Blessed Sacrament and the Blessed Virgin Mary*, first published in 1745,[1] he observes: "Oh, what a delight it is to be in front of an altar and speak familiarly with Jesus in the Blessed Sacrament: asking him to forgive our offenses; to reveal our needs to him, as a friend to a friend; and to ask for his love and the fullness of his grace."[2]

Like the Syro-Phoenician woman in the Gospels who, though not a Jew, longed to find healing for her daughter at the feet of Christ, so too was there a young Episcopalian woman, a beautiful socialite of late eighteenth-century New York, who longed for the solace of bringing her broken heart into the intimate presence of her Redeemer. It was during a sojourn in Italy that Elizabeth Ann Seton (1774-1821) lost her beloved husband and was plunged into inconsolable grief. Amid her sorrow she came to notice that her Italian friends — the Filicchi family with whom she stayed — possessed a consolation she lacked. Telling her sister Ann of it in February of 1804, she wrote:

> My sister dear, how happy would we be if we believed what these dear souls believe, that they possess God in the Sacrament and that he remains in their churches and is carried to them when they are sick; oh my — when they carry the Blessed Sacrament under my window while I face the full loneliness and sadness of my case, I cannot stop the tears at the thought. My God, how happy would I be even so far away from all so dear, if I could find you in the church as they do (for there is a chapel in the very house of Mr. Filicchi); how many things I would say to you of the sorrows of my heart and the sins of my life. . . .
>
> The other day in a moment of excessive distress I fell on my knees without thinking when the Blessed Sacrament passed by

and cried in an agony to God *to bless me* if he were *there*, that my whole soul desired only him. . . .[3]

Some years later, following her entrance into the Catholic faith, Mother Seton recounted the state of her thoughts before her conversion when in her grief she looked to the Catholic belief in the Real Presence for hope and courage: ". . . how many thoughts on the happiness of those who possessed this, the blessed faith of Jesus still on earth with them, and how I should enjoy to encounter every misery of life with the heavenly consolation of speaking heart to heart with Him in His tabernacles, and the security of finding Him in His churches."[4]

Elizabeth Seton returned a Catholic to her native America, where over the course of the nineteenth century, Eucharistic devotion was to flourish under the influence of such figures as Saint John Neumann (1811-1860), who as Archbishop of Philadelphia introduced the systematic observance of the Forty Hours devotion in the United States.[5] A French visitor to our country during this period (pre-1881) has left a touching description of what he observed among the worshipers in a typical Irish-American parish church: "If you wait until the end of mass, you will be further edified. You will see them approach as near as possible to the high altar, before which they bow profoundly, making several genuflections, and frequently remain for a moment almost prostrate to the ground. . . . At the door of the church they take holy water, sign themselves with it repeatedly, and sprinkle their faces with it; then turning to the tabernacle they make a last genuflection, as if to bid farewell to our Lord, and finally withdraw."[6]

For another convert, England's Venerable John Henry Newman (1801-1890), who like Saint Paul became an ardent apostle of the religion he had originally sought to refute, the discovery of the continuing presence of Christ in the reserved Blessed Sacrament came, not before, but rather after, his entrance into Catholicism, serving as an unanticipated consolation of such magnitude that to him the thought of Christian worship devoid of it seemed in retrospect insipid by comparison: ". . . I could not have fancied the extreme, ineffable comfort of being in the same house with Him who cured the sick and taught His disciples. . . . When I have been in Churches abroad [before becoming a Catholic], I have religiously abstained from acts of worship, though it was a most soothing comfort to go into them — nor did I know what was going on; I neither under-stood nor tried to understand the Mass service — and I did not know, or did not observe, the tabernacle Lamp — but now after tasting of the awful delight of worshipping God in His Temple, how unspeakably cold is the idea of a Temple without that Divine Pres-ence! One is tempted to say what is the meaning, what is the use of it?"[7]

On another occasion Newman made a similar observation as he contemplated with unceasing amazement what he later described as "the Great Presence, which makes a Catholic Church different from every other place in the world":[8] "It is really most wonderful to see this Divine Presence looking out almost into the open streets from the various Churches. . . . I never knew what worship was, as an objective fact, till I entered the Catholic Church. . . ."[9]

Over thirty years after his conversion, Newman discovered that a visit to Milan awakened in him not only a closeness to Saint Augustine, Saint Monica, and Saint Ambrose,[10] the drama of whose lives were played out in large measure in this ancient city, but also the recognition that the reserved Eucharist in the tabernacle is a great bond of Christian unity, for it is the same Christ that is found in each and every Catholic church: ". . . here are a score of Churches which are open to the passer by . . . and the Blessed Sacrament ready for the worshipper even before he enters. There is nothing which has brought home to me so much the Unity of the Church, as the presence of its Divine Founder and Life wherever I go — All places are, as it were, one. . . ."[11]

Captivated by "the distant glimmering Lamp which betokens the Presence of our Undying Life, hidden but ever working,"[12] Newman saw in the abiding Eucharistic Presence an occasion to share in the privilege of the first disciples who had walked in the company of Christ and spoken with Him. The sense of wonder that Newman expresses in dwelling under the same roof with Christ in the tabernacle, of which he tells in a letter during his stay at Oscott College (Maryvale) as a new convert in 1846, was to remain with him throughout his life: "I am writing next room to the Chapel — It is such an incomprehensible blessing to have Christ in bodily presence in one's house, within one's walls, as swallows up all other privileges and destroys, or should destroy, every pain. To know that He is close by — to be able again and again through the day to go in to Him. . . ."[13]

The spiritual revolution that transformed the lowly French hamlet of Ars into a center of pilgrimage for thousands began in the still of the night, when Ars's new curé — John Vianney (1786-1859) — would rise from his sleep to spend the long hours before sunrise prostrate in the presence of the Blessed Sacrament, pleading for the salvation of his people: "My God, grant me the conversion of my parish; I am willing to suffer all my life whatsoever it may please thee to lay upon me . . . only let my people be converted."[14] Determined to do his utmost to teach his parishioners the rudiments of the faith, he used the sacristy of his church as a study hall for himself, poring over catechetical, ascetical, and homiletic books in sight of the tabernacle, which he could gaze upon through the open door.[15]

Gradually the shepherd had the consolation of seeing his flock following his example — by 1825, according to the schoolmaster of Ars, "even before the great rush of pilgrims, besides M. le Curé, who spent all his time before the Blessed Sacrament, there were always people engaged in prayer in the church. . . . I cannot recollect a single occasion when, on entering the church, I did not find someone or other in adoration."[16] Among these adorers was a farmer — Louis Chaffangeon — of whom the Curé of Ars was wont to speak time and again, and whose example served to demonstrate that Eucharistic worship was the province of the workingman as well as of the priest and the housewife: "A few years ago there died a man of this parish, who, entering the church in the morning to pray before setting out for the fields, left his hoe at the door and then became wholly lost in God. A neighbour who worked not far from him, and thus used to see him in the fields, wondered at his absence. On his way home he bethought himself of looking into the church, thinking that the man might be there. As a matter of fact, he did find him in the church. 'What are you doing here all this time?' he asked. And the other made reply: 'I look at the good God, and he looks at me.' "[17]

In the years that followed, the influence of Saint John Vianney and of the farmer Louis Chaffangeon could be seen in the row of muddied tools that lined the wall of Ars's church as their owners paused to pray inside.[18]

While many are familiar with the nineteenth-century French sculptor Auguste Rodin, few are aware that this renowned artist pursued his calling upon the advice of one of the greatest apostles of Eucharistic worship in the history of the Church, Saint Peter Julian Eymard (1811-1868).[19] Even as a child Peter Eymard felt drawn to the Real Presence of His Creator in the Blessed Sacrament. Once, when he was five, his sister discovered him in church standing upon a stepladder behind the tabernacle, pressing his ear to the vessel in order, he explained, to hear "Him" better.[20] He grew up to become the founder of an order expressly devoted to the promulgation of Eucharistic adoration — the Society of the Most Blessed Sacrament — consisting of members in three categories: those totally devoted to a life of perpetual adoration, those engaged in a mixed sacerdotal life of action and contemplation, and a "third order" of priests and laity observing a rule consonant with their respective states in life.[21] Not surprisingly it was Father Eymard who promoted the practice of priests committing themselves to spending an hour daily before the tabernacle.[22]

For Peter Julian Eymard the mission of a Eucharistic adorer did not merely begin and end at the door of the church; the adorer was to go forth to live a life consonant with what he had experienced on his knees before the tabernacle. This concept of the adorer as an ambassador of the Eucharistic Christ is made implicit in Peter Eymard's writings on the Blessed Sacrament,[23] which are indeed extensive. He composed reflections upon the Eucharist that in the nearly one and a half centuries since they were first set to paper have lost nothing of their beauty; one example will suffice to demonstrate this:

> . . . Jesus wishes to reign in me; that is His whole ambition. That is the kingliness of His love; that is the end of His Incarnation, of His Passion, of His Eucharist.
>
> To reign in me, to reign over me; to reign in my soul, in my heart, over my whole life, over my love, that is the second heaven of His glory.

> Oh! Yes, Lord Jesus, come and reign! Let my body be Your temple, my heart Your throne, my will Your devoted servant; let me be Yours forever, living only of You and for You![24]

The personage of Saint Thérèse of Lisieux (1873-1897) scarcely needs any introduction — her childlike expression of the wisdom of Carmelite spirituality has made her name almost a household word in twentieth-century Catholic parishes and homes. Yet as in the case of Saint Francis of Assisi, Thérèse's popularity has not led to a sufficient recognition of the depth of her Eucharistic piety. Indeed, the loving trust of God that characterized her thought permeated her prayer before the reserved Blessed Sacrament:

> Frequently, only silence can express my prayer; however, this divine Guest of the Tabernacle understands all, even the silence of a child's soul filled with gratitude![25]
>
> When I am before the Tabernacle, I can say only one thing to Our Lord: "My God, you know that I love You." And I feel my prayer does not tire Jesus; knowing the helplessness of His poor little spouse, He is content with her good will.[26]

Thérèse delighted in the personal dimension of Eucharistic adoration — that Christ remains in the reserved Sacrament not only for the Church as a whole but specifically for each and every soul that comes to Him: ". . . think, then, that Jesus is there in the Tabernacle expressly for *you*, for *you alone*; He is burning with the desire to enter your heart. . . ."[27]

Far from finding Eucharistic adoration an impediment to love of neighbor, Thérèse recognized that in drawing near to Christ in the reserved Sacrament we are in turn drawn nearer to our family and friends — that the tabernacle is the place where the bonds of Christian love and friendship are sustained and renewed. Thus in a letter to her close friend Marie Guerin, Thérèse observed that "the Tabernacle is the house of love where our two souls are enclosed,"[28] while in another letter to her sister Leonie she requested, ". . . think of me in the presence of Jesus as much as I think of you."[29]

In the life of a contemporary of Saint Thérèse's, the young Italian laywoman Saint Gemma Galgani (1878-1903), who like Saint

Francis was a recipient of the stigmata, we find a perfect illustration of the fact that among the saints ardent devotion to the reserved Blessed Sacrament was invariably joined to a love for Mass and Holy Communion. Amidst her daily round of household chores, the two pillars of Gemma's spiritual life were morning Mass with Holy Communion, and in the evening Eucharistic adoration and Benediction, as her spiritual director, the Passionist Father Germanus of St. Stanislaus, testifies in his biography of the girl:

> Although this blessed child was always deep in thought, and always found herself in spirit before the sacred Tabernacle, yet she was not fully satisfied unless she could go to church, and there adore her hidden God. In order to avoid singularity, which she always detested, she contented herself with going to the church only twice a day; in the morning when she went to hear Mass and receive Holy Communion, and in the evening for the public Adoration. . . . On entering the sacred building she turned her first anxious gaze towards the Tabernacle. Then devoutly recollected and as if quite alone before the Altar of the Blessed Sacrament she remained kneeling motionless in prayer. . . . "Oh! what immense happiness and joy," she has said, "my heart feels before Jesus in the Blessed Sacrament! And if Jesus would allow me to enter the sacred Tabernacle, where He, Soul, Body, Blood and Divinity is present, should I not be in Paradise?"[30]

It was in one of her many letters to Father Germanus that Gemma was to ask this haunting question: "Is it possible that there are souls who do not understand what the Blessed Eucharist is? Who are insensible to the Divine Presence. . . ?"[31]

The promulgation of Eucharistic adoration has always depended in large part upon the apostolic zeal of the Church's pastors. Perhaps no better example of this can be found at the threshold of our own century than that of the Venerable John Baptist Scalabrini (1839-1905), who as Bishop of the northern Italian Diocese of Piacenza from 1875 to 1905 distinguished himself not only as a champion of the working classes, of Italian immigrants, and of improvements in catechetical instruction, but also exerted himself with tireless determination to make prayer before the reserved Sacrament part of the very fabric of his people's spiritual life: "When the Lord, in His infinite goodness and mercy, shall grant that I see devotion to the Eucharist deeply rooted in my beloved diocese, then there will be no more for me to do but to exclaim with the prophet Simeon: 'Now thou dost release thy servant, O Master, in peace because my eyes have seen the Savior thou hast given us loved, thanked and venerated by those who are in the time and shall be in eternity my joy and my crown!' "[32]

Beautifully alluding to the Eucharistic Presence in the tabernacle — a word that means "tent" — Bishop Scalabrini described the parish church as "the home of all the faithful, because it is the house of God in which he has pitched his tent in the midst of our tents. . . ."[33] Good shepherd that he was, Scalabrini preached what he himself so intensely lived, spending hours prostrate in prayer before the Blessed Sacrament, and rising even in the middle of the night to visit His Eucharistic Lord in his private chapel.[34] Whenever visiting a church or seminary, he would first direct his steps to the tabernacle in order to greet Him whom he referred to as the "Master of the house."[35] It was before the tabernacle, as well as from his confessor, that the bishop sought guidance, and he was wont to say that it was after visiting the Blessed Sacrament that he was able to arrive at a certainty in his decisions.[36] He likewise implored others to seek discernment at the feet of the Master: " 'I would like you to read this letter before the Holy Tabernacle,' he wrote one priest. 'There you will receive the light and the strength to carry out my advice.' And in letters to others we read phrases like these: 'Kneel for a moment before the Blessed Sacrament and then give me your answer; I will resign myself to the will of God and accept it.' — 'Prostrate yourself before the Tabernacle. . . .' — 'Be of good heart and do not be caught up in vain fears. Do your duty with prudence, but openly. Why be discouraged? Do you not have Jesus Christ in the Tabernacle who keeps saying to you *quare dubitasti'* [Mt 14:31: '. . . why did you doubt?']?"[37]

As in the case of Saint Thérèse of Lisieux, prayer before the Blessed Sacrament possessed a personal and very human dimension for Bishop Scalabrini; at the foot of the tabernacle he experienced the joy of the Communion of Saints, knowing that in the Eucharistic Presence he adored side by side with those of his family who had passed from this world before him: "Adoration! It is no little comfort to me, I confess, when before the Tabernacle I think that all those whom I have loved here on earth are adoring with me the same God — they face to face, I under the mystic veil. Members of the Church Triumphant and the Church Militant, we are kneeling before the same Redeemer, the same Father. My prayer rises to melt into the hymn of love which my dear ones beyond the tomb are lifting around the throne of the Lamb in their eternal dwelling. I meet them again in this sacred assembly."[38]

Scarcely fifty miles to the north of Piacenza, Bishop Scalabrini's field of labor, was the Diocese of Bergamo, where in 1895 a four-teen-year-old seminarian had carefully copied out for himself a series of "Rules of life to be observed by young men who wish to make progress in the life of piety and study"; these rules he would keep the rest of his life. Among the resolutions that the young Angelo Roncalli had written down was the following: "Visit the Blessed Sacrament and some church or chapel where there is a special devotion to the Blessed Virgin, at least once a day."[39]

It was sixty-four years later — on January 25, 1959 — that Angelo Roncalli, as Pope John XXIII (1958-1963), made his historic announcement that he would convene a new council of the Church — Vatican II. During July of that same year, in a message to the National Eucharistic Congress of France, John XXIII stated in no uncertain terms the place he desired Eucharistic adoration to have in the lives of the faithful, even as preparations were under way for a council that would determine the future course of Catholic worship:

> May We offer you yet another suggestion? In addition to the solemn celebration of Holy Mass and the general Communion of different groups of the faithful, is a Eucharistic Congress anything other than a long and fervent "visit to the Blessed Sacrament"? Now you must have observed, as We have, that in our day many souls neglect this touching practice of Catholic life, which is so dear to pious souls and which consists in recollecting oneself in silence at the foot of the tabernacle in order to restock one's soul with God's gifts. There are even some who, led by ideas foreign to traditional piety, seem to look upon this practice as of minor importance.

It is Our fond wish that all participating in the congress at Lyons return to their homes convinced of the excellence of this practice and strive to make it appreciated and loved by others. Pause for a moment and think of the long hours which St. John Vianney spent in the beginning of his pastoral life, alone in his church before the Blessed Sacrament; think of the outpourings of faith and love of this great soul at the feet of his Master, and of the marvelous fruits of sanctity which he and so many others received as a result of these ardent Eucharistic prayers. There is no doubt that a flood of graces would descend on your families and on your country if more and more souls, enlightened and supported by the example of their shepherds, would become docile pupils in the school of the holy Curé of Ars. . . .[40]

Pope John presided over the formal opening of the Second Vatican Council in October of 1962, but he did not live to see its completion. The task of finishing and implementing the work of Vatican II would be left to his successor and close friend, Giovanni Battista Montini — Pope Paul VI (1963-1978). In January of 1964, little more than six months after his accession to the See of Peter, Pope Paul journeyed to the Holy Land and, on the evening of January 5, knelt upon the floor of the room on Jerusalem's Mount Sion traditionally believed to have been the actual site of the Last Supper.[41]

With the memory of the very spot where the gift of the Eucharist had first been given to the world undoubtedly still fresh in his mind, Pope Paul VI issued in September of 1965 his definitive instruction on this sacrament, the encyclical *Mysterium Fidei*. Coming only three months before the close of the council, the document stands as an authoritative expression of the genuine "Spirit of Vatican II" as it applies to the Church's understanding of the Eucharist. Finding it necessary to refute a number of gravely erroneous opinions regarding the nature of the Eucharist that had arisen of late in certain quarters, the Pontiff also sought to reemphasize the continued importance and value of adoring the Blessed Sacrament outside of Mass:

In the course of the day the faithful should not omit to visit the Blessed Sacrament, which according to the liturgical laws must be kept in the churches with great reverence in a most honorable location. Such visits are a proof of gratitude, an expression of love, an acknowledgment of the Lord's presence.

No one can fail to understand that the Divine Eucharist bestows upon the Christian people an incomparable dignity. Not only while the sacrifice is offered and the sacrament is received, but as long as the Eucharist is kept in our churches and oratories, Christ is truly the Emmanuel, that is, "God with us." Day and night He is in our midst, He dwells with us, full of grace and truth. He restores morality, nourishes virtues, consoles the afflicted, strengthens the weak. He proposes His own example to those who come to Him that all may learn to be, like Himself, meek and humble of heart and to seek not their own interests but those of God.

Anyone who approaches this august Sacrament with special devotion and endeavors to return generous love for Christ's own infinite love, will experience and fully understand — not without spiritual joy and fruit — how precious is the life hidden with Christ in God and how great is the value of converse with Christ, for there is nothing more consoling on earth, nothing more efficacious for advancing along the road of holiness.[42]

Pope Paul VI's concept of the Blessed Sacrament in the tabernacle as "the living heart of each of our churches," expressed in his 1968 *Credo of the People of God*,[43] is echoed in the pages of a famous English novel written earlier this century — Evelyn Waugh's *Brideshead Revisited* (1944). For the character Cordelia, who like her mother loved "popping" into the family chapel "at odd times" to visit the Blessed Sacrament,[44] the subsequent removal of the reserved Eucharist was a most painful loss — a loss that she attempted to explain to a family friend, the agnostic Charles Ryder: "They've closed the chapel at Brideshead. . . . Mummy's requiem was the last mass said there. After she was buried the priest came in — I was there alone. I don't think he saw me — and took out the altar stone and put it in his bag; then he burned the wads of wool with the holy oil on them and threw the ash outside; he emptied the holy water stoup and blew out the lamp in the sanctuary and left the tabernacle open and empty, as though from now on it was always to be Good Friday. I suppose none of this makes any sense to you, Charles, poor agnostic. I stayed there till he was gone, and then, suddenly, there wasn't any chapel there any more, just an oddly decorated room. I can't tell you what it felt like."[45]

Years later, after Charles had witnessed the deathbed conversion of the family patriarch, what Cordelia had said on this occasion did finally begin to make sense to him; so it was that while serving as a soldier in World War II, upon finding the Brideshead Chapel a chapel again, with the Blessed Sacrament returned to the tabernacle, Charles the "poor agnostic" knelt to say "a prayer, an ancient, newly learned form of words."[46] Upon leaving he reflected upon the Divine Presence he had found in that chapel and what that Presence has meant to so many other soldiers of ages past and present: ". . . a small red flame — a beaten-copper lamp of deplorable design, relit before the beaten-copper doors of a tabernacle; the flame which the old knights saw from their tombs, which they saw put out; that flame burns again for other soldiers, far from home, farther, in heart, than Acre or Jerusalem . . . there I found it this morning, burning anew among the old stones."[47]

It is truly ironic that, when in the late 1960s and early 1970s the Church eventually issued revised rubrics and instructions governing the various forms of Eucharistic worship outside of Mass, the perception was rife that the Church had made her own the anti-devotional mentality of certain liturgists who frowned upon adoration of the reserved Sacrament as an obsolete and even harmful relic of an unenviable past. Quite to the contrary, the Congregation for Divine Worship's June 1973 instruction *On Holy Communion and the Worship of the Eucharistic Mystery Outside of Mass* provides one of the most eloquent rationales for adoration of the reserved Eucharist ever given:

> The same piety which moves the faithful to eucharistic adoration attracts them to a deeper participation in the paschal mystery. It makes them respond gratefully to the gifts of Christ who by his humanity continues to pour divine life upon the members of his body. Living with Christ the Lord, they achieve a close familiarity with him and in his presence pour out their hearts for themselves and for those dear to them; they pray for peace and

for the salvation of the world. Offering their entire lives with Christ to the Father in the Holy Spirit, they draw from this wondrous exchange an increase of faith, hope and love. Thus they nourish the proper disposition to celebrate the memorial of the Lord as devoutly as possible and to receive frequently the bread given to us by the Father.

The faithful should make every effort to worship Christ the Lord in the sacrament, depending upon the circumstances of their own life. Pastors should encourage them in this by example and word.[48]

Far from imposing new limitations upon Eucharistic devotions, the 1973 instruction actually does away with a number of the pre-Vatican II restrictions as to precisely when and where exposition in a monstrance may take place. What restrictions do remain are largely a repeat of regulations set in place long before the Second Vatican Council. Hence none of these things can honestly be interpreted as a postconciliar "putdown" of Eucharistic devotions. Moreover, both this document and the 1970 *Sacramentary* of Pope Paul VI continue to require those passing before the Blessed Sacrament (whether during Mass or at other times) to honor the Real Presence with the act of *genuflection*.[49]

Three years after the Holy See's new instruction on Eucharistic worship was promulgated, delegates from around the world converged upon the city of Philadelphia for the Forty-first International Eucharistic Congress. On August 3, 1976, the universally loved Mother Teresa of Calcutta, foundress of the Missionary Sisters of Charity, addressed the assembly. Speaking of life in her own religious community, she demonstrated that personal Eucharistic adoration in no way poses a conflict with the postconciliar emphasis upon addressing the material needs of humanity: "To be able to live this life of vows, those four vows, we need our life to be woven with the Eucharist. That's why we begin our day with Jesus in the Holy Eucharist. With Him, we go forward. And when we come back in the evening we have one hour of adoration before Jesus in the Blessed Sacrament, and [at] this you will be surprised, that we have not had to cut down our work for the poor, the ten hours or twelve hours of service that we give have not been cut down. The one hour of adoration is the greatest gift God could give a congregation because it has brought us so close to each other. We love each other better, but I think we love the poor with greater and deeper faith and love."[50]

Among those present in Philadelphia for the 1976 International Eucharistic Congress was the Archbishop of Cracow, Poland: Cardinal Karol Wojtyla. When on the morning of September 29, 1978, he was informed of the death of Pope John Paul I, he immediately sought refuge and strength before the tabernacle in his private chapel[51]; little more than two weeks later he became Pope John Paul II.

In February of 1980, less than a year and a half into his pontificate, Pope John Paul II issued an apostolic letter on the subject of the Eucharist, *Dominicae Cenae*, which, like the encyclical *Mysterium Fidei* of Pope Paul VI, sought to correct and clarify certain misunderstandings regarding the celebration of this sacrament, and with particular emphasis, to reaffirm the Church's commitment to the worship of the reserved Eucharist:

> Adoration of Christ in this Sacrament of love must also find expression *in various forms of Eucharistic devotion*: personal prayer before the Blessed Sacrament, hours of adoration, periods of exposition — short, prolonged and annual (Forty Hours) — Eucharistic benediction, Eucharistic processions, Eucharistic Congresses. . . .
>
> . . . The Church and the world have a great need of Eucharistic worship. Jesus waits for us in this Sacrament of love. Let us be generous with our time in going to meet him in adoration and in contemplation that is full of faith and ready to make reparation for the great faults and crimes of the world. May our adoration never cease.[52]

Implicit in the Holy Father's wish that "our adoration never cease" is the hope that Catholics will always remain acutely conscious of the Real Presence whenever they find themselves near the Eucharistic Species — a consciousness that is expressed in exterior actions as well as within the recesses of the heart. Only a few months before the issuance of *Dominicae Cenae*, on a pastoral visit to Ireland in September of 1979, Pope John Paul II went out of his way to stress the intrinsic value of even the smallest or most routine acts of reverence toward the Blessed Sacrament as professions of faith and love: ". . . dear brothers and sisters, every act of reverence, every genuflection that you make before the Blessed Sacrament, is important because it is an act of faith in Christ, an act of love for Christ. And every Sign of the Cross and gesture of respect made each time you pass a church is also an act of faith."[53]

When under Pope John Paul II the new *Code of Canon Law* was promulgated in 1983, it specifically authorized the continued observation of Corpus Christi processions (with the permission of the local bishop), and required that throughout the year churches be open at least part of the day to facilitate the Eucharistic adoration of the faithful:

> *Canon 944:* Wherever in the judgement of the diocesan Bishop it can be done, a procession through the streets is to be held, especially on the solemnity of the Body and Blood of Christ, as a public witness of veneration of the Blessed Eucharist.[54]
>
> *Canon 937:* Unless there is a grave reason to the contrary, a church in which the blessed Eucharist is reserved is to be open to the faithful for at least some hours every day, so that they can pray before the blessed Sacrament.[55]

Two years later (1985), detailed rubrics for contemporary Corpus Christi processions were issued by the Holy See in a new edition of the *Caeremoniale Episcoporum* — the *Ceremonial of Bishops.*[56]

Adamant in urging the preservation and promulgation of every established form of Eucharistic worship, the Holy Father has revealed in his words on the subject that his commitment to such adoration is personal as well as pastoral; thus in his homily for the Feast of Corpus Christi on June 15, 1995, he shared with those present his own fond memories of the Corpus Christi processions he had participated in as a child and later as a priest and bishop.[57] It is undoubtedly from years of deep reflection upon the rich significance of this annual tradition that

Pope John Paul is able to speak of it time and again with poetic beauty, as he did while celebrating the Feast in Cremona, Italy, in June of 1992:

> In the procession, the public and solemn tribute to the Blessed Sacrament, we expressed visibly the communion to which it commits us and we renewed the prophecy of new times when humanity, united in brotherhood through love, will progress as one on its earthly way, singing praises to its Lord. . . .
>
> Our procession through the streets and between the houses of the city is at the same time a celebration of the pilgrim Church and a shining example of what the Eucharist is meant to accomplish in social life. . . .
>
> Thus our procession together, side by side, listening together to the Word of God, one in heart and mind in our praise and thanksgiving to the Lord, reminds us that *we are a pilgrim Church.*[58]

Drawing upon his own personal experiences in Poland, the Holy Father gave in the course of his June 1995 Corpus Christi homily what is perhaps the most articulate and definitive explanation of the distinct character marking the Eucharistic adoration that takes place throughout the world on the evening of Holy Thursday — the most important of all Eucharistic vigils:

> At the end of the Holy Thursday liturgy, after the Mass of the Lord's Supper, the Blessed Sacrament is placed in a suitable chapel of reposition.
>
> *This Eucharistic procession has a characteristic note:* we pause beside Christ as the events of his Passion begin. We know, in fact, that the Last Supper was followed by the prayer in Gethsemane, by his arrest and trial, first before Annas and then before Caiaphas, high priest at the time. Thus on Holy Thursday we accompany Jesus on the way that leads him to the terrible hours of the Passion, a few hours before he was sentenced to death and crucifixion. In the Polish tradition the place of reposition for the Eucharist after the liturgy of the Lord's Supper is called "the dark chapel," because popular piety links it to the memory of the prison where our Lord Jesus spent the night between Thursday and Friday. A

night certainly not of repose but rather a further stage of physical and spiritual suffering.[59]

Pope John Paul sees Eucharistic adoration as an indispensable wellspring of spiritual renewal that ought to be found in every parish and religious community, a practice that fosters and sustains every state of life in the Church:

> I would also like to repeat my invitation to you to make *adoration of the Blessed Sacrament* a habitual practice in all Christian communities, in accordance with the Church's spirit and liturgical norms. This worship extends and prepares in the best possible way the meeting with Christ in the Sacrifice and Eucharistic Banquet. It is an expression of the whole Christian community's love and worship of its Lord. Priestly, religious, and missionary vocations will stem from this meeting with Christ in the tabernacle, and will bring the light of the Gospel to the ends of the earth; in this crucible of the "Love of loves," will be forged the apostolic spirit of lay Christians, witnesses to Christ amid temporal realities; in the intimacy of the tabernacle, the values that must reign in homes will receive new strength to make *the family a meeting place with God*, a centre that radiates faith, a school of Christian life. In the Bread which came down from heaven, the family will be able to find the support that will keep it united in the face of today's threats and will preserve it as a bastion of life, steadfast against the culture of death.[60]

The Holy Father is not slow to remind priests that in virtue of their sacerdotal vocation, which is primarily ordered to the celebration of the Eucharist, they have a particular obligation to deepen their commitment to Christ at the feet of their Master in the tabernacle:

> To priests the Council [Vatican II] also recommends, in addition to the daily celebration of the Mass, "personal devotion" to the Holy Eucharist, and particularly that "daily talk with Christ the Lord in their visit to the Blessed Sacrament" (*Presbyterorum ordinis*, n. 18). Faith in and love for the Eucharist cannot allow Christ's

presence in the tabernacle to remain alone (*Catechism of the Catholic Church*, n. 1418). Already in the Old Testament we read that God dwelt in a "tent" (or "tabernacle"), which was called the "meeting tent" (Ex 33:7). The meeting was desired by God. It can be said that in the tabernacle of the Eucharist too Christ is present in view of a dialogue with his new people and with individual believers. The presbyter is the first one called to enter this meeting tent, to visit Christ in the tabernacle for a "daily talk."[61]

Far from considering Eucharistic devotions as merely vestiges of a vanishing past reserved for the older generations, Pope John Paul II finds in the adoration of the reserved Sacrament a source of hope for the future. On the first day of the August 1993 World Youth Day weekend held in Denver, the Holy Father invited the young people gathered from around the globe for this event to avail themselves of the opportunity to enter into a heart-to-heart dialogue with Christ exposed for adoration through the coming night: "In *Holy Ghost Church* [Denver] your pilgrimage will lead you to *Christ present in the Holy Eucharist*. Praying before the Blessed Sacrament exposed, you can open your hearts to him, but you should especially listen to what he says to each of you. Christ's special words to young people are the following: *'Do not be afraid'* (Mt 10:31) and *'Come, follow me'* (Mt 19:21). Who knows what the Lord will ask of you, young people of America, sons and daughters of Europe, Africa, Asia and Oceania?"[62]

It was also in 1993, at the Forty-fifth International Eucharistic Congress in Seville, that John Paul II presented his most comprehensive exposition of the Church's teaching and present practices regarding the worship of the Eucharist outside of Mass. Amidst the magnificent setting of Seville's gigantic medieval cathedral, the Holy Father expressed his pronounced desire to see the growth of Eucharistic devotions, including perpetual adoration:

> It gives me great joy to kneel with you before Jesus in the Blessed Sacrament, in an *act of humble and fervent adoration*, in praise of the merciful God, in thanksgiving to the giver of all good gifts and in prayer to the One who "lives forever to make intercession" for us (cf. Heb 7:25). . . .

The continual adoration of Jesus in the Host was the *leitmotiv* of all the work of this International Eucharistic Congress. . . . In fact, the *continual adoration* — which took place in many churches throughout the city, and in some even at night — was an enriching feature that distinguished this Congress. If only this form of adoration, which ends tonight in a solemn Eucharistic vigil, would continue in the future too, so that in all the parishes and Christian communities the custom of some form of adoration of the Eucharist might take root.

Citing the example of a past bishop of Spain, the Holy Father reminded his audience that the abiding presence of our Savior in the tabernacle is a priceless gift that should not be neglected: "Here in Seville we must not fail to remember . . . Don Manuel Gonzalez, the Bishop of the abandoned tabernacles. He strove to remind everyone of Jesus' presence in the tabernacle, to which we sometimes respond so poorly. By his word and example, he never ceased to repeat that in the tabernacle of each church we possess a shining beacon, through contact with which our lives may be illuminated and transformed."

Well aware of the opposition to Eucharistic adoration in some quarters, the Holy Father reasserted the Church's teaching that devotion to the reserved Sacrament is grounded upon pastorally and theologically sound foundations:

Yes, dear brothers and sisters, it is important for us to live and teach others how to live the total mystery of the Eucharist: the sacrament of *Sacrifice,* of the *Banquet* and of the abiding *Presence* of Jesus Christ the Saviour. You know well that the various forms of Eucharistic devotion are both an extension of the sacrifice and of Communion and a preparation for them. Is it necessary to stress once again the deep theological and spiritual motivations which underlie devotion to the Blessed Sacrament outside the celebration of Mass? It is true that the reservation of the Sacrament was begun in order to take Communion to the sick and those absent from the celebration. However, as the *Catechism of the Catholic Church* says, "to deepen faith in the real presence of Christ in the Eucharist, the Church is aware of the meaning of silent adoration of the Lord present under the Eucharistic species" (n. 1379).

Pope John Paul further observed that Eucharistic adoration affords the worshiper with a preeminent means of conversing with God, enriching our own inner life while likewise nurturing a genuine social consciousness in the heart of the believer that can and should translate into actions in the service of our brothers and sisters in Christ: " 'But the hour is coming, and is now here, when true worshippers will worship the Father in Spirit and truth' (Jn 4:23), Jesus said to the Samaritan woman at the well in Sychar. Adoration of the Eucharist 'is the contemplation and recognition of the true Presence of Christ under the sacred species outside the celebration of the Mass. . . . It is a true encounter of dialogue, . . . through which we become open to the experience of God. . . . It is also a gesture of solidarity with the needs and the needy of the whole world' (Basic Document of the Congress, n. 25). And through its own spiritual dynamic, this Eucharistic adoration should lead to the service of love and justice for and with our brothers and sisters."[63]

Perpetual Adoration: Its Past and Present

In virtue of the current resurgence of perpetual adoration in many parishes across the United States and elsewhere, discussed by my distinguished coauthor, Father Benedict Groeschel, in Chapter 6, it would be appropriate to conclude the present chapter with a brief presentation of the rich history of this truly beautiful practice, so deservedly popular in our own day.

As we have seen in the extraordinary case of Lugo, Spain, the practice of perpetual adoration of the Eucharist has roots far deeper in Church history than many may realize — indeed it harks back in spirit to Saint Paul's recommendation to pray without ceasing (1 Thes 5:17). The concept of continuous prayer, prayer without interruption by day and by night, maintained unceasingly by relays of worshipers, arose by the first half of the fifth century. It was at this time that the Eastern monk Alexander the Akoimetos (died circa 430), having first introduced the practice of continuous recitation of the Psalms in Mesopotamia, brought this form of prayer to

Constantinople, where he is said to have founded the Monastery of *Akoimetoi* — the Monastery of "those who do not sleep." His community prayed in eight-hour shifts, twenty-four hours a day.[64] Within a century of Alexander's death, the custom of continuous, uninterrupted prayer appeared in the West, where it came to be known as *laus perennis* — "continuous praise." First instituted between the years 515 and 523 at the Abbey of Agaunum in what is now St.-Maurice-en-Valais, Switzerland, the *laus perennis* spread to other monastic communities in neighboring France, including St.-Denis, Lyons, Chalons, Laon, Remiremont, St.-Germain in Paris, St.-Medard in Soissons, and Luxeuil (where it was introduced in the late sixth century by the famous Irish missionary Saint Columban).[65]

With the church rather than the sanctuary gradually becoming the preferred location for the reservation of the Eucharist, the opportunity arose for such continuous prayer, carried out within the churches, to shift its focus to the sacramental presence of Christ. It seems more than a mere coincidence that Lugo's perpetual adoration is said to have arisen within only half a century or so of the introduction of perpetual prayer at the Abbey of Agaunum. In the year 1226 perpetual adoration of the Blessed Sacrament is known to have been introduced by France's King Louis VIII at a chapel in Avignon. Intended originally as a temporary devotion, Avignon's Eucharistic adoration proved to be so popular with the people that it was extended indefinitely and soon made perpetual, sustained over the centuries by a confraternity of laymen known as the Grey Penitents, who would pray before the Blessed Sacrament in relays, dressed while doing so in coarse gray robes. Although temporarily interrupted by the ravages of the French Revolution, Avignon's perpetual adoration has continued to the present day in a chapel not affiliated with any religious order — serving as a clear refutation to any modern claims that perpetual adoration should be kept out of parish churches.[66]

Although perpetual adoration was introduced elsewhere during the Middle Ages — such as at Portugal's Cistercian Monastery of Santa Maria d'Alcobaça in 1230[67] — the great flowering of this practice came in the seventeenth century. A number of French dioceses at this time took the extraordinary step of establishing perpetual adoration in every parish and chapel within their jurisdiction; such was the case in the dioceses of Chartres and Amiens beginning in 1658, in Lyons (1667), and in Evreux (1672).[68] A new religious order of women arose in France during the same century, instituted for the specific purpose of engaging in perpetual adoration — the Sisters of the Blessed Sacrament, or "Sacramentines," founded in 1639; soon thereafter another French order of women religious, the Benedictine Adoratrices, adopted the practice in 1654.[69]

In the nineteenth century more religious orders devoted to perpetual adoration appeared, including the contemplative branch of Saint Peter Julian Eymard's community of priests and brothers.[70] Other orders already in existence added perpetual adoration to their apostolates, as in the case of the Religious of the Perpetual Adoration, a community of nuns that was founded in sixteenth-century Switzerland but that adopted continuous prayer before the Blessed Sacrament in 1846.[71] By the early twentieth century, perpetual adoration was enjoying great success in Belgium, Germany, Italy, Mexico, Brazil, the United States, Canada, and the "Oceania" region of the Far East.[72]

After a period from the 1960s to the 1980s, when Eucharistic devotions were driven to virtual extinction in many places, a surprising and most welcome renaissance of the various forms of Eucharistic adoration, and in particular, perpetual adoration, has arisen in parishes from Connecticut to California. The enthusiasm with which this practice has been received wherever it is inaugurated is truly remarkable. Thus when in October of 1992 Our Lady of Grace parish in the Gravesend section of Brooklyn became the first parish in New York City to reintroduce perpetual adoration, nearly four hundred people volunteered to participate. In the words of the pastor Father Dominick Cutrone, ". . . we're all looking forward to the time we'll spend praying in the chapel, 'wasting time' with the Lord."[73]

Elsewhere, at the Cathedral of St. Peter in Marquette, Michigan, the inauguration of perpetual adoration in March of 1993 met with immediate success, with over five hundred people participating in just the first week; a holy hour specially designated for young people attracted twenty-four young men and women.[74] At St. Joseph's parish in Camillus, New York, where perpetual adoration was introduced in January of 1992, the late night and early morning hours for adoration have amazingly proved to be especially popular; as the coordinator of another perpetual adoration program at Most Holy Rosary Church in Syracuse, New York, explained, "There's an intimacy late at night that can't be achieved during the day. It's just you and Jesus. . . ."[75]

Perhaps most unexpected was the recent appearance (in January of 1995) of an article on perpetual adoration in *U.S. Catholic*, the same periodical that twenty-five years earlier had published a piece highly critical of Eucharistic devotions (as mentioned in the Introduction). Describing a very successful program of perpetual adoration at Sacred Heart Cathedral in Winona, Minnesota, the author of "Could You Not Wait One Hour with Me?" takes the reader through the different hours of a typical day in the church's Blessed Sacrament Chapel, and tells of the consolation and strength the parishioners have derived from this devotion:

> The 5:15 p.m. Mass has just let out, and as people disperse, a handful head for the chapel. Among them are an older man; a young woman and her two small children; and Lynn Kemmetmueller, a 24-year-old woman who recently received her bachelor's degree in biology. As the children wander around the church, Lynn genuflects before the tabernacle, makes the sign of the cross, and then kneels on the floor. She stays in this position, praying, for 20 minutes. When everyone else has left, she bows down, lying prostrate on the floor before the altar; it's her expression of reverence for the Eucharist.
>
> Lynn struggles with distractions during her hour, as most people do. Sometimes she's so tired, "it seems an effort even to breathe." But she believes that, even when she's unable to concentrate fully, her mere presence is in itself a form of prayer.
>
> "When I'm adoring Jesus, I'm not always aware of his love for me, and I can just imagine Jesus being more pleased with that kind of prayer because it's such an act of faith. When you're going through a time like that, you can just look up and say, 'I know you understand.' "[76]

Why is perpetual adoration, as well as the various other forms of Eucharistic devotion, proving to be so popular again? The late Stanley Joseph Ott, Bishop of Baton Rouge, Louisiana, commenting in August of 1992 upon the spread of perpetual adoration in his diocese, has left us with a very good answer: "Speak to anyone who prays before our Eucharistic Lord on a regular basis. Their joy and enthusiasm I believe will persuade you to give this devotion a try. Get the heart-warming experience of the two Emmaus disciples who exclaimed that 'our hearts were burning inside' when they were in the Lord's presence."[77]

ENDNOTES

1. Frederick M. Jones, CSSR, *Alphonsus de Liguori: The Saint of Bourbon Naples, 1696-1787*, 1992, pp. 190-191.
2. Quoted in Theolule Rey-Mermet, CSSR, *Alphonsus Liguori: Tireless Worker for the Most Abandoned*, 1989, p. 170.
3. *Italian Journal*, Feb. 24, 1804, in Fr. Michael L. Gaudoin-Parker, ed., *The Real Presence through the Ages*, 1993, p. 140.
4. St. Elizabeth Ann Seton, quoted in Madame Helene Bailly de Barberey, *Elizabeth Seton*, 1927, p. 355.
5. Fr. Michael J. Curley, CSSR, *Bishop John Neumann, C.SS.R.: Fourth Bishop of Philadelphia*, 1952, pp. 219-220.
6. Ann Taves, "Context and Meaning: Roman Catholic Devotion to the Blessed Sacrament in Mid-Nineteenth-Century America," *Church History*, Vol. 54, Dec. 1985, p. 482.
7. Letter to Mrs. J.W. Bowden, March 1, 1846, in *The Letters and Diaries of John Henry Newman: XI: Littlemore to Rome, October 1845 to December 1846*, ed. C.S. Dessain, 1961, p. 131.
8. *Loss and Gain: The Story of a Convert*, quoted in Ian Ker, *John Henry Newman: A Biography*, 1988, p. 335.
9. Letter to Henry Wilberforce, Sept. 24, 1846, in Dessain, pp. 252, 253.
10. Ker, pp. 324-325.
11. Letter to Mrs. J.W. Bowden, Oct. 4, 1846, in Dessain, p. 254.
12. Letter to Henry Wilberforce, Sept. 24, 1846, in ibid., p. 252.
13. Letter to Henry Wilberforce, Feb. 26, 1846, in ibid., p. 129.
14. Abbé Francis Trochu, *The Curé d'Ars: St. Jean-Marie-Baptiste Vianney (1786-1859)*, 1927 and 1977, p. 118.
15. Ibid., p. 131.
16. Ibid., p. 183.
17. St. John Vianney, quoted in ibid., p. 184.
18. Ibid., p. 225.
19. Ann Ball, *Modern Saints: Their Lives and Faces*, 1983, p. 61.
20. Ibid., p. 57.
21. Fr. Bernard Kelly, ed., *The Lives of the Fathers, Martyrs and Other Principal Saints: Volume V* (additions to the four volumes of Fr. Alban Butler's *Lives of the Saints*), 1961, p. 347.

22. Ibid., pp. 348-349.

23. See *Eucharistic Prayer Book: For the Members of the People's Eucharistic League* (Eymard Library, Vol. 6), 1948, pp. 171-200.

24. Ibid., pp. 208-209.

25. Letter to Marie Guerin, Nov. 17, 1892, in *Saint Thérèse of Lisieux: General Correspondence*, trans. John Clarke, OCD, Vol. II, 1988, p. 764.

26. Letter to Madame Guerin, Nov. 17, 1893, in ibid., Vol. II, p. 833.

27. Letter to Marie Guerin, May 30, 1889, in ibid., Vol. I, 1982, p. 568.

28. Circa July 27-29, 1890, in ibid., Vol. I, p. 642.

29. Nov. 5, 1893, in ibid., Vol. II, p. 832.

30. Fr. Germanus of St. Stanislaus, CP, *The Life of the Servant of God Gemma Galgani: An Italian Maiden of Lucca*, 1913, pp. 282-283.

31. Ibid., p. 281.

32. Bishop Scalabrini, quoted in Marco Caliaro and Mario Francesconi, *John Baptist Scalabrini: Apostle to Emigrants*, 1977, p. 268.

33. Ibid., p. 264.

34. Ibid., pp. 267-268.

35. Ibid., p. 268.

36. Ibid., p. 266.

37. Ibid., pp. 266-267.

38. Bishop Scalabrini, quoted in ibid., p. 268.

39. Pope John XXIII, *Journal of a Soul*, trans. Dorothy White, 1965, p. 5.

40. Pope John XXIII, Excerpt from a message to the National Eucharistic Congress of France, July 5, 1959, in *The Pope Speaks*, Vol. 6, Spring 1960, p. 192.

41. J.L. Gonzalez and T. Perez, *Paul VI* (English edition by Edward Heston, CSC), 1964, p. 120.

42. Pope Paul VI, *Encyclical Letter of His Holiness Pope Paul VI: Mystery of Faith: Mysterium Fidei*, Sept. 3, 1965 (Daughters of St. Paul edition), p. 26.

43. *The "Credo" of the People of God*, June 30, 1968 (Catholics United for the Faith edition), p. 19.

44. Evelyn Waugh, *Brideshead Revisited: The Sacred and Profane Memories of Captain Charles Ryder*, 1945 and 1973, p. 92.

45. Ibid., p. 220.

46. Ibid., p. 350.

47. Ibid., p. 351.

48. *On Holy Communion and the Worship of the Eucharistic Mystery Outside of Mass*, June 21, 1973, No. 80, in *The Rites of the Catholic Church as Revised by the Second Vatican Ecumenical Council* (Vol. I), 1983, pp. 504-505.

49. Ibid., No. 84; "General Instruction of the Roman Missal," No. 233, in *The Roman Missal: The Sacramentary*, 1974, p. 38.

50. *The Forty-First International Eucharistic Congress, August 1-8, 1976: A History*, ed. John B. DeMayo and Joseph J. Casino, 1978, p. 300.

51. James Oram, *The People's Pope: The Story of Karol Wojtyla of Poland*, 1979, p. 21.
52. Pope John Paul II, *Dominicae Cenae*, Feb. 24, 1980, No. 3, in *Vatican Council II: More Postconciliar Documents* (Vatican Collection, Vol. II), ed. Austin Flannery, OP, 1982, p. 67.
53. Pope John Paul II, Homily during Mass at Phoenix Park, Ireland, Sept. 29, 1979, in *Ireland: "In the Footsteps of St. Patrick,"* ed. Daughters of St. Paul, 1979, No. 7, p. 27.
54. *The Code of Canon Law, in English Translation*, trans./ed. Canon Law Society of Great Britain and Ireland, 1983, Bk. IV, Pt. I, Ch. 2, p. 171.
55. Ibid., p. 170.
56. *Ceremonial of Bishops*, trans. International Commission on English in the Liturgy, Liturgical Press, 1989, Ch. 15, Nos. 385-394, pp. 126-129.
57. *L'Osservatore Romano*, June 21, 1995, No. 2, p. 2.
58. Pope John Paul II, Homily for Eucharistic procession, Cremona, Italy, June 21, 1992, in *L'Osservatore Romano*, July 15, 1992, Nos. 1-2, p. 6.
59. Homily, Solemnity of Corpus Christi, June 15, 1995, in *L'Osservatore Romano*, June 21, 1995, No. 1, pp. 1-2.
60. Pope John Paul II, Message to Archbishop Vallejo of Seville, June 5, 1994, in *L'Osservatore Romano*, June 29, 1994, No. 3, p. 5.
61. Pope John Paul II, General Audience, June 9, 1993, in *L'Osservatore Romano*, June 16, 1993, No. 6, p. 7.
62. Pope John Paul II, Address for World Youth Day Weekend, Mile High Stadium, Denver, Aug. 12, 1993, in *L'Osservatore Romano*, Aug. 18, 1993, p. 11.
63. Pope John Paul II, Homily during Eucharistic Adoration, Forty-fifth International Eucharistic Congress, Seville, June 12, 1993, in *L'Osservatore Romano*, June 23, 1993, Nos. 1-3, 6, p. 4.
64. Alexander Kazhdan, "Alexander the Akoimetos," *Oxford Dictionary of Byzantium*, 1991, Vol. I, p. 59; Alice-Mary Talbot and Fr. Robert F. Taft, SJ, "Akoimetoi, Monastery of," *Oxford Dictionary of Byzantium*, Vol. I, p. 46; J.F. Sollier, "Acoemetae," *Catholic Encyclopedia*, 1907 ed., Vol. I, p. 105; V. Grumel, "Acemetes," in *Dictionnaire de Spiritualité*, Tome I (1937), cols. 169-170; Count de Montalembert, *The Monks of the West, from St. Benedict to St. Bernard*, 1860, Vol. I, Bk. VII, p. 553 (n. 30).
65. H. Leclercq, "Agaunum," *Catholic Encyclopedia*, 1907 ed., Vol. I, pp. 205-206; Montalembert, Vol. I., Bk. VII, p. 553 (text and n. 30); J. Pargoire, "Acemetes," *Dictionnaire d'archeologie chretienne et de liturgie* (ed. Dom Fernand Cabrol and Dom H. Leclercq), Tome I, Pt. I, 1907, col. 314.
66. "The Grey Penitents of Avignon" *The Messenger of the Sacred Heart*, Vol. 29, May 1894, pp. 353-365.
67. Fr. Paul H. O'Sullivan, OP, "Portugal and the Eucharist," in *Thirty-*

First International Eucharistic Congress, Dublin: Sectional Meetings, Papers and Addresses (Vol. II of the Book of the Congress), ed. Very Rev. Patrick Canon Boylan, PP, 1934, p. 307.

68. Joseph H. McMahon, "Adoration, Perpetual," *Catholic Encyclopedia,* 1907 ed., Vol. I, p. 153.
69. Arthur Letellier, "Perpetual Adorers of the Blessed Sacrament," *Catholic Encyclopedia,* 1907 ed., Vol. 11, p. 698.
70. McMahon, p. 154.
71. Letellier, "Perpetual adoration, Religious of the," *Catholic Encyclopedia,* 1907 ed., Vol. 11, p. 698.
72. McMahon, pp. 153-154.
73. Jamie Bamberia, "Someone Always Prays at Gravesend Parish," *The Tablet,* Oct. 31, 1992, p. 3.
74. Joseph Zyble, "Perpetual adoration at St. Peter Begun," *The Upper Peninsula Catholic,* April 9, 1993, p. 3.
75. Colette Guadagnino, "Praying Without *Ceasing,*" *The Post-Standard,* Oct. 9, 1993, pp. C1, C3.
76. Jerry Daoust, "Could You Not Wait One Hour with Me?" *U.S. Catholic,* Vol. 60, Jan. 1995, p. 35.
77. "Bishop's Notebook," *The Catholic Commentator,* Aug. 5, 1992, p. 4.

Epilogue 1

Father Benedict Groeschel

A Labor of Love

As the work on this book draws to a close I recall that I meant it to be more than anything else a labor of love — a votive offering to Christ in the Holy Eucharist, whom I have tried to make the center of my life for many years. These pages, sometimes theological and historical, sometimes psychological, occasionally polemical, are simply the tools I have used to express the devotion and gratitude I feel to our Savior for this wonderful gift, His human presence mysteriously with us in this most Holy Sacrament.

I write these lines in Chicago's O'Hare Airport waiting for the next flight to a preaching assignment. In a quiet corner of this extremely busy airport there is a spacious interfaith chapel, which contains a tabernacle, vigil light, and the reserved Eucharist. I had a long wait at the airport and was delighted to find Him here. I am joined during my holy hour of adoration by a Latino workman in overalls who prays very devoutly. On the other side of the chapel two Muslims genuflect as they make their midday prayer. A few people quietly come and go, mostly acknowledging the mysterious presence of Christ in the tabernacle in traditional Catholic ways.

Today I am tired, concerned about obligations, and I am late. But as I come into the presence of Christ, all these considerations fade away and become silent, like the constant flow of traffic I can see but cannot hear as it encircles the airport. I try to observe the admonition of the Cherubic Hymn of the Eastern liturgy — to put aside all earthly cares as the King of Kings approaches. But He does not come to me as the great King — He comes as my oldest and dearest Friend. ". . . I have called you friends. . ." — "Come to me, all who labour and are heavy laden. . . ."[1] I have always been aware of His presence in many different places, in the mountains and on the subways, in the stars and in the garbage-strewn streets, with the sick and the dying, with the poor and the suffering. I have even caught a glimpse of Him in my enemies when I remembered that He loves them too. But nothing — nothing — can duplicate or come near to His presence in the Holy Eucharist.

Of course this presence begins in the celebration of the Paschal Mystery — the Mass. There the unseen miracle occurs. As Monsignor Robert Sokolowski, a very perceptive commentator presently writing on the Holy Eucharist, suggests — Christ is the Speaker — the celebrant quotes Him:

> Christ, the one who is quoted, speaks with the authority of the incarnate Son of God, as one who has the power to bring about what he declares in his words. . . .
>
> . . . The priest is not there to perform; he is there to accomplish the liturgy as it is written in the Roman Missal. He is there as the servant of Christ and the Church, a servant who becomes quotationally transparent in the words and gestures of the consecration. Christ is the ultimate minister of the Eucharist, and his activity is perceptibly manifest when his words and gestures are quoted at the center of the Church's offering.[2]

Theologians have emphasized in recent years that the reserved Eucharist is the continuation of the celebration of the Paschal Mystery and of the saving sacrifice of Christ. I never thought it was anything else. That's why I am uneasy to this day when the tabernacle is not at the altar where the Mass is offered. What better way to link in one's mind the sacrifice, the sacrament, and the presence of Christ? How wonderful to return to the presence of Christ again during the day and to renew the devotion, resolution, and desire that come at Mass, and to unite myself with my Savior again the next time I have the occasion to offer a little of my complicated life along with our High Priest to the Father.

Although I love to pray alone with the Eucharist, there is something powerful about praying in a place with others who are also meeting the Lord. During the daily holy hour with our friars or with devout Christians on a mission, it is a prayerful reminder that we are all one in Him. I must love Him in them and them in Him. Having thought of myself as one called to serve the poor as a friar since I was a boy, I have never thought of the Eucharist as something private, just for me. I think of all those who pray devoutly before the Eucharist, and of those who would if they were privileged to know about it. The two Muslim workers at the airport are devoutly saying their midday prayer. I don't feel alienated from them at all. I wish that they could know Who it is who is with them and who loves them, but they are doing their best praying with a reverence and devotion that is often not observed in Christians.

The Christ who faith tells me is here is not only the Logos, the transcendent mysterious Word, the Eternal Son. He is Jesus of Nazareth — Body and Blood, Soul and Divinity, as the Church has taught me all my life. I am filled with confidence and hope, because when He walked among us He loved those who did not know Him. He called to those who even hated Him and showed the Father's love to all His children. The Jesus of the Eucharist is the Savior of the world. Nothing makes my responsibility to others clearer to me than the Eucharist, which is the bond of charity, the *vinculum caritatis,* as Saint Augustine called it in the early Church.

Here before the tabernacle I feel at home as in no other place. My sins, my defects, my quirks are all known to Him. There is no secret, nothing to be embarrassed about, no place to hide. I believe (difficult as that may be at times) that He does in fact love me. My self-hate mingled nicely with my self-love (in a familiar sweet-and-sour combination) is defeated for the moment by His presence. With all my failings I have never been afraid to come to Him. In fact, I have run to Him and He has been there for me. In some faint response I have tried to be there for others, but then there are so many, and time and energy give out. But it is not so with Him. "I am with you."

The mystery of a Person present in many places, unseen except for a visible sign, of a Divine Being infinitely good and pure and close to me, all this would deter me — except for one thing: He has said that He comes to me. Sometimes I try to imagine a face, but I am never really successful. I think more of an expression — sometimes tears, sometimes sorrow, often compassion. And when I am sunk in my own self-pity or self-hate, I think of a smile — a quiet compassionate smile, with a gentle touch of admonition.

I love the solemn public moments, the incense, the Latin hymns

— *Tantum Ergo, Adoro Te Devote, Panis Angelicus.* I thrill at a great procession. But not as a steady diet. I love the quiet times, the visit to the Blessed Sacrament and then going with the sacrament to the sick. I love to give out Holy Communion — to meditate on the reverent faces, the devout old people, the children with sparkling eyes. Some are not really well prepared. Some don't even know. But He comes to them as He came by a seeming coincidence to the woman on her way to be stoned, or to the blind beggar of Jericho. I think He smiles at the ignorant who are unprepared. There is a sad smile for those who should not come but do so innocently. And for those not really prepared but who could be, the smile does not turn into wrath but into sorrow. He always was capable of great sorrow. But most of all He was — and is — capable of great mercy and forgiveness.

I feel no need to apologize for my devotion. If some care to call this immature or medieval or obscurantist — I could not care less. I hope I will be merciful in my judgment of those who judge me harshly for my love of His presence so that I would not reject those whom He loves and calls to salvation. When I am in His presence I look at my own life and soul. I have great hope for others because He has given me hope for myself.

Love Is Not Loved

When Saint Francis was newly converted and in the first fervor (which really never left him), he used to go through the streets of Assisi dressed in rags and barefoot, crying, "Love is not loved." I would condemn myself if I did this because love is not loved by me. But I wish I could at this quiet moment go down into the busy aisles and gates of this airport and shout, "Come to the chapel. Love is waiting there for you. Love is a Person, not a thing. He is risen. He is alive. He is waiting for you. Love is not loved." I can't do that, but I can at least try to act like I believe that Love loves those whom I meet — that He calls to them and is there for them, always and everywhere. This mystery lights up the whole of the earth and sky. It sanctifies places far away from where the sacrament is reserved. Bishop James Walsh learned this when he prayed in his prison cell in China. And this I think is what the whole Eucharistic Presence of Jesus of Nazareth is about. It doesn't need to be defended, or even explained very much. The presence of Jesus the Christ needs only to be experienced.

ENDNOTES

1. Jn 15:15; Mt 11:28.
2. These words of Msgr. Sokolowski shed some light on what has become an ever-darkening scene wherein candidates for Holy Orders are often apparently trained for some kind of dramatic presentation in an offensive misuse of the idea of *compositio loci* or sacred drama (Msgr. R. Sokolowski, "Praying the Canon of the Mass," *Homiletic & Pastoral Review*, Vol. 95, July 1995, pp. 11-12).

Epilogue 2

James Monti

It has been my task in the latter chapters of this book to explore the testimony of the past in bringing to light the origins and development of "Eucharistic devotion" — the Church's response of adoration and thanksgiving to the Real Presence of Christ in the Most Blessed Sacrament. In doing so, my purpose has been to bring the reader to a deeper understanding that when we kneel before our Lord in this sacrament we do so in union with "so great a cloud of witnesses" (Heb 12:1) who have come before us, "marked with the sign of faith" (Roman Canon).[1] Their joys and sorrows, their hopes and fears, were not unlike our own. They too found solace and the strength to go on where we find it now — before the tabernacle.

Some, as we have seen, sadly no longer believe they can find such consolation in the adoration of the Eucharist. If after all that has been said in this book they remain unconvinced, perhaps they would be well advised to seek the answer to their questions and doubts in this regard in the pages of our Lord's Last Supper discourse as recorded by Saint John — "I will not leave you desolate; I will come to you. . . . If a man loves me, he will keep my word, and my Father will love him, and we will come to him and make our home with him. . . . Abide in me, and I in you. . . . I am the vine, you are the branches. He who abides in me, and I in him, he it is that bears much fruit. . . . As the Father has loved me, so have I loved you; abide in my love."[2]

In view of such words as these from our God, is it so difficult to understand that simple dialogue of love between the Creator and His creature that is Eucharistic adoration? "I look at the good God, and he looks at me," as it was once described by a humble farmer in the parish of the Curé of Ars.[3] No, Eucharistic adoration is not some obsolete invention of medieval scholastics, encrusted with tawdry sentimentality. It is an invitation to the love of God, a foretaste of the joys of heaven's Wedding Feast of Christ and His Church, because it is an extension of that foretaste of the heavenly joys that is the Mass.

The Mass has always been and always will be the supreme act of Christian worship. Genuine Eucharistic adoration in no way diminishes this unique status of the Eucharistic liturgy; for adoration of the Blessed Sacrament necessarily proceeds from the Mass and ultimately returns the adorer to it. Is it any coincidence that from the seventeenth century onward the great Forty Hours devotion has always begun and ended with the celebration of Mass? Indeed, Eucharistic adoration is at once both an act of thanksgiving for the Eucharistic liturgy, and a preparation for it. When the Christian faithful remain before the Blessed Sacrament beyond the confines of the Mass, they are simply saying to our Lord with the two disciples journeying to Emmaus, "Stay with us, for it is toward evening and the day is now far spent" (Lk 24:29).

Moreover, the Christ found in the Gospels is the very same Christ we will find in the tabernacle; if you want our Lord's Sermon on the Mount, His parables, His miracles of curing the sick and raising the dead, His conversions of sinners, to come alive for you as never before, reflect upon these things before the Blessed Sacrament. In doing so, you will find yourself identifying as never before with the men and women who met our Lord in the New Testament. As for those who strangely complain that Eucharistic adoration is too Christocentric — that in worshiping the Eucharist one somehow neglects praying to the Father — we need look no further than our Lord's answer to Philip's request at the Last Supper that He show His disciples the Father: "Have I been with you so long, and yet you do not know me, Philip? He who has seen me has seen the Father; how can you say, 'Show us the Father'? Do you not believe that I am in the Father and the Father in me?" (Jn 14:9-10).

Having thus journeyed in these pages across nearly two thousand years of the Church's history, we are left to ponder what we, as the sons and daughters of the Church on the verge of a new millennium, are to add to this story of Eucharistic adoration in the pages of our own lives. Christ awaits us in this sacrament of His love — He awaits *all* of us. It is my hope and prayer, as it is of my eminent coauthor, Father Groeschel, that those of you our readers for whom Eucharistic adoration is already an important part of your lives may persevere with a renewed sense of commitment to our Lord in His Most Blessed Sacrament. For those of you as yet unfamiliar with Eucharistic adoration, may we make one final suggestion? "Come and see" (Jn 1:39).

> *. . . give me Thy grace*
> *to long for Thine holy sacraments,*
> *and specially to rejoice*
> *in the presence of Thy very blessed body,*
> *sweet Savior Christ,*
> *in the holy sacrament of the altar. . . .*
>
> — Saint Thomas More[4]

ENDNOTES

1. Eucharistic Prayer I, in *The Roman Missal: The Sacramentary*, 1974, p. 546.
2. Jn 14:18, 23; 15:4, 5, 9.
3. Abbé Francis Trochu, *The Curé d'Ars: St. Jean-Marie-Baptiste Vianney (1786-1859)*, 1927 and 1977, p. 184.
4. "A Devout Prayer," in *St. Thomas More: The Tower Works: Devotional Writings*, ed. Garry H. Haupt, 1980, p. 308.

APPENDIX 1

DECREE OF THE PONTIFICAL COUNCIL FOR THE LAITY
REGARDING THE ESTABLISHMENT OF THE ASSOCIATION OF
PERPETUAL EUCHARISTIC ADORATION
JUNE 2, 1991

PONTIFICIUM CONSILIUM PRO LAICIS

DECREE

With a lively appreciation of the purpose of the "Association of Perpetual Eucharistic Adoration," as an association of the faithful dedicated to promoting Eucharistic worship and devotion, and having as "a particular character of its apostolate of prayer that of perpetual adoration before the exposed Blessed Sacrament" (Statutes: Preamble);

Bearing in mind that the said Association has already promoted, over a considerable number of years, experiences of "Perpetual Eucharistic Adoration" in numerous parishes and dioceses of various countries, always with due respect for the liturgical directives of the Catholic Church and in communion with the Diocesan Ordinaries and the parish priests concerned;

Considering also that the said Association intends to develop communication and cooperation with other approved associations of Christ's faithful that pursue similar purposes;

After receiving the testimony of Bishops of various countries who know, appreciate and encourage the "Association of Perpetual Eucharistic Adoration";

After having studied and revised the statutes of the Association and having found them to be in harmony with the doctrine and discipline of the Catholic Church;

Observing that "competent ecclesiastical authority alone has the right to erect associations of the Christian faithful which set out to teach Christian doctrine in the name of the Church or to promote public worship or which aim at other ends whose pursuit by their nature is reserved to the same ecclesiastical authority" (CIC Can. 301, 1).

THE PONTIFICAL COUNCIL FOR THE LAITY DECREES

The erection of the Association of Perpetual Eucharistic Adoration as a universal and international public association of the faithful, with juridic personality, in accordance with Book II, Part I, Title V of the Code of Canon Law, and the approval of its *Statutes*, the original text of which has been deposited in the Archives of the Pontifical Council for the Laity.

PAUL J. CORDES   EDUARDO CARD. PIRONIO
Vice-President   President

From the Vatican, 2nd June, 1991, Solemnity of the Body and Blood of Christ.

APPENDIX 2

"PERPETUAL EXPOSITION OF THE BLESSED SACRAMENT"
STATEMENT IN THE *NEWSLETTER* OF THE COMMITTEE ON THE
LITURGY OF THE NATIONAL CONFERENCE OF CATHOLIC
BISHOPS
JUNE 1995, VOLUME XXI
pp. 21-22

Perpetual Exposition of the Blessed Sacrament

Over the past several years a number of questions have been raised regarding the practice of perpetual exposition of the Blessed Sacrament. The Liturgy Committee discussed the issues raised several times and decided to submit a series of questions regarding perpetual exposition to the Congregation for Divine Worship and the Discipline of the Sacraments. The following responses were received from the Congregation at the beginning of July. As these responses indicate, those who are responsible for perpetual exposition should carefully review the norms contained in nos. 82-100 of Holy Communion and Worship of the Eucharist outside Mass.

Should perpetual adoration or exposition of the Blessed Sacrament take place in parishes?

RESPONSE: The Roman Ritual: *Holy Communion and Worship of the Eucharist outside Mass* (HCWEOM), no. 90, states that, according to their constitutions and regulations, some religious communities and other pious groups have the practice of perpetual eucharistic adoration or adoration over extended periods of time. If by "perpetual eucharistic adoration" is meant prayer before the Blessed Sacrament in the tabernacle, this involves no special permission. However, if by "perpetual eucharistic adoration" is meant adoration of the Blessed Sacrament exposed in the ciborium or monstrance, the permission of the local Ordinary is required.

Perpetual exposition of the Blessed Sacrament is a devotion and practice which is permitted to those religious communities that have it as an integral part of their communal life and to pious associations of the laity which have received official recognition.

If a pious association of the laity, which has perpetual exposition as a part of its constitution, is established within a parish, the activity of that association should be seen as separate from that of the parish, although all members of the parish are free to participate in it.

May perpetual exposition take place in the parish church?

RESPONSE: Because perpetual exposition is a devotional practice of a religious community or a pious association, it should normally take place in a chapel of that religious community or association. If for some good reason perpetual exposition must take place in a parish church, it should be in a chapel distinct from the body of the church so as not to interfere with the normal activities of the parish or its daily liturgical celebrations.

When Mass is celebrated in a chapel where the Blessed Sacrament is exposed, the eucharist must be replaced in the tabernacle before the celebration of Mass begins.

May perpetual exposition take place twenty-four hours a day, 365 days a year?

RESPONSE: Groups authorized to have perpetual exposition are bound to follow all the liturgical norms given in *Holy Communion and Worship of the Eucharist outside Mass*, nos. 82-100. Under no circumstances may perpetual exposition take place during the Easter Triduum. There should always be a sufficient number of people present for eucharistic adoration before the Blessed Sacrament exposed (see HCWEOM, no. 88). Every effort should be made to ensure that there should be at least two people present. There must absolutely never be periods when the Blessed Sacrament is exposed and there is no one present for adoration. It may prove necessary to expose the Blessed Sacrament for adoration only at stated times when members of the faithful are present.

Who is responsible for overseeing perpetual exposition?

RESPONSE: The local Ordinary has the responsibility for the regulation of perpetual exposition. He determines when it is permissible and establishes the regulations to be followed in regard to perpetual exposition of the Blessed Sacrament. He normally entrusts the superior or chaplain of religious communities or the local pastor or chaplain, in the case of pious associations, with the responsibility of seeing that the liturgical norms and his regulations are followed.

Must the local bishop permit perpetual exposition?

RESPONSE: The bishop is responsible for all matters pertaining to the right ordering of the celebration of the Eucharist and adoration and devotion to the Eucharist outside Mass. It is his duty to promote and guide the liturgical life of the diocese. Consequently, he alone determines the pastoral appropriateness of perpetual exposition in his diocese and accordingly may permit it or not and may limit the number of places where it takes place.

BIBLIOGRAPHY

Acta Sanctorum. Ed. Bollandists. 67 vols. Antwerp, 1643ff; rpt. Paris: Victor Palme, 1863ff.

Allies, M.H. "Blessed Juliana of Cornillon and Corpus Christi." *Irish Ecclesiastical Review*, 14, 3rd series (Nov. 1893), pp. 1010-1017.

Andrieu, Michel. "Aux Origines du Culte du Saint-Sacrement: Reliquaires et Monstrances Eucharistiques." *Analecta Bollandiana*, 68 (1950), pp. 397-418.

Armstrong, Rejis J., OFM Cap. *St. Francis of Assisi: Writings for a Gospel Life.* New York: Crossroad Publishing Co., 1994.

Augustine, St. *The Confessions of St. Augustine.* Trans. Frank J. Sheed. New York: Sheed and Ward, 1943.

_____. *St. Augustine: The City of God: Books VIII-XVI.* The Fathers of the Church, Vol. 14. Trans. Gerald G. Walsh, SJ, and Mother Grace Monahan, OSU. New York: Fathers of the Church., Inc., 1952.

_____. *A Select Library of the Nicene and Post-Nicene Fathers of the Christian Church: Volume VIII: Saint Augustin: Expositions on the Book of Psalms.* Ed. A. Cleveland Coxe. 1888; rpt. Grand Rapids, Mich.: William B. Eerdmans Publishing Co., 1974.

Bailly de Barberey, Madame Helene. *Elizabeth Seton.* New York: The Macmillan Co., 1927.

Ball, Ann. *Modern Saints: Their Lives and Faces.* Rockford, Ill.: Tan Books and Publishers, Inc., 1983.

Bamberia, Jamie. "Someone Always Prays at Gravesend Parish." *The Tablet*, Oct. 31, 1992, p. 3.

Barbiero, Giuseppe. "L'Origine delle Confraternite del SS.mo Sacramento in Italia." In *Studia Eucharistica: DCC Anni a Condito Festo Sanctissimi Corporis Christi, 1246-1946.* Antwerp: Uitgeverij Paul Brand, Bussum de Nederlandsche Boekhandel, 1946, pp. 187-215.

Berenger, Jean. "The Austrian Church." *In Church and Society in Catholic Europe of the Eighteenth Century.* Ed. William Callahan and David Higgs. New York: Cambridge University Press, 1979, pp. 88-105.

Bernardi, Claudio. *La Drammaturgia della Settimana Santa in Italia.* Milan: Vita e Pensiero, 1991.

Bishop, P., and M. Darton. *Encyclopedia of World Faiths*. New York and London: Facts on File; London: MacDonald Co., 1987.

Black, Christopher. *Italian Confraternities in the Sixteenth Century*. Cambridge and New York: Cambridge University Press, 1989.

Bonnin, T., ed. *Registrum Visitationum: Journal des Visites Pastorales d'Eude Rigaud, Archeveque de Rouen*. Rouen, France: Auguste le Brument, 1852.

Bouyer, Fr. Louis. *Liturgical Piety*. Liturgical Studies, Vol. 1. Notre Dame, Ind.: University of Notre Dame Press, 1955.

_____. *The Church, the Word and the Sacraments in Protestantism and Catholicism*. New York: Desclee Co., 1961.

Bridgett, Fr. T.E., CSSR. *A History of the Holy Eucharist in Great Britain*. London: T. Fisher Unwin; Burns and Oates, 1908.

Brilioth, Yngve. *Eucharistic Faith and Practice: Evangelical and Catholic*. London: S.P.C.K., 1965.

Britt, Fr. Matthew, OSB. *The Hymns of the Breviary and Missal*. New York: Benziger Brothers, 1922.

Brown, Sydney N., trans. *The Register of Eudes of Rouen*. Records of Civilization, Sources and Studies, No. 72. New York and London: Columbia University Press, 1964.

Burchard, Johann. *Diarium sive Rerum Urbanarum Commentarii (1483-1506): Tome Premier (1483-1492)*. Ed. L. Thuasne. Paris: Ernest Leroux, Editeur, 1883.

Burton, Fr. Harold. *The Life of St. Francis de Sales*. 2 vols. London: Burns, Oates and Washbourne, Ltd., 1925, 1929.

Butler, Fr. Alban. *Butler's Lives of the Saints*. Edited, revised, and supplemented by Fr. Herbert Thurston, SJ, and Donald Attwater. New York: P.J. Kenedy and Sons, 1956.

_____. *The Lives of the Fathers, Martyrs and Other Principal Saints*. Ed. Fr. Bernard Kelly. London and Dublin: Virtue and Co., Ltd., 1961.

Cabie, Robert. *The Church at Prayer: An Introduction to the Liturgy: Volume II: The Eucharist* (Series ed., Msgr. A.G. Martimort). Collegeville, Minn.: The Liturgical Press, 1986.

Caliaro, Marco, and Mario Francesconi. *John Baptist Scalabrini: Apostle to Emigrants*. New York: Center for Migration Studies, 1977.

Canon Law Society of Great Britain and Ireland, ed. *The Code of*

Canon Law: In English Translation. London: Collins Liturgical Publications; Grand Rapids, Mich.: William B. Eerdmans Publishing Co., 1983.

Capella, Fr. Andrew. *A Manual of Spiritual Exercises* (English translation). St.-Omer, France: John Heigham, 1625; rpt. Menston, Yorkshire, England: Scolar Press (English Rescusant Literature, 1558-1640, Vol. 59, which also contains Edward Weston, *The Repaire of Honour*), 1971.

Cargnoni, Constanzo. "Quarante-Heures." *Dictionnaire de Spiritualité*. Vol. 12, Tome II, 1985-1986, cols. 2702-2723.

Catechism of the Catholic Church. Libreria Editrice Vaticana, 1994 (English edition).

Catholic Truth Society, ed. *The Holy Bible: Revised Standard Version: Catholic Edition*. London: Catholic Truth Society, 1966.

Caussade, Fr. Jean-Paul de, S.J. *Abandonment to Divine Providence*. Trans. John Beevers. Garden City, N.Y.: Image Books, Doubleday and Co., Inc., 1975.

Ceremonial of Bishops. Trans. International Commission on English in the Liturgy. Collegeville, Minn.: Liturgical Press, 1989.

"Charles II of Spain." *Ave Maria*, 2 (Dec. 22, 1866), pp. 805-806.

Cherubini, Laertius, ed. *Magnum Bullarium Romanum, A.B. Leone Magno usque ad S.D.N. Clementem X: Tomus Primus*. Lyons, France: Laurentius Arnaud and Peter Borde, 1673.

The Companion to the Catechism of the Catholic Church. San Francisco: Ignatius Press, 1994.

Congregation of Sacred Rites. *Decreta Authentica Congregationis Sacrorum Rituum*. 5 vols. Rome: Typographia Polyglotta, 1898-1901.

Corbin, Solange. *La Déposition Liturgique du Christ au Vendredi Saint: Sa Place dans l'histoire des rites et du théâtre religieux*. Collection Portugaise. Paris: Société d'Éditions 'Les Belles Lettres,' 1960.

Corblet, Abbé Jules. *Histoire Dogmatique, Liturgique et Archeologique du Sacrement de l'Eucharistie*. 2 Vols. Paris: Société Generale de Librairie Catholique, 1885.

Corpus Christianorum, Series Latina: CLXXV: Itineraria et Alia Geographia. Turnhout, Belgium: Typographi Brepols Editores Pontificii, 1965.

Cruz, Joan Carroll. *Relics.* Huntington, Ind.: Our Sunday Visitor, Inc., 1984.

Curley, Fr. Michael J., CSSR. *Bishop John Neumann, C.SS.R.: Fourth Bishop of Philadelphia.* Philadelphia: Bishop Neumann Center, 1952.

Currer-Briggs, Noel. *The Shroud and the Grail: A Modern Quest for the True Grail.* New York: St. Martin's Press, 1987.

"Custodia." *Enciclopedia Universal Ilustrada.* 1958 ed. Vol. 16, pp. 1295-1298.

Daly, Card. Cahal. "Eucharistic Devotion." In *Understanding the Eucharist.* Ed. Patrick McGoldrick. Dublin: Gill and Macmillan, 1969, pp. 77-110.

Daoust, Jerry. "Could You Not Wait One Hour with Me?" *U.S. Catholic,* 60 (Jan. 1995), pp. 33-36.

Deikman, A.J. "Experimental Meditation." In *Altered States of Consciousness,* ed. Charles Tart. Garden City, N.Y.: Anchor Books, Doubleday, 1972.

Deiss, Lucien, C.S.Sp., ed. *Early Sources of the Liturgy.* Collegeville, Minn.: The Liturgical Press, 1975.

DeMayo, John B. and Joseph J. Casino, ed. *The Forty-First International Eucharistic Congress, August 1-8, 1976: A History.* Pennsauken, N.J.: DeVlieger Associates, 1978.

Diederich, Fr. Everett, SJ. "Eucharistic Worship Outside Mass." In *The New Dictionary of Sacramental Worship,* ed. Rev. Peter Fink, SJ, 1990, p. 459.

Eckhart, Meister. *Meister Eckhart: A Modern Translation.* Ed. Raymond B. Blakney. New York: Harper Torchbooks, The Cloister Library, Harper and Row, Publishers, 1941.

Eliot, T.S. *Collected Poems: 1909-1962.* New York: Harcourt, Brace and World, 1963.

Erikson, Erik H. *Childhood and Society.* New York: W.W. Norton and Co., Inc., 1964.

"Eucharistic Presence: Introduction" (editorial). *Commonweal,* 122 (Jan. 27, 1995), p. 10.

Euchologium Ratisbonense sive Ordo Sacri Ministerii Servandus in Processionibus cum S.S. Eucharistiae Sacramento et in Sacris Officiis Publicisque coram eodem Exposito Praecendis. Regensburg: Frederick Pustet, 1876.

Fehren, Fr. Henry. "Where is the Dining Room?" *U.S. Catholic*, 35 (Sept. 1970), pp. 40-43.

Fehring, Fr. Fabian, OFM Cap. "Capuchin Origin and Propagation of the Quarant' Ore." *Round Table of Franciscan Research*, 17 (Jan. 1952), pp. 15-22.

Felder, Fr. Hilarin, OFM Cap. *The Ideals of St. Francis of Assisi.* New York: Benziger, 1925.

Fitzpatrick, P.J. *In Breaking of Bread: The Eucharist and Ritual.* Cambridge: Cambridge University Press, 1993.

_____, and Paul Baumann. "Signs & Disguises: Sorting Out Transubstantiation." *Commonweal*, 122 (Jan. 27, 1995), pp. 18-21.

Flannery, Austin, OP, ed. *Vatican Council II: More Postconciliar Documents.* Vatican Collection, Vol. II. Northport, N.Y.: Costello Publishing Co., 1982.

Fortini, Arnaldo. *Francis of Assisi.* New York: Crossroad Publishing Co., 1992.

Freestone, W.H. *The Sacrament Reserved: A Survey of the Practice of Reserving the Eucharist, with Special Reference to the Communion of the Sick, During the First Twelve Centuries.* Alcuin Club Collections, No. 21. London: A.R. Mowbray and Co., Ltd.; Milwaukee: The Young Churchman Co., 1917.

Frossard, André. *I Have Met Him: God Exists.* New York: Herder and Herder, 1971.

Gaudoin-Parker, Fr. Michael L., ed. *The Real Presence through the Ages: Jesus Adored in the Sacrament of the Altar.* Staten Island, N.Y.: Alba House, 1993.

Germanus of St. Stanislaus, Fr. *The Life of the Servant of God Gemma Galgani: An Italian Maiden of Lucca.* London and Edinburgh: Sands and Company; St. Louis, Mo.: B. Herder, 1913.

Gilliat-Smith, Ernest. *Saint Anthony of Padua, according to His Contemporaries.* London and Toronto: J.M. Dent and Sons Ltd.; New York: E.P. Dutton and Co., 1926.

Giovagnoli, Canon Anthony Francis. *The Life of Saint Margaret of Cortona.* New York: P.J. Kenedy and Sons, n.d. (1800s).

Gonzalez, J.L., and T. Perez, *Paul VI* (English edition by Edward Heston, CSC), 1964.

"The Grey Penitents of Avignon." *The Messenger of the Sacred Heart*, 29 (May 1894), pp. 348-365.

Grumel, V. "Acemetes." *Dictionnaire de Spiritualité.* Tome I (1937), cols. 169-175.

Guadagnino, Colette. "Praying Without Ceasing." *The Post-Standard,* Oct. 9, 1993, pp. C1, C3.

Guardini, Romano. *The Humanity of Christ.* New York: Pantheon Books, 1964.

Guerin, Msgr. Paul. *Les Petits Bollandistes: Vies des Saints.* 17 vols. Paris: Bloud et Barral, 1872-1874.

Guibert, Joseph de. "Capilla (André)." *Dictionnaire de Spiritualité.* Tome 2, Pt. 1, 1937, cols. 117-119.

Gundersheimer, Werner L., ed. *Art and Life at the Court of Ercole I d'Este: The 'De triumphis religionis' of Giovanni Sabadino degli Arienti.* Travaux d'Humanisme et Renaissance, No. 127. Geneva: Libraire Droz, 1972.

Habig, Marion A., OFM. *The Franciscan Book of Saints.* Chicago: Franciscan Herald Press, 1959.

_____, ed. *St. Francis of Assisi: Writings and Early Biographies: English Omnibus of the Sources for the Life of St. Francis.* Chicago: Franciscan Herald Press, 1973.

Haimerl, Dr. Theol. Xavier. *Das Prozessionswesen des Bistums Bamberg im Mittelalter.* Munchener Studien zur Historischen Theologie, Vol. 14. Munich, Germany: Verlag Kosel-Pustet, 1937.

Hammarskjöld, Dag. *Markings.* New York: Knopf, 1970.

Hardison, O.B., Jr. *Christian Rite and Christian Drama in the Middle Ages.* Baltimore: John Hopkins Press, 1965.

"Higuera (Geronimo Roman)." *Biografia Eclesiástica Completa.* Ed. B.S. Castellanos de Losada. Madrid: D. Alejandro Gomez Fuentenebro. Vol. 9 (1855), pp. 1021-1023.

Hirn, Yrjo. *The Sacred Shrine: A Study of the Poetry and Art of the Catholic Church.* London: MacMillan and Co., Ltd., 1912.

Holder-Egger, Oswald, ed. *Chronica Fratris Salimbene de Adam, Ordinis Minorum.* Monumenta Germaniae Historica, Scriptorum, Vol. 32. Hannover and Leipzig: Impensis Bibliopolii Hahniani, 1905-1913.

The Holy Bible: Douay Rheims Version. Baltimore, Md., 1899; rpt. Rockford, Ill.: Tan Books and Publishers, 1971.

Hontoir, Fr. M. Camille, OCR. "Le Devotion au Sacrement chez les Premiers Cisterciens (XII-XIII siecles)." In *Studia Eucharistica:*

DCC Anni a Condito Festo Santissimi Corporis Christi 1246-1946. Antwerp: Uitgeverij Paul Brand, Bussum de Nederlandsche Boekhandel, 1946, pp. 132-156.

Hopkins, Gerard Manley. *Poems of Gerard Manley Hopkins.* 3rd ed. New York: Oxford University Press, 1948.

Howell, C.W. "Monstrance." *New Catholic Encyclopedia.* 1967 ed. Vol. 9, pp. 1070-1071.

International Commission on English in the Liturgy, trans. *The Rites of the Catholic Church as Revised by the Second Vatican Ecumenical Council* (Vol. I). New York: Pueblo Publishing Co., 1976 and 1983.

Irenaeus of Lyon, St. *Irenée de Lyon: Contre les Hérésies, Livre V: Tome II: Texte et Traduction.* Ed. Adelin Rousseau. *Sources Chretiennes,* Vol. 153. Paris: Les Editions du Cerf, 1969.

Jaki, Fr. Stanley, OSB. *The Road of Science and the Ways to God.* Chicago: University of Chicago Press, 1978.

Jastrow, Robert. *God and the Astronomers.* New York: W.W. Norton and Co., Inc., 1978.

John XXIII, Pope. Excerpt from a message to the National Eucharistic Congress of France, July 5, 1959. In *The Pope Speaks,* 6 (Spring 1960), p. 192.

_____. *Journal of a Soul.* Trans. Dorothy White. New York: McGraw-Hill Book Co., 1965.

John of the Cross, St. *The Collected Works of St. John of the Cross.* Trans. Kieran Kavanaugh, OCD, and Otilio Rodriguez, OCD. Washington, D.C.: ICS Publications, 1979.

John Paul II, Pope. *Ireland: "In the Footsteps of St. Patrick"* (talks delivered during the papal visit to Ireland, Sept. 29-Oct. 1, 1979). Ed. Daughters of St. Paul. Boston: Daughters of St. Paul, 1979.

_____. Homily following Eucharistic procession, Cremona, Italy, June 21, 1992. *L'Osservatore Romano,* July 15, 1992, p. 6.

_____. General Audience, June 9, 1993. *L'Osservatore Romano,* June 16, 1993, p. 7.

_____. Homily at Eucharistic Vigil, Forty-fifth International Eucharistic Congress, Seville, June 12, 1993. *L'Osservatore Romano,* June 23, 1993, p. 4.

_____. Address for World Youth Day Weekend, Mile High Stadium, Denver, Aug. 12, 1993. *L'Osservatore Romano,* Aug. 18, 1993, pp. 7, 11.

_____. Message to Archbishop Vallejo of Seville, June 5, 1994. *L'Osservatore Romano*, June 29, 1994, p. 5.

_____. Homily, Solemnity of Corpus Christi, June 15, 1995. *L'Osservatore Romano*, June 21, 1995, pp. 1-2.

Jones, Frederick M., CSSR. *Alphonsus de Liguori: The Saint of Bourbon Naples, 1696-1787*. Westminster, Md.: Christian Classics, Inc., 1992.

Jorgensen, Johannes. *Saint Francis of Assisi: A Biography*. Garden City, N.Y.: Image Books, Doubleday and Co., Inc., 1955, p. 314.

Jungmann, Fr. Josef Andreas, SJ. *The Mass of the Roman Rite: Its Origins and Development*. 2 vols. Trans. Rev. Francis A. Brunner, CSSR. New York: Benziger Brothers, Inc., 1951 (Vol. I), 1955 (Vol. II).

_____. *Pastoral Liturgy*. New York: Herder and Herder, 1962.

_____. *The Place of Christ in Liturgical Prayer*. Staten Island, N.Y.: Alba House, 1965.

Justin, St. *The Ante-Nicene Fathers: Volume I: The Apostolic Fathers with Justin Martyr and Irenaeus*. Ed. Rev. Alexander Roberts and James Donaldson, revised by A. Cleveland Coxe. 1885; rpt. Grand Rapids, Mich.: William B. Eerdmans Publishing Co., 1973.

Kazhdan, Alexander. "Alexander the Akoimetos." *Oxford Dictionary of Byzantium*. A. Kazhdan et al., ed. New York: Oxford University Press, 1991, Vol. I, p. 59.

Keifer, Ralph A. *Blessed and Broken: An Exploration of the Contemporary Experience of God in Eucharistic Celebration* (*Message of the Sacraments* series, Vol. 3). Wilmington, Del.: Michael Glazier, Inc., 1982.

Kelly, Fr. Bernard, ed. *The Lives of the Fathers, Martyrs and Other Principal Saints: Volume V* (additions to the four volumes of Fr. Alban Butler's *Lives of the Saints*). London and Dublin: Virtue and Co., Ltd., 1961.

Kennedy, V.L., CSB. "The Date of the Parisian Decree on the Elevation of the Host." *Medieval Studies*, 8 (1948), pp. 87-96.

Ker, Ian. *John Henry Newman: A Biography*. Oxford: Clarendon Press, 1988.

King, Archdale. *Eucharistic reservation in the Western Church*. London: A.R. Mowbray and Co., Ltd., 1965.

Knowles, David, trans./ed. *The Monastic Constitutions of Lanfranc.* New York: Oxford University Press, 1951.

Knox, Fr. Thomas F., trans. *The Life of Blessed Henry Suso, by Himself.* London: Burns, Lambert, and Oates, 1865.

Larranaga, Fr. Ignacio, OFM Cap. *Sensing Your Hidden Presence: Toward Intimacy with God.* Garden City, N.Y.: Image Books, Doubleday and Co., Inc., 1987.

Leclercq, H. "Agaunum." *Catholic Encyclopedia.* 1907 ed. Vol. I, pp. 205-206.

Lefebvre, Dom Gaspar, OSB. *Saint Andrew Daily Missal: With Vespers for Sundays and Feasts.* St. Paul, Minn.: E.M. Lohmann Co., 1943.

Letellier, Arthur. "Perpetual adoration, Religious of the." *Catholic Encyclopedia.* 1907 ed. Vol. 11, p. 698.

_____. "Perpetual Adorers of the Blessed Sacrament." *Catholic Encyclopedia.* 1907 ed. Vol. 11, pp. 698-699.

"Liutprando." *Biografía Eclesiástica Completa.* Ed. B.S. Castellanos de Losada. Madrid: D. Alejandro Gomez Fuentenebro. Vol. 12 (1862), pp. 458-459.

Lockton, W. *The Treatment of the Remains at the Eucharist after Holy Communion and the Time of the Ablutions.* London: Cambridge University Press (New York: The Macmillan Co.), 1920.

"Lugo." *Enciclopedia Universal Ilustrada.* 1958 ed. Vol. 31, pp. 568-577.

MacErlean, A.A. "Lugo." *Catholic Encyclopedia.* 1907 ed. Vol. 9, pp. 417-418.

Mansi, J.D., ed. *Sacrorum Conciliorum Nova et Amplissima Collectio.* 36 vols. Florence: Antonius Zatta, 1757-1798; rpt. Paris and Leipzig: Huberto Welter, 1901.

Mariotti, Fr. Candido, OFM Cap. *L'Eucaristia ed I Francescani.* Fano, Italy: Societa Tip. Cooperativa, 1908.

Martene, Dom Edmund. *De Antiquis Ecclesiae Ritibus.* 2nd folio ed. 4 vols. Venice: Baptistae Novelli, 1763-1764.

Martimort, Msgr. A.G. *La Documentation liturgique de Dom Edmund Martene.* Studi e Testi, No. 279. Vatican City: Biblioteca Apostolica Vaticana, 1978.

Martinez, Fr. Enrique Llamas, OCD. "El Culto Mariano en España, a través de las Iglesias y Santuarios dedicados a la Virgen María, antes del Siglo XII." In *Du Cultu Mariano Saeculis VI-XI: Acta Congressus Mariologici-Mariani Int. in Croatia Anno 1971 Celebrati, Vol. V: De Culto Mariano saeculis VI-XI apud Varias Nationes et Secundum Fontes Islamicos*. Rome: Pontificia Academia Mariana Internationalis, 1972, pp. 171-206.

Martos, Joseph. *Doors to the Sacred: A Historical Introduction to Sacraments in the Catholic Church*. Garden City, N.Y.: Doubleday and Co., Inc., 1981.

Mary Alphonsus, Sr., OSSR. *St. Rose of Lima: Patroness of the Americas*. St. Louis, Mo.: B. Herder Book Co., 1968.

McDonnell, Ernest W. "Beguines and Beghards." *New Catholic Encyclopedia*. 1967 ed. Vol. 2, pp. 224-226.

_____. *The Beguines and Beghards in Medieval Culture, with Special Emphasis on the Belgian Scene*. New Brunswick, N.J.: Rutgers University Press, 1954.

McDonnell, Fr. Kilian, OSB. "Eucharistic Exposition: An Obsolete Relic?" *America*, 160 (Feb. 25, 1989), pp. 166-169.

McKenna, Fr. Joseph. "Quarant' Ore or the Forty Hours' Prayer." *Clergy Review*, 6 (Sept. 1933), pp. 186-199.

McMahon, Joseph H. "Adoration, Perpetual." *Catholic Encyclopedia*. 1907 ed. Vol. I, pp. 152-154.

Mershman, Francis. "Corpus Christi (Body of Christ)." *Catholic Encyclopedia*. 1907 ed. Vol. 4, pp. 390-391.

Migne, J.-P., ed. *Patrologia Graeca*. 161 vols. Paris: Garnier Fratres, 1857-1865.

_____. *Patrologia Latina*. 221 vols. Paris: Garnier Fratres, 1878-1890.

Mitchell, Nathan. *Cult and Controversy: The Worship of the Eucharist Outside Mass (Studies in the Reformed Rites of the Catholic Church*, Vol. IV). New York: Pueblo Publishing Co., 1982.

_____. "Who Is at the Table? Reclaiming Real Presence." *Commonweal*, 122 (Jan. 27, 1995), pp. 10-15.

Moloney, Fr. Raymond, SJ. "Eucharistic Devotions Today." *The Furrow*, 45 (Sept. 1994), pp. 503-508.

Montalembert, Count de. *The Monks of the West, from St. Benedict to St. Bernard* (Boston: Thomas B. Noonan and Co., 1860), Vol. I.

Monti, James. *The Week of Salvation: History and Traditions of Holy Week*. Huntington, Ind.: Our Sunday Visitor, Inc., 1993.

_____. "Sacred Vessels." *Catholic Heritage*, 4 (May-June 1995), p. 14.

More, St. Thomas. *The Tower Works: Devotional Writings*. Ed. Garry H. Haupt. New Haven: Yale University Press, 1980.

Nelson, Rt. Rev. Msgr. Joseph A., ed. *Roman Breviary in English: Summer*. New York: Benziger Brothers, Inc., 1951.

Newman, Ven. John Henry. *Discourses Addressed to Mixed Congregations*. London: Longmans, Green and Co., 1899.

_____. *The Idea of a University, Defined and Illustrated*. London: Longmans, Green and Co., 1901.

_____. *The Letters and Diaries of John Henry Newman: XI: Littlemore to Rome, October 1845 to December 1846*. Ed. C.S. Dessain. London: Thomas Nelson and Sons, Ltd., 1961.

Nichols, Fr. Aidan. *The Holy Eucharist: From the New Testament to Pope John Paul II*. Oscott Series, No. 6. Dublin: Veritas, 1991.

O'Briain, Felim, OFM. "The Blessed Eucharist in Irish Liturgy and History." *In Studia Eucharistica: DCC Anni a Condito Festo Sanctissimi Corporis Christi, 1246-1946*. Antwerp: Uitgeverij Paul Brand, Bussum de Nederlandsche Boekhandel, 1946, pp. 216-245.

O'Brien, Fr. Roger G. "Preconciliar Agenda Seems to Surface" (letter to editor). *Catholic Northwest Progress*, Oct. 19, 1995, p. 8.

O'Callaghan, Joseph. *A History of Medieval Spain*. Ithaca, N.Y.: Cornell University Press, 1975.

O'Connor, Msgr. James T. *The Hidden Manna: A Theology of the Eucharist*. San Francisco: Ignatius Press, 1988.

Ojeda, Juan Angel Onate. *El Santo Grial: Su historia, su culto y sus destinos*. Valencia, Spain: Tipografia Moderna, 1952.

Olin, John C. *The Catholic Reformation: Savonarola to Ignatius Loyola*. New York: Fordham University Press, 1992.

Optatus of Mileve, St. *S. Optati Milevitani Libri VII*. Corpus Scriptorum Ecclesiasticorum Latinorum, Vol. 26. Ed. Carolus Ziwsa. Prague and Vienna: F. Tempsky; Leipzig: G. Freytag, 1893.

Oram, James. *The People's Pope: The Story of Karol Wojtyla of Poland*. San Francisco: Chronicle Books, 1979.

O'Reilly, E. Boyle. *Heroic Spain*. New York: Duffield and Co., 1910.

Osborne, Kenan, OFM. *The Christian Sacraments of Initiation: Baptism, Confirmation, Eucharist*. New York and Mahwah, N.J.: Paulist Press, 1987.

O'Sullivan, Fr. Paul H., OP. "Portugal and the Eucharist." In *Thirty-First International Eucharistic Congress, Dublin: Sectional Meetings, Papers and Addresses* (Vol. II of the Book of the Congress). Ed. Very Rev. Patrick Canon Boylan, PP. Wexford, Ireland: John English and Co., 1934, pp. 304-318.

Ott, Bp. Stanley Joseph. "Bishop's Notebook." *The Catholic Commentator*, Aug. 5, 1992, p. 4.

Pargoire, J. "Acemetes." *Dictionnaire d'archeologie chretienne et de liturgie*. Ed. Dom Fernand Cabrol and Dom H. Leclercq. Paris: Librarie Letouzey et Ane, 1907, Tome I, Pt. I, cols. 307-321.

Paul VI, Pope. *Encyclical Letter of His Holiness Pope Paul VI: Mystery of Faith: Mysterium Fidei*. Boston: St. Paul Editions, Daughters of St. Paul, n.d.

_____. *The "Credo" of the People of God*. New Rochelle, N.Y.: Catholics United for the Faith, Inc., n.d.

Pedrayo, Ramon Otero. *Galicia: Una Cultura de Occidente*. Madrid: Editorial Everest, S.A., 1985.

"Perpetual adoration of the Blessed Sacrament: Clarification." National Conference of Catholic Bishops, *Committee on the Liturgy: Newsletter*, 23 (Jan. 1987), p. 50.

"Perpetual Exposition of the Blessed Sacrament." National Conference of Catholic Bishops, *Committee on the Liturgy: Newsletter*, 22 (June-July 1986), pp. 24-25.

"Perpetual Exposition of the Blessed Sacrament." National Conference of Catholic Bishops, *Committee on the Liturgy: Newsletter*, 31 (June 1995), pp. 21-22.

The Persecution of the Catholic Church in the Third Reich: Facts and Documents Translated from the German. New York: Longmans, Green and Co., 1940.

Peter Julian Eymard, St. *Eucharistic Prayer Book: For the Members of the People's Eucharistic League*. Eymard Library, Vol. 6. New York: Eymard League, 1948.

Preston, William. *The Blessed Sacrament and the Church of St. Martin at Liège*. New York: The Catholic Publication Society Co.; London: Burns and Oates, 1890.

Rahner, Karl. *The Church and The Sacraments*. New York: Herder and Herder, 1963.

_____. *Mission and Grace: Essays in Pastoral Theology.* Vol. I. London: Sheed and Ward, 1963.

_____. *Everyday Faith.* New York: Herder and Herder, 1967.

_____. "Eucharistic Worship." In *Theological Investigations: Volume XXIII: Final Writings.* New York: Crossroad, 1992, pp. 113-116.

Reinhold, Fr. Hans Ansgar. *The American Parish and the Roman Liturgy.* New York: Macmillan Co., 1958.

Rey-Mermet, Theolule, CSSR. *Alphonsus Liguori: Tireless Worker for the Most Abandoned.* Brooklyn, N.Y.: New City Press, 1989.

Righetti, Mario. *Manuale di Storia Liturgica.* 4 vols. Milan: Editrice Ancora, 1949-1955.

The Roman Missal: Lectionary for Mass. New York: Catholic Book Publishing Co., 1970.

The Roman Missal: The Sacramentary. New York: Catholic Book Publishing Co., 1974 and 1985.

Rosa, Mario. "The Italian Churches." In *Church and Society in Catholic Europe of the Eighteenth Century.* Ed. William Callahan and David Higgs. New York: Cambridge University Press, 1979, pp. 66-76.

Roustang, François, SJ. *An Autobiography of Martyrdom: Spiritual Writings of the Jesuits in New France.* St. Louis, Mo.: B. Herder, 1964.

Rubin, Miri. *Corpus Christi: The Eucharist in Late Medieval Culture.* Cambridge: Cambridge University Press, 1991.

Sands, Leo, CSB. "The Blessed Sacrament After Vatican II." *Canadian Catholic Review,* 12 (Feb. 1994), pp. 32-34.

Scanlan, Olive M. *St. Anthony of Padua.* Dublin: Clonmore and Reynolds Ltd., 1958.

Scheeben, Matthias. *The Mysteries of Christianity.* St. Louis, Mo.: B. Herder Book Co., 1961.

Schnackenburg, Fr. Rudolf. *Belief in the New Testament.* New York: Paulist Press, 1974 (English trans.).

Secretary General, Diocese of Lugo. "Santuario Eucarístico y Mariano." Manuscript submitted for publication in forthcoming book, 1995, p. 3.

Simcox, Carroll, ed. *A Treasury of Quotations on Christian Themes.* New York: Seabury Press, 1975.

Skinner, B.F. "Origins of a Behaviorist." *Psychology Today*, 17, No. 9 (Sept. 1983), pp. 22-33.

Sokolowski, Msgr. Robert. *Eucharistic Presence: A Study in the Theology of Disclosure.* Washington, D.C.: Catholic University of America Press, 1993.

_____. "Praying the Canon of the Mass." *Homiletic & Pastoral Review*, 95 (July 1995), pp. 8-15.

Sollier, J.F. "Acoemetae." *Catholic Encyclopedia.* 1907 ed. Vol. I, p. 105.

Staniforth, Fr. Oswald, OSFC. *The Saint of the Eucharist: Saint Paschal Baylon.* London: R.& T. Washbourne, Ltd., 1908.

Stoddard, Charles W. *The Wonder-Worker of Padua.* Notre Dame, Ind.: The Ave Maria Press, 1896.

Stone, Darwell. *A History of the Doctrine of the Holy Eucharist.* 2 vols. London: Longmans, Green and Co., 1909.

_____. *The Reserved Sacrament.* Handbooks of Catholic Faith and Practice. London: Robert Scott; Milwaukee: The Young Churchman Co., 1917.

Sumption, Jonathan. *Pilgrimage: An Image of Medieval Religion.* Totowa, N.J.: Rowman and Littlefield, 1976.

Symons, Dom Thomas, trans. *Regularis Concordia: The Monastic Agreement of the Monks and Nuns of the English Nation.* Medieval Classics. New York: Oxford University Press, 1953.

Talbot, Alice-Mary, and Fr. Robert F. Taft, SJ. "Akoimetoi, Monastery of." *Oxford Dictionary of Byzantium.* A. Kazhdan et al., ed. New York: Oxford University Press, 1991, Vol. I, p. 46.

Taves, Ann. "Context and Meaning: Roman Catholic Devotion to the Blessed Sacrament in Mid-Nineteenth-Century America." *Church History*, 54 (Dec. 1985), pp. 482-495.

Thérèse of Lisieux, St. *Autobiography of St. Thérèse of Lisieux.* Trans. Ronald Knox. New York: P.J. Kenedy and Sons, 1958.

_____. *Saint Thérèse of Lisieux: General Correspondence.* Trans. John Clarke, OCD. 2 vols. Washington, D.C.: Institute of Carmelite Studies, 1982 (Vol. I), 1988 (Vol. II).

Thomas Aquinas, St. *The Three Greatest Prayers: Commentaries on the Lord's Prayer, the Hail Mary, and the Apostles' Creed.* Manchester, N.H.: Sophia Institute Press, 1990.

_____. *Divinity I Adore Thee: The Hymns and Prayers of St. Thomas Aquinas. Trans. R. Anderson and J. Moser. Manchester, N.H.: Sophia Institute Press, 1993.

_____. *Summa Theologiae: Volume 57: Baptism and Confirmation (3a.66-72)*. Ed. James J. Cunningham, OP. Cambridge: Blackfriars; New York: McGraw Hill Book Co.; London: Eyre and Spottiswoode, 1975.

_____. *Summa Theologiae, Volume 58: The Eucharistic Presence*. Ed. William Barden, OP. Cambridge: Blackfriars; New York: McGraw Hill Book Co.; London: Eyre and Spottiswoode, 1965.

_____. *Summa Theologiae, Volume 59: Holy Communion (3a.79-83)*. Ed. Thomas Gilby, OP. Cambridge: Blackfriars; New York: McGraw Hill Book Co.; London: Eyre and Spottiswoode, 1975.

Thurston, Fr. Herbert, SJ. "Our Popular Devotions: IV.-Benediction of the Blessed Sacrament: II.-Exposition." *Month*, 98 (July 1901), pp. 58-69.

_____. "Our Popular Devotions: IV.-Benediction of the Blessed Sacrament: III.-The Benediction." *Month*, 98 (Aug. 1901), pp. 186-193.

_____. "Easter Sepulchre, or Altar of Repose?" *Month*, 101 (April 1903), pp. 404-414.

_____. *Lent and Holy Week: Chapters on Catholic Observance and Ritual*. London: Longmans, Green and Co., 1904.

_____. "The Early Cultus of the Blessed Sacrament." *Month*, 109 (April 1907), pp. 377-390.

_____. "The Blessed Sacrament and the Holy Grail." *Month*, 110 (Dec. 1907), pp. 617-632.

_____. "The Early Cultus of the Reserved Eucharist." *Journal of Theological Studies*, 11 (Jan. 1910), pp. 275-279.

_____. "Reservation in its Historical Aspects." *Month*, 130 (Sept. 1917), pp. 233-243.

_____. "The Transition Period of Catholic Mysticism." *Month*, 139 (June 1922), pp. 526-537.

Thwaites, Reuben Gold, ed. *The Jesuit Relations and Allied Documents: Travels and Explorations of the Jesuit Missionaries in New France 1610-1791: Vol. XXVIII: Hurons, Iroquois, Lower Canada, 1645-1646*. Cleveland: The Burrows Brothers Co., 1898.

Trochu, Abbé Francis. *The Curé of Ars: St. Jean-Marie-Baptiste Vianney (1786-1859)*. London, 1927; rpt. Rockford, Ill.: Tan Books and Publishers, Inc., 1977.

Valcarcel, Fr. Amador Lopez. "Lucus Augusti, Locus Sacramenti: El Culto Eucarístico en Lugo. Notas para su historia." *El Progresso*, June 8, 1969, rpt. in *Historias Luguesas*, Excma. Disputación Provincial de Lugo, ed. Lugo: Excma. Disputación Provincial de Lugo, 1975, pp. 39-49.

_____. *La Catedral de Lugo*. Lugo, Spain: Servicio de Publicaciónes, Excma. Disputación Provincial, n.d., n.p.

Van Dijk, S.J.P., OFM, and J. Hazelden Walker. *The Myth of the Aumbry: Notes on Medieval Reservation Practice and Eucharistic Devotion*. London: Burns and Oates, 1957.

_____. *The Origins of the Modern Roman Liturgy: The Liturgy of the Papal Court and the Franciscan Order in the Thirteenth Century*. Westminster, Md.: Darton, Longman and Todd, 1960.

_____. *Sources of the Modern Roman Liturgy: The Ordinals of Haymo of Faversham and Related Documents (1243-1307)*. 2 vols. Leiden, Netherlands: E.J. Brill, 1963.

Vassalli, G. "Santissimo Sacramento." *Dizionario degli Instituti di Perfezione*. Vol. 8, 1988, cols. 819-838.

Very, Francis G. *The Spanish Corpus Christi Procession: A Literary and Folkloric Study*. Valencia, Spain: Tipografia Moderna-Olivereta, 1962.

Von Balthasar, Hans Urs. *New Elucidations*. San Francisco: Ignatius Press, 1986.

_____. *"You Crown the Year with Your Goodness": Radio Sermons*. Trans. Graham Harrison. San Francisco: Ignatius Press, 1989.

Walsh, Thomas, ed. *The Catholic Anthology: The World's Great Catholic Poetry*. New York: Macmillan Co., 1942.

Walsh, Most Rev. W. *Eucharistica; or a Series of Pieces, Original and Translated, of the Most Holy and Adorable Sacrament of the Eucharist*. New York: T.W. Strong, Late Edward Dunigan and Brother, 1854.

Waugh, Evelyn. *Brideshead Revisited: The Sacred and Profane Memories of Captain Charles Ryder*. Boston: Little, Brown and Co., 1945; rpt. n.d.

Weiser, Fr. Francis X., SJ. *Handbook of Christian Feasts and Cus-*

toms: *The Year of the Lord in Liturgy and Folklore.* New York: Harcourt, Brace and Co., 1958.

Wilkinson, John, trans./ed. *Egeria's Travels.* London: S.P.C.K., 1971.

Willis, John R. *The Teachings of the Church Fathers.* New York: Herder and Herder, 1966.

Young, Karl. *The Drama of the Medieval Church.* 2 vols. Oxford: Clarendon Press, Oxford University Press, 1933.

Zyble, Joseph. "Perpetual adoration at St. Peter Begun." *The Upper Peninsula Catholic*, April 9, 1993, p. 3.

INDEX

(*Note:* Due to a number of considerations, this index does not conform to conventional styles; for example, some entries appear with first and last names in that order — as in Thomas Aquinas, St., instead of Aquinas, St. Thomas. Some entries have cross references while others do not. Still other entries will include pages where the concept rather than the specific entry is explained, clarified, or expanded. Other modifications are more or less self-evident.)

E

M

Z

23

34 1648 Chas II of Spain

38 Justin Martyr